W9-BCZ-637

By the same author

The Circle Tour

The Crazy Years

Disappearances

The Wolf Is Not Native to the South of France

K

Ballads, Blues and Swan Songs

The Great Good Place

AMERICAN EXPATRIATE WOMEN IN PARIS

William Wiser

W·W·NORTON & COMPANY
New York · London

Printed in the United States of America.

The text of this book is composed in Goudy Old Style
with the display set in L'Auriol.
Composition and manufacturing by the
Haddon Craftsmen Inc.
Book design by Jacques Chazaud.

First Edition.

Library of Congress Cataloging-in-Publication Data

Wiser, William
The great good place : American expatriate women in Paris / William Wiser.
p. cm.
Includes bibliographical references and index.
I. Title.
PS3573.I87G74 1991
813'.54—dc20 90-22763

ISBN 0-393-02999-9

W.W. Norton & Company, Inc., 500 Fifth Avenue, New York, N.Y. 10110
W.W. Norton & Company, Ltd., 10 Coptic Street, London WC1A 1PU

1 2 3 4 5 6 7 8 9 0

For my sister, Jean

Contents

Introduction

My first hotel in Paris was across rue Jacob from the mock Greek temple in Natalie Barney's enclosed garden, the Temple à l'Amitié, where, from the turn of the century through the twenties, Colette and the painter Romaine Brooks might meet, where the doomed spy Mata Hari entertained and Natalie Barney kept rendezvous with Oscar Wilde's niece, Dolly. One block away from my hotel was the rue Bonaparte hotel Janet Flanner referred to when she wrote for *The New Yorker:* "We settled in the small hotels on the Paris Left Bank near the Place St. Germain des Prés. . . ." A short walk across the boulevard St. Germain took me to the address of Shakespeare and Company, the congenial bookshop founded by Sylvia Beach. Before coming to Paris, a beginning writer that winter of 1960, I had worked in a Manhattan bookstore, which partly explains my attraction to Sylvia Beach, a dedicated purveyor of literature—and my admiration extended to her generosity of spirit as midwife to the masterpieces of James Joyce. From Shakespeare and Company, just the other side of the Jardin du Luxembourg, once lived another expatriate, Gertrude Stein, who caught my interest and held it all these years with her playfully original *Autobiography of Alice B. Toklas* which echoed pervasively whenever I attempted to perceive a Paris of my own.

In a first non-fiction work I wrote about these women, along with a kaleidoscopic cast of expatriates with an affinity for this city, who for reasons economic and artistic, as well as to live sexually liberated lives, chose exile in Paris. They have been written about extensively and in greater detail elsewhere, though perhaps the most rewarding testament to their lives was written by themselves—and I discovered that Gertrude Stein came more successfully to life when I cast her as a fictional character in a novel.

My research into the lives of these figures of the 1920s, and my personal acquaintance with contemporary expatriate women during my long sojourn in France (I live here still) led me to conclude that women, more so than male expatriates, came early to Paris and stayed late; they learned the language and made their adjustment to the French—assimilation is not so much at issue in Paris as adjustment to Parisians—married or formed liaisons here, died and were buried in exile.

Why did they come to Paris, what made them stay, how did the city affect their lives? Five women expatriates who passed the most critical or significant years of their lives in France engaged my interest and provoked these questions as I went looking for the common thread of connection to Paris, or to one another. There was no clear thread. I came to accept the truth of Hemingway's statement: "the memory of each person who has lived in Paris differs from that of any other," and learned that Paris was for each of these women a dramatic break with the commonplace: in the variety of their expatriate experiences, none lived in the same city.

In *fin-de-siècle* France, the painter Mary Cassatt was the expatriate pioneer of her time and gender: anomaly of anomalies, she was an American woman working with a radical group of independent male painters, the Impressionists. Her life and circumstances in Paris aroused my curiosity; I chose to write about her and also about another woman, patrician born, the writer Edith Wharton. Both were attracted early to the arts and to the relative freedom of Paris at a time when it was difficult for women to pursue independent aspirations at home, and few would risk the adventure abroad.

The generation of Mary Cassatt and Edith Wharton, the Age of Innocence, was shattered by World War I, its complacent protocol challenged by the younger, less inhibited twenties woman typified by Caresse Crosby. Less known than her death-haunted husband, Caresse Crosby was the loving wife and distracted mother who, in the delirious Paris of the twenties, attempted to share Harry Crosby's dilettante dreams along with his drug and sexual excesses. Later Caresse discovered her true vocation as a small-press publisher of avant-garde work, yet never quite escaped the influence of her late husband or the ethos of the 1920s.

Another twenties figure, remembered best as the wife of F. Scott Fitzgerald, Zelda Fitzgerald came to France not long after her marriage to the rising star of American letters; she watched her husband's star obscured and hoped to light up the heavens on her own. The art of the dance was for Zelda a desperate and ruinous obsession that came too late in middle age, then precipitated her tragic decline.

The most reluctant and unlikely visitor to Paris of any, Josephine Baker, came upon the same 1920s scene to make of the music-hall stage a medium of personal fulfillment and public acclaim. Josephine Baker's success was sustained during a lifetime in Paris, and the illiterate teenage chorus girl from St. Louis became the closest of any expatriate woman to a changeling hybrid Parisienne while remaining, as did the others, forever American.

In the Afterword to her novel *The Cubical City,* Janet Flanner makes a remark in her deeply felt yet offhand way: "I spent much of my adult life in France and thus know how true it is that humans from different civilized races and educations remain alien to each other, even in love." It occurs to me that this truth is a recurrent theme in these five alien lives, a truth I attempt to illustrate along with other themes, only as far and with whatever opportunities the literal record allows. Nevertheless, several scenes, interior thoughts, and spoken dialogues are pieced together from letters, memoirs, and random comment—gossip, that is—to dramatize those moments the archival records neglect for lack of data. Some authorities will quarrel with my method, for I cannot promise that any any of my quintet spoke or acted precisely as I have assumed she would in the undocumented instances. Biography has been called a novel that dare not speak its name; this novelist, a familiar of the streets and interiors of Paris, a student of its history and a congenital browser of the city's bookstalls along the Seine, has but his oblique approach to character and events to offer as credentials for a meddler's attention to these several lives.

Mary Cassatt in 1913,
when she was nearly blind,
and just before she stopped painting.

I

Mary Cassatt

1844–1926

There has never been a question of money.
I am very indifferent to that as I have
all the comforts I need and more money
than I feel I ought to have. France is still
the easiest and cheapest place to live in.

As young George Biddle bicycled through the wet-green untouched and placid terrain beyond Paris there echoed all the while an uneasy rumbling in the distance, like thunder. He pretended it *was* thunder—or tried to ignore the ominous reverberation to the northeast. He was traveling the countryside that brought to life the landscapes of Pissarro and Monet he had seen in Paris. The young American painter so valued his tentative acquaintance with Mary Cassatt, the *grande dame* of the Impressionists, that he was willing and even eager to risk a bicycle journey to visit her during this early critical moment of World War I. What he heard ahead of him was the sound of heavy artillery. The Somme offensive had begun, and the field of battle was dangerously close to Mesnil-Théribus and the château de Beaufresne.

At age seventy the primly unpredictable Mary Cassatt had taken on a kindly tolerance toward young American painters in France, though not necessarily tolerant of their work. Friendship with her was not an easy or natural process. To remain in the good graces of Cassatt called for another kind of tolerance on the part of the friend. Her illogical crotchets were known to the Paris art world, and young Biddle was as aware of her volatile temperament as of the thunder to the north.

When he first met her at the apartment in Paris (he would always think of the stately sedate rue Marignan as *her* street), she had rattled off a barrage of blunt comment about art and artists that could only excite the mind of a young and impressionable painter. Some of her opinions were outrageous—but not to young Biddle, who was trying to work up some original outrage of his own. He was frustrated by the balanced analytical insistence of his teachers so far: Mademoiselle

Cassatt's rigidly personal and instinctive approach to art was refreshing and invigorating. The very eccentricity of her mind and character inspired him . . . to what end? To think, and to paint—and that was everything.

Despite the span of years between them, Mary Cassatt was to George Biddle a natural and attractive force. In her presence, or standing before one of her oils (the bold blues and yellows of *The Boating Party,* with its odd but exciting Japanese composition, displaced for a moment the tender shades of green and strict double line of populars along the road), he knew she was, well, *grande.* The French term seemed more appropriate: she raged against the word "great," especially when applied to herself. How different she was from Gertrude Stein, whom George Biddle had also met, and who considered herself a genius. Mary Cassatt was a puzzle: why the repeated theme of mother and child from a painter who was not a mother and, in Paris, appeared to care only for her own mother? As far as he could tell she took only passing notice of children, if she noticed them at all, and then only for their possibilities as models. Incongruent as her character was, she was somehow an inspiration, and he would have given away a part of himself to be the painter she was. These thoughts impelled him on as he cycled through the war-threatened zone toward the village of Mesnil-Théribus.

Mary Cassatt herself, with her two sour-faced miniature dogs, met him at the graveled drive to her estate. The two agitated griffons yapped at his approach, but his hostess lifted a thin arm in greeting.

"They have taken Mathilde from me," she explained immediately. Mathilde was the servant closest to her during Mary Cassatt's expatriate years, and had now been expelled from France. "She is from Alsace, my Mathilde, and technically, the way they see it, a German national. That is their notion of winning the war, sending off our foreign domestics who might be enemy spies."

She did not often smile, but smiled now as her stern features came alive in greeting. The hand she extended was long and thin and vibrant with electric force.

The young man dismounted. The griffons snapped nastily at his heels as he held his bicycle upright with one hand and took the old woman's strong painter's hand in the other. It was the French style of formal embrace—the two spoke English together, but if they had spoken French he would have used the *vous* form of respect and the title "Mademoiselle." His thought was that he could love her ("love" was the word, and he would record this in his journal), truly love this Philadelphia spinster if it were possible, if one could love with a purely detached enthusiasm in the way he loved Paris, as he loved art.

On her side, Mary Cassatt took a strong and lively interest in these late-blooming liaisons with the young. The young were so spontaneously affectionate; but not she, she had not herself had time to be young. Or she could not remember being young in the easy insouciant way they were. She understood his facade of guarded respect: his hand trembled with suppressed feeling while hers remained firm. The young man's attachment brought on strong sensations in her breast, rekindled ancient fires. She reflected on the varieties of love, love as it was then and now. She had indulged the same adulation for Manet, from afar, then Degas at closer range. She loved France, above all Paris, though she had become impatient with the French; she indulged a nostalgia for the United States but guarded few illusions about the country of her birth. Art, the love of her family, had taken up so much room—was that not as much love as we are allowed in a lifetime?

Although she was obliged to ration the time spent with acquaintances, American or French—just as she must carefully spare her failing eyes—she could allow for special dispensation in this instance. The occasion called for a respite from her customary discipline. Mr. George Biddle had begun his studies at her own school, the Philadelphia Academy of Arts; the Biddles were known to the Cassatts—families were important, background did mean something—the old values were handed down through the ranks of good families. (Degas had been an example of superior breeding, but those inherited qualities of refinement were spoiled by the man's excessive self-assurance, and finally arrogance of spirit.) This young Biddle was in Paris to devote himself to painting, his gifts as yet to show themselves; but he was young, and devotion counted for much.

Time was running out. She had become seventy without quite knowing how, the past swallowed up in work. No matter that time slipped away so treacherously, one must get on with the job. Did the faint cannonade in the background mean that the Germans had crossed the Somme? She needed Beaufresne as a sanctuary at this period in her life; she needed the tranquil work time away from Paris. The war had got in her way, but she intended to stand fast. Only an invading army could drive her from her easel: any day now the military authorities would clear this region of resident civilians and not even her longstanding friendship with Clemenceau would spare her from the general evacuation.

But right now Mr. Biddle was here to see her. She would bring up from the *cave* a rare bottle of wine for the occasion, a Château Margaux from the case her brother Aleck had sent.

There was what appeared to be a greenhouse on the grounds, but it was a kind of glassed-in hangar, with ropes that dangled from pulleys into a deep trench: it was in this outdoor studio that Mary Cassatt had painted the massive mural triptych for the Women's Pavillion at the Chicago Exposition. Had she worked the heavy rope pulls herself, George Biddle wondered—the hearty handshake he received from her suggested that she had.

As his hostess moved ahead of him, leaning slightly against her cane (but otherwise with rigid dignity, as stiff as the cane itself), the young man felt a sensation of emptiness once they had moved past the door into the foyer. She led him through barren rooms—too many rooms for one aged infirm artist slowly going blind—rooms with stark white walls, but walls admirably suited to the several Cassatt works he glimpsed in transit: children, in the arms of their nursemaids or mothers, as if to tenant the empty rooms with "her" children. There was her first version of *The Boating Party,* an engraving in the Japanese manner, and several original Japanese prints which had inspired her gravures. She had also shrewdly and passionately collected her fellow Impressionists—no paintings as far as he could observe by Degas (those were in the apartment in Paris), but there was a Pissarro that reminded him of the countryside he had just passed through. The paintings—except for the works of Mary Cassatt herself, which seemed to call for a bourgeois setting—showed to so much better effect in this spacious château than in the overfurnished apartment on the rue Marignan.

"Sixteen hectares, that would be about forty acres," she explained, defining the extent of her private domain, once the family seat of l'Amiral de Grasse. "He was, you know, a most valued ally of the Yankees in that famous victory at Yorktown."

No, admitted young Biddle, he did not know.

"Then you did not know that his own countrymen arrested him on his return, for some so-called misadventure in the Indies."

During lunch it had become apparent to George Biddle that Mary Cassatt, for all her years—most of her adult life—spent in France, had developed an aversion to the French. His own wary attitude toward the Parisians he had met, the awkwardness of getting on with the Gallic temperament, corresponded only in part to her situation and sentiments—but her distaste had developed over a longer span, and ran deeper. She must in the beginning have been charmed by all that was French, as he had been, and especially charmed by the city of Paris at first sight. Something in the American character was at odds with the French temperament, and yet the original enchantment persisted. Becoming a permanent resident but never a *concitoyen* was the common fate of long-term expatriates here. Nevertheless, expatriates seemed oddly comfortable and perversely resigned to the ambivalence France aroused in them.

The young man had come to Paris in the midst of an artistic ferment that excited yet repelled him, and he was encouraged by his hostess to admit to his confusion: "Their Matisse?" she asked him narrowly, "and this Picasso?"

"Yes. I mean, I don't know . . . " He confessed to a dislike of the jackrabbit art scene in Paris at the moment: "Leaping and darting in every direction. In search only of the unexpected and anxious only to leave the pack panting heavily up the wrong scent."

Though she smiled approvingly at his example, Mary Cassatt did not know about *that.* "The pack, in my day, followed no scent at all. They panted heavily after whatever l'Ecole des Beaux-Arts insisted was the proper direction. I have known French art at its best, and then it is very good indeed. You can ignore their talk about art. That is what does them in, these revolutionaries in art, the talk. You are seeing the decline of what the Impressionists properly began. I was part of that, but never part of the talk, except with Degas." She paused; her sharp gaze faded and the sight-dimmed eyes turned inward. "They talked, oh the talk, but I did not. They met at the Guerbois and such cafés in Montmartre and the only women present were *grisettes* or they thought of you as a *grisette* if you went there. Or models sat with with them in the cafés, but not I." For all her condemnation of the café scene, George Biddle's eyes were alight; he was thinking what it must have been like to be part of all that. His young man's disillusionment with the new art in France was very likely premature; his regret was having been born too late to experience the glorious time of the Café Guerbois.

"If the passion was oftentimes drained away in café talk," she went on, "there was always the work. Work was everything then. The work was what earned our respect and *our* respect was the only thing that counted. The *pompiers* of the Academy were being displaced, finally, and there we were."

An idle thought passed through the young man's mind that the Impressionists were now the Old Guard, and the younger painters were bent on displacing *them,* but he dismissed this heresy in the excitement of her declaration. By remaining silent he was urging her on. She spoke of the Impressionists, of Pissarro, "a dear man, he was loved by all, and like myself not technically French—which may have been his saving grace—Danish, I believe, and a Jew. An anarchist Jew, but a sweetness of heart in his socialist notions. Degas turned against him. That was Degas for you, he vilified poor Pissarro. *Pissarro,* our founding father—but that was how hateful Degas could be. He was the best of us, after all."

He did not know if she was referring to Pissarro or Degas as "the best of us" nor when she said "those marvelous hands" (pausing to look at the backs of her own hard-worked hands) whose hands she meant. She had gone into reverie again, then swiftly she returned to the luncheon table and urged more eggplant on her guest. A vegetarian herself, she nevertheless served lunch in the French tradition, including a perfectly prepared viande despite wartime austerity. The dogs had been allowed into the dining room and scrambled beneath the table at the young man's feet, scenting the cutlet on his plate. The eggplant was an American legume, not yet cultivated in France: Mary Cassatt was tenacious in her American tastes.

"My brother Aleck sends me seeds. He would send over Virginia ham and canvasback duck when I was still a meat-eater. I have corn, which the French know nothing about except as cattle fodder." The roses she grew in such abundance were as close to American varieties as she could cultivate at Beaufresne. "And apples, alas, no more." She would ration the apples to herself and others, that delightful windfall from Aleck, a nostalgic sample of home. "He would send a basket of winesap apples at Christmas. The war, of course, has ended the shipments of that dear bounty."

Her brother, George Biddle recalled, was president of the Pennsylvania Railroad.

From apples and corn she shifted to the Dreyfus Affair: "Disgraceful. It brought out the worst side of Degas, it showed him at his most vile. We stopped speaking. I am not for the Jews, but I cannot abide injustice." It was difficult to keep her on the subject, for Mary Cassatt's mind circled and digressed through a kaleidoscope of memories only she could reassemble, and pertinent only to her. Since she had mentioned Degas, George Biddle attempted to interject a question.

"Wasn't Degas your teacher?"

"My dear boy, the Louvre was my teacher. The Louvre was the first most important teacher of us all. And nature was, for the Barbizon painters—but I was never drawn to landscape, nor was Degas. But Degas, yes—he was an important moment in my life." Ever so briefly her eyes slipped back into that moment, then returned. "He was the first to recognize what I had attempted to do. He *knew.* It was he, you know, who invited me to show with the Impressionists. The Louvre was my first teacher. Degas was . . . later."

She was looking at her hands again, and he wondered about the stories he had heard in Paris. Even as she spoke about Degas's shabby behavior there was that inward turning of her eyes, and he could almost believe her eyes had moistened. They had not: Mary Cassatt refused to allow herself this sentimental indulgence. The inevitable question: "Was he ever your lover?" could not be asked of her, ever. The rumor was that she had burned his letters, and he hers. The young man would like to have known if this were true, but of course could never put such a question to his gracious but steel-willed hostess. Anyway, she was talking again, about the Steins.

"They came to Paris poor and without connections, but they are not Jews for nothing." She had mistaken the brother and sister, Leo and Gertrude Stein, for man and wife, and was also in error about their wealth and connections, but George Biddle saw no reason to offer correction. He knew Gertrude Stein, and was intrigued by her and her collection of art, though it would be inappropriate to say so.

"No sound artist ever looked except with scorn at these Cubists and Matisse. The Steins have bought up Matisse's pictures cheap and now pose as amateurs of the only real art. *Arrivistes* and speculators are what they are, and that is what rules the art market today." She snapped her fingers to dismiss them, and hardly paused for breath or reflection before going on: "Forty years ago when Degas and Monet, Renoir and I first exhibited, the public did not understand. Only the elite bought, and time has proved their taste correct. This Gertrude Stein wears sandals on her feet as a novelty, for she has discovered novelty only."

She was fumbling with her lace collar, then took one of the homely little dogs into her lap to fondle it behind the ears. "He found a breeder of Belgian griffons for me, he brought me flowers when my leg was broken, he once said, 'I will not admit that a woman can draw so well.' "

These thoughts—was she speaking of Degas?—and a jumble of remembered slights and old resentments had come to dominate her philosophy and sour her last years of exile in France. This time Biddle was certain her eyes, for one vulnerable moment, had filled. As he watched her softly touch each eye in turn with her folded napkin, George Biddle felt a surge of affection for this prim old Philadelphia spinster.

He ate his cake, Philadelphia White Mountain Cake—Lord, where had she got it?—and drank down the aged vintage in the drafty dining hall to the thump and rumble of cannon fire. He risked no blunt inquiries of his touchy hostess: her briefly moist eyes were no indication of easy sentiment. Mary Cassatt had long learned to keep herself to herself, her sentiments in check. The ruffled collar came to the hard line of chin, white curls showed beneath a quaint dust cap, she continued to hold herself rigorously erect.

Mary Cassatt, of the Huguenot Cossarts, however genetically tempered by the distant French strain, was of stern Puritan-American stock. The corset of self-control was her pride. Prints and paintings, the work and collection of a lifetime, hung a little to one side of the middle distance: the young man had only an oblique awareness of the art works as he sipped the rare Bordeaux and fingered the crumbs of his cake and contemplated emptiness, the vast unpainted space surrounding one sight-dimmed determined *grande dame.*

ii

Robert Cassatt was a restless success in the New World tradition, moving out of house after house and selling the property for a profit every time. For two years he had been mayor of Allegheny City, where Mary was born in 1844. The Cassatts moved across the river to Pittsburgh (Mother complained of the soot, how do you keep five children clean in Pittsburgh?), then to a farm in Lancaster County where the children took to horses like red Indians—especially little Mary.

Until the family moved to France, Mary found childhood a boring and monotonous prospect. Her father noticed that she was quiet as a rabbit in company, her thoughts her own. She fought with her brothers—even with Aleck, the oldest and her favorite—when the boys tried to put something over on her. Mary was no tomboy, she cared about clothes, but she did seem to prefer the company of boys, and she rode as well as Aleck for her age. She seemed to want to get her growing-up years over with and to turn to something serious enough to match the serious expression she habitually wore.

The Cassatts would of course go to Europe. The frontier spirit is only one side of the American character: a sense of the abandoned past lingers in the psyche, a perpetual conundrum that can only be solved by reattaching the missing link of lineage. The original French name was Cossart. The enterprising Robert Cassatt had been a successful man, by the lights of Philadelphia, and now determined to revisit with his wife and five children their obscure place of origin.

Robert Cassatt's plans were vague, the length of their stay indefinite—another difficult uprooting for his wife. As he saw it, the spa waters abroad would do wonders for little Robbie, sickly and fragile, and for older sister Lydia of equally delicate constitution (Mother had lost two babies within a month of birth—but then little Mary, tough as Pittsburgh steel, had survived). The Old World was medically advanced, far ahead of Philadelphia's quacks and cranks. An education at foreign schools would impress the Panjamdrums on Wall

Street when the time came for the boys to be brokers, like himself. His wife would get some good out of all those French lessons she took for so long—from a Parisian teacher, too. As for Mary, she'd benefit from travel as well, even at age seven; languages and culture never hurt a girl's prospects. Who would have thought that Mary, of all the children, would become miserably sick aboard ship? Her father advised her that seasickness was all in the mind, but Mary recovered only when her feet touched terra firma at Le Havre.

The trip by boat-train through the north of France restored Mary's enchantment with the prospect ahead. Paris was to be the largest and longest-lasting excitement of her young life.

The second half of the nineteenth century had just begun when the Cassatts settled into the antique luxury of the Hôtel Continental. Her father liked to walk the streets of Paris alone, and Mary would have loved to explore those streets of central Paris along with him, but she caught her own Alice-in-Wonderland flavor of Paris from the floor-to-ceiling hotel windows or in fiacres with her mother, from behind the fat rumps of cab horses. On foot, her mother took her for short excursions on rue Castiglione to the jewel-box enclosure of the place Vendôme, or the opposite way to the Tuileries Gardens, where she was treated to tame pony rides through the dappled light beneath ancient trees planted to shade royalty. Along the graveled walks she puzzled over the monumental statuary, stone gods and goddesses illustrating a mythical past she knew nothing of, and was just as curious about flesh-and-blood creatures in extravagant costumes, especially the lavishly feathered hats of the women, sharing the pathways with her. She lingered beside the *bassins* where schoolboys in blue smocks with identical berets set their toy craft afloat on the tranquil waters of an oval pool. Their concentrated play and incomprehensible babble made her feel shy and alone until Robbie was given a boat to sail in the *bassin,* and would sometimes share with her—but little girls did not sail boats, they clutched their dolls close and watched their brothers sail boats. What she dearly loved was to watch the flash and color of *la garde Républicaine* with their burnished helmets pass the gardens, and the clatter of their magnificent steeds down the rue de Rivoli. One morning the dashing parade did not take place and Mary wondered if it were a holiday.

Next day her father came in from his morning leg-stretching constitutional to announce to the family with some fervor: "Well, Louis's done it!"

Done what? Mary wondered. The streets were abuzz with the news, and although Robert Cassatt had difficulty taking in the simplest phrase in French he could not fail to understand that Louis Napoléon had declared a bloodless coup d'état and pronounced himself emperor of France. Robert Cassatt approved: he liked a man of spirit and grit.

Despite the lip service paid to the sentiment of liberté-egalité-fraternité, France's heritage from the Revolution, there persisted a streak of aristocratic nostalgia in the French. In 1852 Louis Napoléon responded to that nostalgia, and offered the further promise of a return to the glories of half a century before, the golden era of his uncle Napoléon Premier. The Cassatts had arrived in France at a stirring moment. Mary Cassatt was a child witness to the complete transformation of the city of Paris, though her immediate concern, at age eight, was that the Tuileries might now be barred to the public and the gardens revert to the private domain of the royal family.

Baron Georges-Eugène Haussmann was appointed préfet de la Seine by Louis Napoléon, and thenceforth Mr. Cassatt's wide-ranging promenades on the Right Bank of the Seine would alter daily. Haussmann, according to the Parisians of his time and since, was either a far-sighted genius or a demonic assassin of historic Paris. He was of a new breed of urbanist, detached from nostalgia and directed more by pragmatic than aesthetic considerations. He surely understood but discounted the great loss of much of the unplanned beauty of Paris, the loss of the very spirit of the ancient city.

More objectively, the imperial city planner was a relentless and sometimes reckless force, with his ambitions and obsessions for the grand vista. His was an eye for sweep and grandeur in rectilinear perspective. He envisioned mass transit and controlled traffic; he boldly cut through the heart of the city with spacious arteries of majestic parade. He saw to the outward-opening of the Grand-Châtelet area to the boulevard de Sébastopol, and at the same time created two ornate theatres (still in operation) where Mary's mother and father attended the spectacles of the day—but the theatre was not the place for the younger Cassatts, and Mary glimpsed only the scaffolding of the monumental fountain in the center of the square and the stone facades of the two flanking theatres as she passed with her mother in horse-cab excursions down the rue de Rivoli.

Haussmann created the unbroken line of identical appartment buildings on both sides of wide boulevards, with their *bombé* zinc roofs and unadorned stone facades replacing the eighteenth-century and medieval structures to achieve the unity of design most comforting to the sensibility of the *haute bourgeoisie.* Robert Cassatt was in favor of such progress and might have wanted Haussmann to do the same for Pittsburgh and Philadelphia.

The gradually recreated city was the Paris Mary Cassatt would adopt and love and contend with—a vista essentially fixed, except for Eiffel's tower added at the turn of the century—for the remainder of her life there. As a child she had only glimpsed the antique Paris Haussmann had marked for annihilation. At midcentury she was looking on with her large serious eyes at the before and after. She watched from the steps at the end of the Tuileries as the moats around the place de la Concorde were filled in, and the ring of ornate gas lamps added (the touch that gave Paris the title of City of Light). Where her mother had first shopped, until the Cassatts engaged a cook, in the menacing quarter of les Halles with its brooding fortress walls and stone colonnades around the executioner's square, Haussmann had the happy thought to open the marketplace to light and air by way of Baltard's ironwork hangars—or rather, the imperial city planner abided by the injunction of Louis Napoléon himself: "What we need [at les Halles] are parasols." Under the sheltering spanned ironwork, with her mother, or later in the company of a servant or cook, Mary experienced the crowded chaos of the marketplace, the geometrical design of fruit stalls and pyramids of *légumes,* carcasses of beef and sheep, and the daintier arrangements of cheeses and *charcuterie,* the central market Zola would call "the belly of Paris."

Much of what Haussmann accomplished was of enduring utility and harmonious splendor: several of the sweeping stone spans across the

Seine were his doing, as was the graceful garden edge of Notre Dame where a great mass of ivy trails down a sheer wall to the water. Haussmann's intent may have been aesthetic in principle, in the debatable taste of a self-proclaimed royal court, but the strategy behind much of his urban renewal was Louis Napoléon's desire to avoid counterrevolution by shifting certain troublesome neighborhoods "of the people" to outlying districts where the paving-stone barricades of the working class would have little effect. This Haussmann accomplished brilliantly by razing many of the sixteenth- and seventeenth-century dwellings of laborers and artisans that honeycombed the heart of Paris. The central arteries of the city became wide boulevards intersecting at monumental focal points like l'Etoile and the place de la Nation. The popular neighborhoods, with their troublemaking *ouvriers,* and the poor, were now dispersed into smaller and more manageable units. The broad new avenues could accommodate entire troops of gendarmes and were thus more easily policed.

Before the police department could push ahead with its gruesome and altogether inappropriate decision to place the city morgue at that loveliest of points, the tip of the Ile de la Cité where the Seine divides into two gracefully confluent streams; and before Haussmann could reach beyond the newly constructed spans (bridges worthy of a better man) to dissect then blight further sections of the Left Bank, the enterprising baron was dismissed by the emperor. His downfall, Robert Cassatt would note sourly, was fiscal mismanagement—when finances, according to the Philadelphia financier, should have been the primary consideration of this far-sighted pragmatist.

The changes wrought by the city planner's conception of Paris would profoundly affect Mary Cassatt's future. Beauty had been declared and carried out by fiat. During Haussmann's tenure and because of his official enterprise in recreating a vast imaginative cityscape with municipal funds, the Parisian bureaucracy won its overwhelming dominance in deciding matters artistic. Not only would the city of Paris take on the physical appearance approved by the administration, but l'Ecole des Beaux-Arts would henceforth determine the standards of art by which painters would be obliged to conform or else languish in obscurity.

Upper-middle-class standards were the acceptable criteria of the day, but artists have a way of undermining the acceptable and the official. In the bosky groves near Fontainebleau, a dissident band known as the Barbizon painters had broken with the frozen traditions of the Beaux-Arts and in defiance of the abiding committee-approved classicism, a break that was to lead to a splendid detour in the nineteenth-century direction of French art. This bloodless coup was unknown to the apprentice artist Edgar De Gas, ten years older than Mary Cassatt, completing his final year at the prestigious Lycée Louis-le-Grand, winning notice but no prizes for his first sketches taken from plaster models the school provided.

Meanwhile, the American child knew nothing of art except for the oil portrait of the boys commissioned by Robert Cassatt just before the family left for France. The girls, Lydia and Mary, were not included in the portrait, which gave Mary an opportunity to watch and reflect: the little girl was fascinated by the performance of an indifferent Philadelphia artist, James Reid Lamdin, dabbing at his palette with a brush, then rendering the frozen likenesses of her brothers on a square of canvas. Yes, her brothers were the focus of the painter's eye, but she was a fascinated child-gazer absorbed by the process.

iii

At ten the eyes were wide and intense, with a shade of the adult in her guarded stare. She did not smile often, and did not smile now, for the camera. The small, sharp chin would grow all the more pointed and determined. She never liked her photographs, and had no intention of looking back on her static childhood except for this one image: the little girl with braids looped in twin beribboned whorls, German-style—the photograph was taken in Heidelberg. She saved this one snapshot, perhaps because it reminded her of the time Robbie was still alive.

Her father had taken his brood to Germany in 1854, first to Heidelberg where he commissioned a second family portrait-sketch in pencil, including the girls this time, then to Darmstadt, an up-and-coming steel town like Pittsburgh, to investigate the best schools for Aleck and to find a proper doctor for Robbie who was suffering from a disease of the knee joint. The clinics, the doctors, were of no use—in Darmstadt Robbie died of his mysterious ailment. He was buried there "far from home" (though it was difficult to know where "home" was), and Mary suffered the loss of her little brother harder and longer than anyone knew. It was all the more grievous to leave him behind in another country, buried in foreign soil.

For reasons as mixed and now obscure as his purpose in coming to France in the first place, Robert Cassatt brought his family back to Pennsylvania. During the years when the United States was torn asunder by a bloody civil war, the adolescent Mary Cassatt tamely resigned herself to the Pennsylvania Academy of Fine Arts. She did not enter the study of art because it was a fashionable and respectable pursuit for young women; she actually applied for admission to the Academy at the earliest possible date for fall and looked forward to the prospect with rare enthusiasm. Robert Cassatt shared her enthusiasm; he was aware that a young woman's marriage opportunities were greatly enhanced by a gift for drawing and a delicate touch with the watercolor brush. But his teenage daughter was not in the least interested in adding these female accomplishments to the domestic arts.

Mary had caught the mysterious fever for art from that first sojourn in Paris. Even from a child's naive perspective, the Louvre was a picture palace of awesome complexity and rare delight; her glimpses of the streets of Paris, the style of Parisian interiors, further conditioned her dawning sense of color and design. It remained unclear how she might have been affected or inspired by the minor artists engaged by her father to produce those early likenesses, but she had been in Paris in 1855 during the celebrated Exposition Universelle, and even at nine years of age she could not have failed to hear of the furor aroused by the exhibition of more than five thousand "approved" paintings. It was in France that she first learned art could be an exciting cultural issue: that the rivalry of Ingres and Delacroix for the gold medals awarded by Louis Napoléon was an item of widespread newspaper coverage as well as for the salon gossip of *le tout Paris.* The public took sides in the scandal over Gustave Courbet's Pavillon du Réalisme, the artist's defiant sideshow built at his own expense next door to the Palais des Beaux-Arts. Here Courbet flaunted a one-man show of some fifty of his paintings, including *L'Atelier du peintre,* rejected by the conservative Exposition jury. The Pavillon du Réalisme became the true center and vital meeting place of those young talents outside traditional acceptance by the Academy: for all his love of the formal beauty expressed by Ingres, the young beginner Edgar De Gas prowled these unholy precincts, finding the subversive work of Courbet exciting and passionate in ways that strict classicism could not offer.

At first Mary Cassatt must have believed that the same passion for art would pervade Philadelphia's official sanctuary for painters. The central hall of the Pennsylvania Academy was a copy of the French Panthéon, as if this architectural duplication might invoke the institutionalized glory of its counterpart, a monument and mausoleum for the illustrious dead. Classrooms were the repositories of plaster casts and dried paint, anatomical charts and dust. Women were reluctantly permitted the study of anatomy from the works of Vesalius and Gray, but drawing from the live male or female model would have been too shocking for young women students. Beginning students of either gender were required to master the drawing of finite details in repeated exercises that were a reminder of primary school penmanship classes. Early on, Mary Cassatt showed her impatience with the cramped academic approach by taking up brushwork on her own (at her stage of instruction, the use of oils was forbidden) to make a beginner's copy of one of the heads in Wittkamp's crowded depiction of *The Deliverance of Leyden.*

Her contemporary, the American artist Thomas Eakins, was also a student at the Philadelphia Academy (and for a short time taught there, but was fired for keeping corpses in his atelier), so Mary Cassatt was not alone in her frustration with the rigidity of attitudes toward the study of art. Nor did her contemporaries in Paris—Monet, Renoir, Cézanne, Bazille, Jongkind from Holland, and the Englishman Sisley—escape the labor under this same uninspired drill. Their fathers subsidized the apprenticeship with far more reluctance than Robert Cassatt, for the choice of painting as a career for a son was considered the most frivolous of intentions. Invariably the hard requirement was that the son study with an acceptable maître sanctioned by the Académie des Beaux-Arts, or family support would be withdrawn immediately.

The banker Auguste De Gas, descendant of both French and Italian nobility, relented early to his son's determination to make painting instead of the law his life's work, but it was with bitterness and infinite regret that he arranged for the funds necessary to allow Edgar to study as he wished. The young De Gas enrolled at l'Ecole des Beaux-Arts as he was required to do, but he was seldom seen at classes or in the official ateliers. He did frequent the cafés where rebellious young talents let off steam after studio hours, and he paid constant homage and drew illimitable instruction from the masterpieces in the Louvre. "The Louvre!" shouted Fantin-Latour, urging Renoir to copy there. "The Louvre! There is only the Louvre!" But Philadelphia had no Louvre, and Mary Cassatt was without that close company of young artists except for her friend Eliza Haldeman: the two, along with other female students at the Academy, were called upon to stitch together, apparently as part of their artistic instruction, an enormous American flag.

As Mary Cassatt turned into a slim and graceful young woman, she found herself as bored with the swains of Pennsylvania as she had been by her childhood. Though she dressed exceedingly well, in the latest Paris mode (her mother was the model for that, her father provided the money), she was not pretty in the conventional way, and she knew this. The young men she met on strained and formal occasions found her dauntingly outspoken, and they did not wish to challenge her a second time. Her father's strategy of allowing Mary's artistic graces to develop as a matrimonial enticement was misguided.

The older daugther, Lydia, tended to be a homebody—and that was fine with Robert Cassatt. No, Mary was not pretty, nor was she winningly conversant enough with young men to show promise of imminent wedlock. A pity, but she had her art lessons as an attractive distraction. Now that the two boys had ventured onto paths of great expectation in a business way—Aleck was starting out with the Pennsylvania Railroad, Gardner into banking—their father was easing into the mental comfort of affairs taken care of and a future secure. He further enjoyed the Victorian pleasure of having three women (Mary perhaps his secret favorite of the three) to look after him, and up to him, at home.

At the Pennsylvania Academy, Mary Cassatt may have acquired a rudimentary sense of craft and an accommodation to scheduled discipline, but her schooling constituted the closest possible experience to the cloistered life. The French windows at the Hôtel Continental that had permitted her to look out into the rue Castiglione to the Jardin des Tuileries were a fixed but distant memory of Paris otherwise lost to her; meanwhile she breathed only the Academy's dust.

The history of Impressionist art is something of the history of fathers versus sons, and one daughter. Robert Cassatt was at his newspaper, spectacles low on the bridge of his nose. His wife, who had been allowed in her day to take up the daring study of French, attempted to intercede on Mary's behalf, speaking up guardedly in her daughter's defense. Mary's determination was reflected in her expression, with the scowl that contributed to her reputation as crab-apple "sour," and the sharp chin in its defiant projection set against her all-powerful father and his newspaper.

"I do not wish to continue at the Academy," she announced, the charcoal traces of drawing class still on her fingertips. "There is no teaching, it is useless, and I am unhappy there. I want to study art on my own. In Paris."

"I would rather," he said, without looking up from his newsprint, "see you dead."

iii

"Miss Cassatt and I are about as 'forte' as any there taken all and all, and we really have more prospect of improving rapidly than they have. . . ." Eliza Haldeman was writing to her father from Paris, 1866: "they" were the other students at Charles Chaplin's atelier, where Mary Cassatt and Eliza Haldeman were permitted by their fathers to study. Breaking down Robert Cassatt's resistance had been a tedious process, and the success set the standard of persistence and determination by which Mary Cassatt would work henceforth. She had got to Paris that way, and into an acceptable atelier: even the dreadful seasickness she suffered on the New York–Le Havre voyage was worth the stubborn campaign.

The young women were naturally under the restrictions their fathers imposed: they were to study with a recognized maître at an atelier approved by the Académie; and the French painters—still unknown to Mary, for none of her later associates studied with Chaplin—were under the same obligation to their fathers, and had waged an even more difficult campaign to earn the right to paint at all. Camille Pissarro had twice run away from home in St. Thomas, the Danish West Indies, before his father gave in to the meager allowance that would permit his son a limited period of study in Paris. Paul Cézanne, awkward, introverted iconoclast from Provence, won begrudging permission from his banker father to give up the study of law for painting. Also from the South, Frédéric Bazille was allowed to enter the Gleyre studio with his father's strict proviso that he spend at least half time at his original choice of career in medicine. When Claude Monet was called up for military service, his father offered to buy him out, that is, to pay for a substitute who would volunteer in his place if he would renounce "dabbling in paint" altogether. Oddly enough, Monet was actually drawn to the dash and spirit of soldiering and the adventure of being posted in North Africa, but by 1862 he fell ill in Algiers and was obliged to return to metropolitan France for a period of recuperation. During Monet's convalescence (cared for by Bazille in the region of Barbizon, where the two painted in the woods together) his father was finally convinced of the young man's resolve and so decided to buy him out of military service with the injunction: "I will do this only if you agree to attend an atelier under the discipline of a well-known and established master. At the very first hint you have resumed your 'independence,' I swear I will cut you off without another centime."

When these sons of the bourgeoisie set off for the ateliers of Paris they had, by this gesture alone, made the first substantial break with their fathers. Mary Cassatt had no such family rupture in mind. She was devoted to her father yet traditionally conditioned to a father's final and decisive word: she need only convince Robert Cassatt of the rightness of her determination. She meant to please rather than defy him—to please, in her unorthodox fashion, by way of artistic accomplishment.

"Miss Cassatt and I are friends again. We met at the door of the Louvre one day . . . took a walk on neutral ground [the garden of the

Tuileries] and had a talk." There were gaps and breaks in any friendship with Mary Cassatt, and Eliza Haldeman had discovered how touchy her temperamental companion might be. But that day in the Tuileries the two women were reunited after a spat. They chose to be companions again, for they could not very well have continued on alone in Paris, and celebrated their renewed friendship by the odd ceremony of observing the French, on the feast of Toussaint, place bouquets and wreaths against the solemn upright mausoleums of Père Lachaise Cemetery.

Mary Cassatt's letters from this period are scarce, but her friend wrote regularly to both her own and Mary's family, and gave spirited accounts such as a typical Sunday dinner: "First soup, cant say what kind as french soups are always a mysterious compound. Then what they call boeuf braisé or stewed with beans and radishes. Next goose done with olives, next a hare and peas. We had a cream cake for dessert, fruit and raisins and after that cheese and wine, after all café noire." Often Eliza referred to Mary's illnesses, possibly a result of such elaborate cuisine. One letter, during a long week's constant illness, reflects Mary's certainty of mind: "Mary wishes to be remembered to you, she laughed when I told her your message and said she wanted to be *better* than the old masters."

By 1868 Eliza Haldeman was making pronouncements on the Parisian art scene, speaking of the French school going through a phase. "They are leaving the academy style and each one seeking a new way consequently everything is Chaos." The chaos had begun in 1863 while both young women were still at the Philadelphia Academy. That year the Salon jury had seen fit to exclude over four thousand paintings, and the murmurs of indignation had reached the imperial throne. Here was a disturbing element not even a philistine emperor could ignore: his majesty decided to review the rejected works personally. In the royal opinion, many of the paintings excluded from the official show were as good as those selected for the Salon, therefore he decreed that the entire lot of rejects be given a separate exhibit, called the *Salon des Refusés:* let the public be the judge. This show was of course a scattershot display ranging from competent work to the raggedly amateur, from the eccentric to the manic, but—Louis Napoléon's taste aside—there were also works of genuine merit far superior to most of the Salon choices. The Salon of the Rejected became a democratic forum, however limited and sometimes laughable, for non-conforming artists of fresh new vision and personal flair. It did not enter Mary Cassatt's mind to participate in any exhibit that bore the onus of rejection.

At this stage, she was single-mindedly concerned with recognition by the official Salon she had worked two years to enter. In 1868 she succeeded. This first artistic acknowledgement by the Salon des Beaux-Arts encouraged her as much as her guarded nature allowed; both she and Eliza Haldeman had paintings accepted for the Exposition. The belief that the exhibit was unusually poor that year ("as there has [sic] been 1200 more pictures accepted than usual in fact almost anything would have passed") largely undercut their accomplishment, and Eliza went on gamely to admit, "Mary has also been successful even more so than I as her picture is well hung." By this, her friend meant that *La Mandoline*—portrait-study by Mlle Stevenson (for reasons of her own, Mary chose to sign her mother's maiden name to that first canvas)—was hung on-the-line, at eye level, rather than closer to the ceiling where Eliza Haldeman's entry was part of the chock-a-block display, one frame touching the next in a crowded mass of color rising past the notice of viewers.

Meanwhile, a certain degree of calculated socializing with the gentlemen of the press and other useful elements of the art world appeared to be a necessary strategy for a young painter attempting a breakthrough in Paris. Mary Cassatt did, through Eliza's friend Mrs. Simmons, meet a man named Ryan on *The New York Times* who wrote a brief but favorable notice of *La Mandoline.* It was doubtful, in the light of Eliza's comment, that Mary actually cultivated Mr. Ryan for his usefulness: "Mary calls it moral depravement, for really talking oneself into the opinion of the Publick is not the most genteel of occupations."

Although Mary Cassatt's first unveiling to the public was an apprentice work, unexceptional in technique, *La Mandoline* did show an attempt at psychological insight in her portrayal of the sad peasant girl with mandolin—a work she accomplished under the direction of the painter Thomas Couture, an academic genre painter who had nevertheless distanced himself from the Academy, at least by several kilometers to the north of Paris in the Barbizon region. This shift of maîtres was an initial tentative dissatisfaction with Chaplin's florid conformity, though she did at first accept Chaplin's advice to paint an academic nude with gravy-stained palette for Salon approval—it was rejected, that first nude, and Mary Cassatt would never paint another.

Instead of the disciplined attendance at the Chaplin atelier, Mary had by now turned for instruction to the Louvre—"the greatest art teacher in the world," she wrote her father. Haussmann had added two flanking wings to the Louvre, on the quai du Louvre and along the rue de Rivoli, vastly increasing the scale and wall space of the museum. She wandered the kilometers of parquet flooring transported from one century to the next, feeling a strange visual rapport with artists who had come before her: the Louvre was forever that hallowed temple of Parisian culture. She registered for a permit to copy there. Sisley, Bazille, and Renoir were copying at the Louvre, as was De Gas, his name now written as Degas, already a youthful cynic but one who had found the galleries of the Palais du Louvre a private sanctuary in the midst of public treasure, an art student's second home.

Of the group of young radical painters who met regularly at the Brasserie des Martyrs, only Monet found the exercise of copying indoors too confining and not to his purpose: he painted exclusively out of doors. Monet was the natural heir to the Barbizon *plein air* painters, a student of the effect of light in nature with an affinity for depciting the luminous reflections of water surfaces. For a time Mary Cassatt also pursued the exercise of *plein air* painting, exploring the countryside around Paris, especially in the Barbizon region. She settled with Eliza Haldeman in small rented houses, and the two young women carried their paints and portable easels into the wood to work at landscape painting. However, Mary did not find the outdoors a congenial subject, although she admitted to Eliza—and this may have inspired her attempts at the genre—that Americans were particularly fond of landscapes and bought them, if they bought anything. While this was not the driving force behind her efforts, commercial possibilities were ever a part of the Cassatt design: Mary was ambitious about the pursuit of art, but she also intended her paintings to reach the marketplace. Despite her frequent illnesses and by now a disinclination toward the painting of landscape, her retreats into the French countryside to paint paint paint was exactly the idyllic circumstance she had dreamed of when confined to the Philadelphia Academy. In 1870 the idyll came to an abrupt end with the outbreak of the Franco-Prussian War. Men and their wars. The Civil War in the United States was still an ugly memory; was there no end to the destructive mischief men imposed upon one another? Mary Cassatt's belief was that the only hope for peace in the world was through the influence of women.

She would have to go home again. She was just beginning to discover the mysteries of light and dark rendered in color, the power of brush stroke against canvas; and she had just barely heard of other apprentice painters, Frenchmen, who had got beyond her own tepid attempts to express the seemingly inexpressible. But many of the young rebellious spirits who had come to Paris to study and change the course of art were now subject to mobilization. Pissarro and Monet chose to flee France for civilian haven in England, where they joined Sisley, a British subject, in London. Cézanne managed to avoid a call to arms by returning discreetly to Aix once again. Renoir was as anti-military as the others, but quixotically enlisted in the cavalry—on impulse only, for he cared nothing about horses and could not in fact ride. Degas and Manet had become friends, partly out of the *snobisme* of both having come from the right sort of background. They dressed in the manner of dandies and went to the Café de Bade, favored by the pedigreed set, or they attended the races together. The two young men also joined the Paris National Guard together: if they must fight, they would at least take their patriotic stand defending the city both dearly loved.

Paris was the city that Mary Cassatt, too, had come to love in ways the outsider would not or could not express. As a young unmarried woman and foreign national, however, she was unable to remain in France during the hostilities, so Mary resigned herself once again to Philadelphia, this time in a mood of optimism. She had never intended to sever family ties; she loved each Cassatt dearly, and rebelled only against the culture-starved background of her origins. She determined that culture and art would be advanced by her efforts and in her time. Mary Cassatt had shown at the Salon in Paris, and this was likely to impress her compatriots. Now seemed the moment to draw from a reassuring sense of professional accomplishment a remnant-memory of the Parisian experience, and to make the best of whatever opportunities the New World offered.

Unfortunately, the home scene in no way provided the atmosphere and inspiration she had become accustomed to in Paris, and almost immediately even the most practical concerns blocked her progress. It had never occurred to her that she would be unable to find adequate studio space or even basic painting materials: "I have run out of colors," she wrote her painter friend Emily Sartain, "& have sent to town for more but they have not arrived yet. Do you know where I can get some good rough canvas . . . I cannot tell you what I suffer for want of seeing a good picture."

Experienced models were impossible to engage, but Mary was content to begin a portrait of her father, a hopeless and frustrating project because he kept falling asleep during the pose. A mulatto servant was an exotic model (rendered on the same canvas with the unfinished portrait of her father, for canvas was dear and Robert Cassatt expected his daughter to be self-sufficient in her chosen field as the boys were in theirs), but the sittings ended when the model left the Cassatts to marry. "I commenced a study of our mulatto servant girl but just as I had the mask painted in she gave warning. My luck in this country! I was amused at her finding that I had not made her look like a white person."

Mary's next attempt was a portrait of her two-year-old nephew, Edward, in velvet suit with lace collar, the first of her portraits of children. It was the work of a skilled student of art with no evidence of the mastery she would in time achieve in child portraiture, but she was strangely affected by the challenging process of painting a two-year-old. Actually, the notion of painting Edward's portrait was a gesture of conciliation toward her sister-in-law, Lois, who had always thought Mary pretentious and overbearing. Then Lois could praise the picture as a very good likeness of her son, which it was, while the two antagonists enjoyed a temporary interval of sisterly rapport. The gesture on Mary's part, and its appreciation by Lois, camouflaged the source of their mutual dislike: the competitive affection for husband-brother Aleck Cassatt. Here was another disadvantage of living "at home": these family frictions and petty concerns had never bedevilled Mary's spirit during student life in France.

At home she watched her brothers pursue the American way of wealth and success. Their direct accession to affluence and position was so in contrast to the niggling spider-like tradition of a Frenchman's rise in business: both Gardner and Aleck prospered—not only to their father's undisguised pride, but to Mary's as well. "The wealthy," she declared more than once, "are the only true supporters of art." Properly informed and patiently educated, the well-to-do *would* buy paintings, not always for reasons Mary Cassatt might hope for; at any rate she intended to initiate the Cassatts and other successful families along the Eastern seaboard into an appreciation for the one commodity they did not yet recognize, a collection of works of art.

Mary could sell none of the paintings she had executed in Paris; there was no market of any consequence in the United States at that time. She intended to change all that, and would. Meanwhile there was no use to brood over the deplorable lack of American interest in fine arts. She would concern herself with the immediate practicalities. She heard of a part-time so-called art dealer in Chicago who might be interested in her paintings. Accompanied by her mother she made the trip to Chicago, but the timing was unfortunate. A group of Mary Cassatt's earliest paintings was delivered to the dealer just before the great Chicago fire in 1871. Aleck wrote the news of the disaster to his wife Lois; he seemed to imply that Mary's luggage, and her mother's (including the Parisian frocks both delighted in), survived the fire, fortunately, "but Mary's pictures were lost. I am glad they got off so easily."

V

That same year, 1871, Paris too was in flames.

"Paris is burning. A vast cloud of smoke covers the city, burnt papers and cinders have been carried by the wind. It is like a volcano erupting . . . if Monsieur Degas could be roasted in the fire, it would be what he deserves!" Berthe Morisot's mother apparently believed Edgar Degas was one of the rebels who could not accept the humiliating defeat of the Second Empire at Sedan, when Louis Napoléon and

100,000 of his troops were captured by the Germans. The "undefeated" established the Commune of Paris as an independent state—which Paris had always been, in spirit if not in form.

A few years earlier the Confederacy had attempted its bloody secession from the United States, without Mary Cassatt's sympathy; the Paris Commune, however, was closer to her heart. "Poor Paris!" she wrote to her friend Emily Sartain. "I enclose a plea for the Commune which I wish you would read, I think it does them more justice than most of the newspaper correspondents."

Mary would have heard that Gustave Courbet, the defiant challenger to the establishment with his Pavillon du Réalisme in 1855, was appointed Commune Councilor in charge of the Beaux-Arts. This was a violent and ironic reversal of the establishment culture that had maintained its stagnant influence before the Commune: during Courbet's mandate the centerpiece of the place Vendôme, its majestic column honoring Napoléon I, was declared a symbol of Empire—as well as an example of retrograde art—then pulled down in triumphant riot.

When the Commune was brutally suppressed by official troops stationed at the temporary French capital at Versailles, landmarks of Paris were put to the torch by the Communards, including the magnificent seventeenth-century Hôtel de Ville, where the *Apotheosis of Napoléon I,* the work of Ingres, was destroyed. The Palais des Tuileries was burned, and Mary Cassatt's beloved Louvre was in flames but saved by the arrival of a contingent of volunteer *pompiers* and loyalist troops from Versailles. Monsieur Degas was not as politically engaged as appeared, and certainly he would have had no part in the desecration of the Hôtel de Ville and consequent loss of a painting by his adored Ingres. True, both Degas and Manet were part of the National Guard supporting the Commune, but during the days of chaos and carnage Degas was steadily sketching and painting as always. He eventually managed to join Manet at the barricades during the final Week of Bloodshed, where Manet was working on drawings for lithographs of the slaughter. The dedicated soldier-artists of Paris were artists first.

Forty thousand Communards were captured then force-marched to Versailles for sentencing to exile, imprisonment, or death. Courbet was held personally responsible for the destruction of the Vendôme column, and received the relatively light sentence of six months in prison and a fine of 500 francs. In prison packets of paints and canvas were smuggled to him by friends, and he managed to continue painting those works that had early excited Mary Cassatt's admiration and inspired her defense of Courbet and the iconoclast Barbizon painters. "These men were kept back for years," she declared. They were kept back because the Imperial Director of Fine Arts, Count Nieuwerkerke, believed their work was the painting of democrats and "of those who don't change their linen, who want to put themselves over on men of the world."

With her conservative upbringing and Victorian cast of mind, Mary Cassatt would in some respects echo the narrow sentiments of the dictatorial count; but in matters of painting she was convinced "we need a new system, the old one is used up," and she was willing to associate with those who did not change their linen if the artistic vision was changed.

Hardly had the smoke cleared from the holocaust than Mary Cassatt was back in Paris, the faint stench of burning still perceptible in certain narrow streets. Again, Mary would require a female companion, and Emily Sartain happily obliged in order to make possible the required respectable twosome, the only means by which such women could travel abroad apart from their families. In the year the Commune was suppressed, Mary Cassatt received a commission by the bishop of Pittsburgh to execute two copies of European artwork for the cathedral, a commission that allowed her to return to Paris prepared to bear her own expense. The Sartains backed Emily's travels financially, but this was Mary Cassatt's second painting sojourn in Europe, and her father reminded her that self-support was the surest form of independence: look at her older brothers! Mary was equally determined to be independent, fiscally and otherwise, so the bishop's commission was a stroke of good fortune and a first encouraging step.

"The ruins appeared more desolate yet," wrote Emily Sartain,

> from the caps of snow the piles of stone wore. The Hotel de Ville seems like a Roman ruin, the standing arches looked very fine—only the public buildings attract attention as ruins on the north side of the Seine, but on going up the rue du Bac on the other

> side we saw stretching on each hand a street in ruins. We expected to see the destroyed quarter near the Bastille . . . but the fog was so thick everything was lost at fifty feet off. I could barely see the pictures at the Louvre it was so dark.

The two women did not linger in the darkened city with its reminder of smoldering devastation mixed with snow. "It thawed most slushily our last two days in Paris, but men were busy opening the gutters and carrying away the snow, so we were not quite drowned." They sought the warmth of Parma where Mary was caught up in a new passion, printmaking. She studied engraving with Carlo Raimondi, of the Art Academy of Parma—a tedious and demanding art, worthy of the Cassatt gift and energies. Soon she was alone in Parma, knowing no Italian but pleased enough to be the only American there, for Emily Sartain returned to Paris ahead of time. In Mary's case, it was common that these arrangements of mutual chaperonage satisfy appearances only, both parties eventually going their separate ways. This had happened with Eliza Haldeman during that first sojourn: the Cassatt temperament did not make for congenial exchange under all circumstances, and Mary's advanced opinions had begun to clash with those of her more conventional-minded friend, Emily Sartain. "I by no means agree with all Miss C's judgments, she is entirely too slashing, snubs all modern Art, disdains the salon pictures of Cabanel Bonnat and all the names we are used to revere—but," Emily then generously allows, "her intolerance comes from the earnestness with which she loves nature and her profession."

In Italy, Mary Cassatt did complete three paintings of her own, one of which, *Pendant le Carnaval,* she submitted to the 1872 Paris Salon. The carnival scene was accepted and hung, but this time not "on-the-line": she was to learn the price of independence, for the best eye-level exhibit spaces were reserved for favored pupils of politically astute maîtres. *Pendant le Carnaval* was again attributed to Mlle Mary Stevenson. Her father, meanwhile, proud as he was of her second success, was impatient to see his family name on one of his daughter's canvasses.

After the Salon show, Mary left Paris once more, traveling on her own this time, following the same peripatetic trail Degas had taken five years before. Degas had concluded that the Paris art world had become *une bourse,* a stock exchange dealing in the fluctuating reputations of fashionable painters according to market calculations. Despite her successful access to the official Salon, Mary Cassatt had soured on the French art scene; little had changed since Louis Napoléon's reign: neither war nor revolution could unseat the rigid bureaucracy that controlled the fine arts. The Impressionists, a dissident band of Parisian painters Mary Cassatt did not yet know, had withdrawn from Salon competition altogether—except for Renoir, whose two paintings were both rejected. Mary felt the need, like Degas before her, to flee the heady but misleading excitement of the *bourse* in Paris and plunge back into the deeper sources of art, to draw sustenance and reassurance from the masters of the Renaissance rather than accept the influence of the latest favorites of the Salon.

In Italy she savored the independence of living completely alone, copying from the masters (and conscientiously sending off a copy ordered by the bishop of Pittsburgh), charmed and inspired by the madonnas of Corregio. She went off to Spain with less money than she knew she would need, regretting the pair of gloves she had bought in Parma which further reduced her reserves. In Madrid she haunted the Prado, where she learned much and accumulated an inventory of techniques from the study of the works of Murillo, Goya, and El Greco. She particularly fell under the spell of Velásquez, and appeared to feel his presence in the Prado gallery (as later when she took up a belief in psychic phenomena, she would *feel* the presence of the dead) by addressing his shade with the words: "Velásquez oh! my but you knew how to paint!"

While the fever to study and copy was on her, she traveled to the Low Countries, lingering in Haarlem long enough to work on a painstaking rendition of Frans Hals's crowded *Meeting of Officers of Cluveniers-Doelen*—a daunting enterprise few journeyman painters would have contemplated with anything but dismay; but she had discovered that self-imposed discipline among the masters of the past was far more valuable than submitting to the rote and confinement demanded by the maîtres of Paris.

The spirit of Velásquez worked its way into her *Torero and Young Girl,* another acceptance by the Salon jury the following year, one of Mary Cassatt's few successful attempts at painting the male figure. She was also much influenced by Goya—the Goya of the drawing room, not the underground Goya of terror and grotesquerie—and attempted a balcony scene in the manner of his similarly posed *Majas*, with foreshortened heads of the three figures, so difficult to pose for that one of the Spanish models asked her, "Do your models live long?"

Though the thought of the French art world was a persistent irritant, Paris was not, and she frequently returned to the city as a touchstone to renew her sense of the rightness of things. When the marketplace ambiance became too frustrating Mary Cassatt traveled on, sketching and copying from the European treasurehouse of classics, recording in her sharp memory a museum-by-museum catalogue of masterpieces. Not only did she enlarge her own useful backlog of inspiration, she would someday draw from this personal inventory of art work when she set about the transfer of art from the Old World to the New.

This ambulant period of study drew her again and again to the classic Madonna-and-Child motif. Mary Cassatt was not religious in the accepted and acceptable sense of her time, but the spirituality depicted so naturally in these paintings, the baby Jesus held by his mother, impressed itself upon her. She never ceased moving through this European gallery of mirrors, reflecting some timeless vision she seemed to have dreamed or anticipated in a recurrent *déjà vu*, variations from one century to the next on the miracle and mystery of a mother holding a child in her arms.

For the third consecutive year, 1874, the Salon accepted a painting submitted by Mary Cassatt; her *Mme Cortier* was the first undeniable evidence of her mastery in portraiture, an accomplishment she decided to acknowledge openly with her first Cassatt signature. Strolling the aisles of this crowded show was Joseph-Gabriel Tourny, a minor painter and lithographer, accompanied by his younger friend, Edgar Degas. The two had been in Italy together, and had managed to remain friends despite Degas's bearish manners and sarcastic tongue—Degas's opinionated superiority had managed to alienate many another friend, excepting the loyal Manet.

Degas stopped and began to examine the rendering of *Mme Cortier* in the mass and confusion of a far-too-inclusive exhibition. He stood before the work longer than his patience at the Salon ordinarily endured.

"*Tiens.* This is genuine, the real thing. Now *here* is someone in this cluttered show who feels as I do."

"I know the painter," said Tourny. "I met her in Antwerp."

"Her?" Degas squinted at the card below the frame: *Mlle Mary Cassatt,* then again at the painting, surprised and disconcerted to discover the work had been executed by a woman.

vi

Joseph-Gabriel Tourny, whom she had first met in Antwerp and not thought much of (a Parisian dilettante, Mary thought, for she was beginning to know the type), was standing at her atelier door accompanied by a friend. Over her dress she wore a torn smock, and a muffler at her throat.

Tourny made his formal excuse for disturbing her at her work, then announced: "Mademoiselle Cassatt, Monsieur Edgar Degas."

She was undeniably excited, but would not allow her feelings to show. Degas took her hand, murmured that he was enchanted, and with a slight bow touched the back of her hand with his lips. Her knuckles, she realized, were stained with paint, but he would not, she knew, be concerned with that.

She invited the two men, their *chapeaux melons* in hand, into the atelier. If the painter was untidy, the atelier was not; Mary had decorated the large studio on the rue de Laval in the style of a comfortable salon, for she spent most of her waking hours here. Her guests sat beneath a great antique hanging lamp; "statues and articles of *vertu* filled the corners," Tourny recalled, for Mary Cassatt thought of the decor of interiors as an extension of painting—a way, in her words, "of making pictures with real things." Degas's eyes ranged the walls for bits of her work, preliminary sketches and the copies she had made as a student, while Tourny's gaze was upon the two artists he had brought together.

Mary Cassatt knew Degas's work; she had discovered his pastels in a gallery window on the boulevard Haussmann. The gallery was closed and she had stood with her nose pressed against the glass: *It changed my life. I saw art then as I wanted to see it.* As for the painter himself, Mary Cassatt did not know what she thought of Monsieur Degas. Before her stood a small man of some forty years (ten years older than she) with rather exotic features and unusual coloring. More Italian, she would have thought, than French. Some women would find his appearance all the more attractive for the dark Italian strain—but French he was, in manner and attitude: he bore himself with the distinction and self-assurance of a much taller man. (Instinctively, she compared him with her taller American father and brothers.) She detected in his supercilious smile an air of presumption as if, behind his facade of perfect manners, he was here to tell her a good joke. In his manner of speech there was an exaggerated, even for a Frenchman, self-satisfaction.

Mary Cassatt was susceptible to praise if sincerely expressed and from a source she could respect. Degas's remark about her painting, "Now *here* is someone . . . who feels as I do," had got back to her, and pleased her more than she liked to admit. She wished the painting he had admired was in the studio, to remind him of his interest in her work, instead of the portrait of her sister Lydia, the one she had altered. The year after she had shown *Mme Cortier* the Salon accepted another Cassatt portrait, *Mlle E. C.*, but declined the one of Lydia because a member of the jury told her the colors were "too bright." He advised Mademoiselle Cassatt to tone down her coloring and resubmit. I will not, she had thought at the time, but after some weeks of aesthetic debate and ethical consideration, Mary Cassatt did play with the coloring to achieve a different but not altogether satisfying effect, one that a conservative jury would likely approve. She entered the repainted portrait the following year and the jury obliged by acceptance—to Mary's initial satisfaction but eventual shame.

She might have offered the gentlemen tea, but Monsieur Degas immediately made known the reason for his visit.

"Mademoiselle, I am—as you have heard from our mutual friend—much impressed with your work. And I speak for our little group of independent painters when I say that you appear to be working in the same independent way as we." (She wished she had turned the altered canvas to the wall, but Monsieur Degas appeared not to have studied it with any interest.) "The current *bourse* for painting is a vulgar bazaar, it annoys and disgusts me, it disgusts us all. We beg you to consider the possibility that you might join our group and exhibit your work alongside ours."

She could never afterward quite explain the delight with which she exclaimed, "I accept."

Before very long Degas was to discover that Mary Cassatt's explicitly expressed views were not very different from his own sharp opinions. Even when they disagreed, he was aroused to something more than admiration, invariably mixed with exasperation, by the qualities of her mind. This American was so different from any Frenchwoman he had ever known. No passivity here, nor did she concede the male prerogative. No wonder she had not married: her bons mots were clever but cutting, her attitudes apparently fixed, like his own, for all time. She did not and could not flirt: the feminine strategy of provoking a proposal, either to marry or join the independents, was evidently not for her. She was frankly ambitious, though not coy about it, and rather too anxious to sell and be recognized, to his mind. Mademoiselle would have to discount the suspect homage of the Salon and rid herself of Salon conventions. But not even Berthe Morisot had this unexpected force and artistic drive, along with the undeniable talent—but Berthe, after all, was afflicted with the weaknesses of womankind.

Degas had never married. "A married man," Courbet maintained, "is a reactionary in art." Degas thought Courbet a blundering fool in politics, but the man was right about marriage. Degas also agreed with Delacroix, who warned one of his students: "Even if she is pretty and you *love* her, your art is dead. An artist must have no passion except for his art."

Women were for Degas creatures whose mysterious beauty it was necessary to contemplate from aside, then render just as mysteriously in line and color. He spoke of models as *objets,* and he considered them so—Mary Cassatt could understand this ethereal remove, this sense of model as object, for she too had stared at human form and quite forgotten the person. Degas had even spoken of models as *outils,* and when informed that a model could not work that day, complained, "I am deprived of my tool."

Yes, Degas confessed to his café cronies, women were useful in that other way as well, but such a relapse from art diminished one's vitality and distorted perception. (At this Monet and Renoir laughed together, and Monet made a crude rejoinder.) But it was quite true, and those who laughed could not even rely on the extra-legal concubinage so common to this metier, the free-love relationship of a painter and his model. There would be babies, oh yes, and she would confront you with her misery, bewail her social degradation; she would drag you to the altar on one pretext or the other. Pissarro was doomed, whether he knew it or not, as were Monet and Renoir with their models and the *maîtresses* they must eventually marry. Nor could an artist depend on the casual sexual release granted by a passing *petite amie* or the professionals of a *maison close:* look at Manet, diseased, and no cure for *that.* (Berthe, the empty-headed thing, was in love with Manet but must marry his brother.) None of this could be mentioned to Mademoiselle Cassatt, but she understood it nevertheless.

Women were to be looked at, and painted.

Let them laugh or snicker in Degas's presence when the subject of celibacy came up. The word had gone round the Café Guerbois, when the Independents moved from the Brasserie des Martyrs, that he was as unnatural as that repellent writer who had come over from England, Monsieur Wilde. Now the group had taken to meeting at the Nouvelle Athenée—but Degas could not stay away from them, he needed to feed his bilious anger on their raging theories of art, and the word was that he was impotent. It was Manet, he knew, who started that slander. What then must they think of his association with the aristocratic Mademoiselle Cassatt?

Even the American accent charmed him. She spoke tolerable French, with the peculiar rhythm and flatness of pronunciation Americans must learn from the red Indians. Her aristocratic bearing and manner also appealed to him: he and she were of the same set—as much as Americans can be of any social class, the distinctions apparently based on wealth alone—therefore they could be comfortable in one another's company.

Degas was formally accepted by Robert Cassatt when received at their home in Montmartre, for the family had come over to live with Mary: her father, mother, and sister Lydia. The sixth-floor apartment at 13, avenue Trudaine adequately accommodated the four Cassatts and their servants. The building faced the steep *escalier* leading to the butte Montmartre, and their street was populated by tradesmen, working artisans, and the resident bourgeoisie, enlivened sporadically by a strolling concertina player or window-plate repairman with glass panels strapped to his back, and his cry of *Vi-tr-ièeere!* The Pigalle region would seem a disreputable quarter for the well-born Cassatts to settle in, but Degas lived there himself. The lively demimonde element was only apparent after dark and concentrated nearer the intersection of the place and the boulevard Rochechouart, for it was a characteristic of Paris that such districts reverted to solid working-class and middle-class neighborhoods during the daylight hours.

Degas would prowl the meaner streets at night (and later, his protégé Toulouse-Lautrec would paint his nightclub and brothel scenes here), but this was a world removed from the daylight respectability of the Cassatt family. Degas would sometimes see Cassatt *père* enjoying the same daily constitutional he had taken in the place Vendôme district ten years before. He was aging, and avoided the breathless uphill streets beyond boulevard Rochechouart, but did walk as far as the place de Clichy, and Degas caught a glimpse of him often enough on his own rue Victor-Massé.

Unlike other fledgling artists anxious for a break with family background, Mary flourished in this close family situation, perhaps because she had already lost any interest in a menage of her own; and she was more than delighted to add her invalid sister Lydia, who often modeled for her, to the curiously displaced family ensemble. Whatever the differences in their characters and tastes, these expatriate Cassatts took comfort and sustenance from one another in their isolation and exile. Degas found the father a bit stuffy—forever concerned with the cost of models or the price of *frames* ("The frame is pretty of carved wood & would cost at home I suppose 100 to 120 $, but Mame paid only 200 fcs for it in Rome second hand. . . ."), but the two had a common interest in the hippodrome and could discuss horses together—Degas avoided the subject of painting with dilettantes of any nationality.

One thing Degas had not told the other Independents (he detested the label "Impressionists") who thought him a wealthy man—let them think what they liked, their resentment over his financial "independence" was evident—he could at least inform Mademoiselle Cassatt: in truth, he had felt obliged to pay up his father's considerable debt after bankruptcy proceedings, a debt of honor. He had nearly beggared himself to do so. For this, Mademoiselle Cassatt, who was also endowed with a sense of duty and honor, had expressed her admiration. It was the kind of gesture she herself would have made.

The Impressionists, except for Caillebotte, also believed Mary Cassatt to be a woman of great wealth, an American *richissime.* She could not dress as stylishly and expensively as she did without all those American dollars. Actually, Mary was considering every centime and working toward an independence of income they would have thought foolish. True, she would never be hardpressed for food and lodging, as most of the others constantly were: she was a woman, with the support of a father and brother to rely on. Nevertheless, since her paintings were beginning to sell for modest prices, she took upon herself the expense of studio, models, and supplies; and when possible she would contribute to the family budget ordinarily managed by her father. She wanted and needed the sense of earning her way. Robert Cassatt's cash reserves could accommodate a style of living that included servants, at the scale of wages in French francs, but the funds were not inexhaustible. "Mame," as her father called her, was made to know that the sooner her metier achieved solvency, the better.

Her father wrote to Aleck that Mame was afraid she might be forced to paint "pot boilers" to earn money. A French collector, Victor Choquet, had bought one painting and had ordered another; nevertheless, Robert Cassatt wrote that the financial situation was uncertain, even grim. He did not express himself about Mame's decision to join the outlaw band of Impressionists, but he was beginning to take a new look at the world of art—at least a look at the economic side. Without Salon showings, Mary had little chance to reach the limited marketplace for paintings. At one point her father wrote to Aleck: "Mame is working away as diligently as ever, but she has not sold anything lately and her studio expenses with models from 1 to 2 francs an hour! are heavy."

The sixth-floor walkup on the avenue Trudaine became too strenuous for Mary's aging father, her mother who had a heart condition, and the invalid Lydia, so—with the financial aid from Aleck (now president of the Pennsylvania Railroad)—the Cassatts leased excellent new quarters at 10, rue Marignan, just off the Champs-Elysées. There was the luxury of a creaking, cagelike hydraulic lift, and rooms for servants so essential to the Cassatt way of life.

They sometimes painted together—at first with Lydia as model (and superfluous chaperone)—in Degas's studio, or at Mary's, a professional intimacy neither would have allowed another painter. Degas could be certain their conversation, if conversation there was, would concern craft, and not the airy trivia of the ordinary female mind. Another advantage was that Mademoiselle accepted his counsel: she was aware that her own art was in a state of flux; the apprenticeship years were behind her, as were her twenties, but the accomplishments so far were still those of a *débutante.* Degas noted only one sign of humility in his American friend: Mademoiselle Cassatt acknowledged his mastery, and she was willing to learn.

Ingres had passed the word on to his young admirer, Edgar De Gas: "Draw lines, young man, *des lignes!* Draw. Draw from memory and from nature. It is in this way you will become a great artist." Now Degas passed the word on to Mary Cassatt, that good painting came from drawing, from *des lignes.*

Degas did actually help Mary Cassatt paint the unusual and challenging *Le Salon Bleu.* She spoke to him of the problem of light through curtained windows, the atypical pose of the child with her skirt drawn up sprawled provocatively in a blue armchair, with three similar armchairs scattered oddly about the salon, and in a letter to the dealer Ambroise Vollard she admitted: "It was the portrait of a child of a friend of Monsieur Degas. I had done the child in the armchair and he found it good and advised me on the background and he even worked on it." Degas took from her the brush already tipped with blue and made a hasty stroke to the armchair. Absorbed, he went on. Mary Cassatt nodded, watched, was fascinated by the odd pattern that evolved from the flat gray floor and the chairs cropped in Degas's style at the edge of the painting. The background was becoming as she might have wished. Later she added her own little dog, a Belgian griffon, asleep in the next chair, counterpoint to the little girl, but left intact the background Degas had painted during this spontaneous collaboration she could never explain nor would ever deny.

vii

At their first Durand-Ruel–sponsored exhibit in 1864 the Independents were to acquire the name they were never afterward to shake, *Impressionistes,* from the art critic Louis Leroy, writing in the satirical journal *Charivari* of Monet's painting entitled *Impression—Sunrise.* Leroy mused in print: " 'Impression,' I was sure of it. I had just been telling myself that as I was impressed there must be some impression to it all—why, wallpaper in its earliest stages is more finished."

Despite the diversity of styles displayed by Monet, Pissarro, Renoir, Sisley, Degas, and Berthe Morisot at the exhibit on the rue Daunou, just off the rue de la Paix, it was Leroy's play on the word "impression" that labeled the group as Impressionists thereafter. Manet was asked to join them, but as he had little sympathy with any of the so-called Impressionists except for Degas, and as he was beginning to achieve some notice through official channels (a silver medal at the Salon that year) and dreaded any association with this motley band of outcasts, he refused to be part of the rebellion. Cézanne was drawn philosophically to any group working against the bourgeois art establishment, and would consent to show with them on occasion, but he too was wary of being called an Impressionist: he went his own independent way apart from the Independents, which was not to show at all.

Mary Cassatt had eagerly and "with pleasure" committed herself to the Impressionist band, despite the indignation and mockery the first three Impressionist shows had aroused. A review she read in an American journal summed up the general attitude: "We cannot in fact understand the purpose of the new school. It is founded neither on the laws of Nature nor the dictates of common sense. We can see in it only the uneasy striving after notoriety of a restless vanity, that prefers celebrity for ill doing rather than an unnoted persistence in the paths of true Art." The reviewer concluded by suggesting one would do better to "see an exhibition of pictures painted by the lunatics of an insane asylum."

The hope of any financial return was as grim. "Gold is not exactly flowing into their pockets," Cézanne reported to his friend Zola. "Their pictures in fact are rotting on the spot." A small collection of money was earned from charging an admission fee of one franc to see the exhibits, and those few paintings sold brought ridiculously low prices—around 100 francs each, approximately $20—for desperate artists already operating at poverty level. In 1875 Pissarro's wife was expecting a child; Monet could not afford a doctor or medicine for his wife who was gravely ill (she later died from poverty and the consequent medical neglect). Temporary help came from a new member to the group, the wealthy Gustave Caillebotte, a marine engineer and Sunday painter, who took upon himself much of the expense of organizing the shows, and made a private charity of Monet's case: he even put up the money and helped Monet build a boat on which to paint, the ideal floating ark-atelier for a painter obsessed with the play of light on water surfaces of the Seine.

After the first flush of elation at being asked to join this unhappy band of insolvent painters, Mary Cassatt began to fear the motive behind their acceptance of her had to do with the possibility that she might, like Caillebotte, be prepared to offer financial support to the group. Later she was convinced that the others—not Degas of course, she trusted him—were more interested in her purse than her palette.

Mary Cassatt did not quite know what to think of this other newcomer, Paul Gauguin, who had been discovered by Pissarro. Despite his bourgeois metier (a broker, as her father had been), his sarcastic expression and brutal profile suggested a certain lack of the refinement she found essential in someone like Degas or Caillebotte, either of whom she could confidently invite to 10, rue de Marignan. Gauguin, too, might have aroused expectations of a possible source of income, since he was a member of the Paris *bourse,* but the 1874 stock-market crash had made his financial contribution unlikely. Gauguin, in any case, made no gesture toward investing anything in the Impressionist movement except his own paintings.

Durand-Ruel had also been hurt by the 1874 market collapse, so, when all else failed, Degas secretly and Caillebotte openly financed the fourth annual exhibit. Even with word of this windfall of funds, Sisley and Renoir simply decided it was no longer possible to celebrate their independence in desperate poverty, and declined to show. Cézanne further distanced himself from the group by going back to Aix, as he so often did when feeling frustrated in Paris.

For the first time since Degas had invited her, two years ago, Mary Cassatt was a participant in an Impressionist exhibition. In the 1879 show she contributed eleven works, many of them influenced by her close association with Degas. Her decision to join the Impressionists was, in spite of all logic, a fortuitous career move for her, but did little for the advancement of the movement itself. Only Mary Cassatt, and her mentor Degas, received favorable notices from the press.

"M. Degas and Mlle. Cassatt," wrote George LaFenestre in *Revue des Deux Mondes,*

> are perhaps the only artists who distinguish themselves in this group of "dependent" Independents, and who give the only attractiveness and excuse to this pretentious display of rough sketches and infantile daubing, in the middle of which one is almost surprised to come across their neglected works. Both have a lively sense of fragmented lighting in Paris apartments; both find unique nuances of color to render the flesh tints of women fatigued by late nights and the rustling lightness of worldly fashions.

The usual scorn was heaped upon the rest of the group, and the public came to the show as it had done to the three previous shows, to mock.

Nevertheless, on the day of the opening the mocking paid off in revenue. The painters, including Mary, lingered in the gallery to count the first day's receipts: "We are saved!" declared Caillebotte. They had counted up more than 400 francs, mostly in coin from the modest admissions fee. Saved they were, at least from the repeated disaster of the earlier exhibits. The Impressionists were still attracting attention, even if of the wrong kind. The predictable response of *le tout Paris* remained as hostile and misguided as ever.

Naturally Mary's father picked through the reviews of LaFenestre, Huysmans, and Duranty (the latter most generous to "the diversity of expression" at the show) for any favorable mention of his daughter's work. F.-C. de Seyne's in *L'Artiste* was the most flattering notice of all:

> There isn't a painting nor a pastel by Mlle. Mary Cassatt that is not an exquisite symphony of color. Mlle. Mary Cassatt is fond

> of pure colors and possesses the secret of blending them in a composition that is bold, mysterious and fresh. *The Woman Reading* [Mary's mother], seen in profile, is a miracle of simplicity and elegance. There is nothing more graciously honest and aristocratic than her portraits of young women, except perhaps her *Woman in a Loge* [Lydia] with the mirror placed behind her reflecting her shoulders and auburn hair.

When the final pot of 6,000 francs was divided among the exhibitors, Mary's share came to 439 francs, all of which she invested in the purchase of two paintings from the show, one each by Monet and Degas.

Robert Cassatt wrote immediately to Aleck that Mame was the toast of the Parisian art scene, enclosing generous samples of this first trickle of critical praise. "She is now known to the Art world as well as to the general public in such a way as not to be forgotten again as long as she continues to paint!! Every one of the leading daily French papers mentioned the Exposition & nearly all named Mame—most of them in terms of praise, only one of the American papers noticed it and *it* named her rather disparingly!!!"

Mary Cassatt would seem to have far outstripped her new colleagues in this most successful debut at a private exhibit. She harbored an instinctive distrust of reviewers, enforced by Degas's disdain for critics of any stripe. What did she think of the Parisian applause?

"Too much pudding," said she.

viii

Light, and the distorting way it fell upon the real, shown transparent in the choice of color applied to faces and forms and illuminated interiors: this was her daily challenge, and she worked at it until the light failed. To brighten her darkening studio she might set a vase of lilacs against the sloping skylight or a brightly striped piece of fabric over a chair. Degas had complained that her ground-floor atelier was inappropriate for a woman, and the street-level light was unreliable. She no longer worked out of doors; landscapes or still life were framing devices or pertinent background to her central interest. Light was the great mystery to be solved with each individual brushstroke, the light of Paris, the interior light. Her sister Lydia obligingly posed for her, and her mother and father were in-house models; servants and neighbors posed, and then children were recruited.

For many months the Paris atmosphere was one of gloom. There were only variations of gray—and gray was not a staple of the Impressionist palette—diffused through a sooty pigeon-splattered skylight: she might yearn for the sharper outlines, flat planes, and open skies of Spain or Italy, but there was no explaining the Paris light and its subtler patterns of gray. Unable to find words to express the difference of Paris gray from the grays of Philadelphia, she remained silent in the authoritative presence of Degas. Understanding came visually only, from the constant application of paint to what she saw and sensed.

Those late winter days of interminable rain when shadows lost color and even lamplight was deceptive she might accept a rare interruption to indulge that other passion, a shopping excursion to the *grands magasins* behind l'Opéra, or to her dressmaker, or especially to Reboux for another fantasy in fabric and egret feathers to add to her collection of fashionable hats.

Oddly enough, Monsieur Degas wanted to accompany her on these tours and fitting sessions. How different from most men, Mary realized—her father and brothers would have detested time squandered in a mirrored salon full of ladies trying on hats. But Degas was discovering the hidden world of dressmakers' apprentices beyond the curtained fitting rooms, just as he had explored the backstage domain of preadolescent ballerinas to sketch *les petits rats* of the Opéra. With Mademoiselle Cassatt he entered the equally private world of simple working women, the *ouvrières* "with their rough red hands." He was a student of hands, as well as a secret observer of the unassumed poses of young women stitching garments or leaning upon their blunt steam irons to press a skirt's final pleats.

Meanwhile his American friend held forth on the client's side of the curtain, seated before a modiste's mirror—mirrors were an important motif, and appeared often in Mary's painted compositions. In this world of fashion, Mademoiselle Cassatt herself became the subject of a Degas study when she agreed to pose in a mass of flowered bonnets for his painting *Chez la Modiste (At the Milliner's).*

Mary Cassatt had never been drawn to the commonplace or inspired by such subject matter as seamstresses and workshop apprentices. Degas believed that through the artist's perception and style, even the sloppy tilting posture of the drudge was redeemed and made beautiful. As for the delineation of style, Mary once declared of a painter known to them both, "That picture lacks style."

"Women," Degas shot back at her, "should never attempt to be critics—what do they know about style?"

She suppressed a rejoinder at the time, but long after, with the echo of Degas's sour comment still in mind, she painted an ungainly servant girl tending a braid of hair, very much in the manner of Degas. It was an atypical Cassatt for the time, yet one of her most successful works. When Degas saw the completed painting, he exclaimed, "What drawing, what *style!*" Instead of reminding him of his earlier remark, Mary exchanged her painting for one of his pastels. Degas kept the painting in his collection for the rest of his life, and years after the exchange Mary Cassatt would have the further satisfaction of seeing her *Girl Arranging her Hair* identified by an auctioneer as one of Degas's great paintings.

By 1880 Mary Cassatt was a fixed star in the Impressionist constellation, and the only painter in the sixth Independent exhibition of 1881 to receive featured notices. Again, the others were lavishly denigrated, including this time, Degas. Degas was the one Impressionist who sold regularly, but critics and buyers now stood aside. What aroused the antipathy of critics—and the amusement of the public for anything unexpected or innovative—was Degas's wax statuette of a young ballet dancer with a much-ridiculed pink tutu attached to the figurine. The same Albert Wolff who praised Mary Cassatt as a "veritable phenomenon" condemned Degas as "the god of failure." For all Degas's irascible character and readiness for argument, he accepted with rare good grace the published reports of Mary Cassatt's rising reputation and his own apparent steady decline.

At Degas's suggestion and her own inclination, Mary began to concentrate almost exclusively on the theme of mother with baby and portraits of children posed in timelessly intimate drawing rooms. By the sixth annual Impressionist show, the critic Huysmans referred to the charm of her bourgeois Parisian interiors, admitting he felt "chez moi" as he entered her pictures, even though here was an American woman depicting the interior life of his own city. "She achieves something none of our painters could express—the happy contentment, the quiet friendliness, of an interior." Only a woman, wrote Huysmans (the remark annoyed Mary Cassatt) could so successfully paint children.

Children were central to Mary Cassatt's art. She responded to them in her own fashion, on her own terms. By this constant association with the young she learned to deal shrewdly with their volatile formative natures: she sought to express an unsentimental radiance she discerned in their faces. The affection she felt for her young models was genuine enough and far more complicated than the sublimation amateur psychologists attributed to some repressed maternal instinct. Beyond whatever personal attraction she had to babies and children, there was first and foremost an objective aesthetic consideration of their pictorial qualities.

The model was often chosen from among Mary Cassatt's own nieces and nephews. If a young model proved intractable, Aunt Mame managed to fascinate or distract at least long enough for a preliminary pose. She chose for them the most natural and expressive positions, taking advantage of a child's inclination to be the center of interest or the object of an adult's attention. On one notable occasion, however, her nephew Gardner Jr., too rigidly positioned or held to a pose beyond endurance, abruptly spat in the painter's face. Mary Cassatt was momentarily shocked, but the boy's mother was horrified. As a punishment she shut him in a closet, but Aunt Mame released the young prisoner, presented him with a millefeuille pastry, and soon had him posing again.

The handling of Edgar Degas was another matter. Only Mary Cassatt managed to tolerate Degas's bluntness and vitriol or could abide his company for any extended period. Now that her father was aging, Degas remained a formidable figure in her life. She herself possessed a sharp tongue, but in Degas's presence kept her trenchant comments to herself.

Among the rowdy crowd from Durand-Ruel's gallery gossiping

at the Nouvelle Athenée, speculation about the quaint relationship between Edgar Degas and Mademoiselle Cassatt led to many a sly joke. The American woman was not attractive of face, but perhaps Edgar found other qualities in her, the term *autres qualités* made to sound as suggestive as possible. Degas did find qualities, and quite serious ones: a rare talent (in a woman, he always added) and an edgy temperament equal to his own. She posed for him, always of course fashionably dressed, as in the painting of the skewed-angle figure of an art lover at the Louvre, seen from the rear and leaning on her umbrella. Only Edgar could make so much of such an awkward composition, and all the more so in Mademoiselle Cassatt's long face and torso in another pose, leaning forward with a hand of cards. It was bizarre, yet effective, and (all agreed) strangely charming.

Perhaps he intended to marry her. Degas had once stated his fear that a wife might see a new painting perched on his easel and exclaim, "*Tiens.* Now there's a pretty picture." Clearly, this American woman would never utter such a banal remark.

The undecipherable intent and attitude was equally obscure in Degas's relationship with his fellow painters. While he regularly purchased their work and appeared to respect them as artists and colleagues, he argued bitterly with every member of the group. Everyone argued with everyone else as well, but the principal source of dissension was Degas himself, his outrage catalyst to most of their violent disputes. His bombastic sarcasm was particularly damaging to the group's fragile unity.

"A great wrangler," commented the poet Paul Valéry, "and a formidable arguer—especially excitable on the subject of politics, or drawing. He would never concede a point. And very quickly he would reach the point of ranting. He would toss out the most scathing remarks, harsh to the point of insult, then abruptly he would break off as if in total scorn or loathing for his verbal opponent. One sometimes wondered if he did not *like* being intractable and having a reputation as such."

The greathearted peacemaker of the group was Pissarro, whose mature authority seemed to emanate from his vast Old Testament beard, whose kindness and loyalty were natural endowments. He practiced an extreme diplomacy in dealing with fellow artists, the reliable center of calm in their frequent storms. Pissarro could not perceive unmixed evil in individuals—only in systems; in this he was like Courbet, but Pissarro did not act on his anarchistic beliefs. Like most of the Impressionists, he was a painter first and a politician not at all—except that every painter was a politician in matters of art. When the issue arose of dropping Degas from the group, Pissarro stood by him, however reluctantly. Degas was an unsettling element in their midst—"He's a terrible man," Pissarro had to admit, then added, "but frank." Pissarro hesitated, trying to think of another quality, ". . . and loyal."

Loyalty—to friends, family, and to the painters she cared about—was a virtue Mary Cassatt also cultivated. The others did not know Degas as she did; they could not discern that essential humanness to his character. Would they have believed that the man they pretended to despise was capable of a letter to his friend the count Lepic in a gracious style that truly represented the other Degas, and his feeling for her:

> I think it is in good taste to warn you that the person who desires [a Belgian griffon], is Mlle. Cassatt, who approached me as I am known for the quality of my dogs and for my affection for them as for my old friends etc. etc. The person who requests the dog, whom you know for a good painter, is at this moment engrossed in the study of the reflection and shadow of flesh or dresses, for which she has the greatest understanding. . . . This distinguished person whose friendship I honor, as you would in my place, asked me to recommend to you the age of the animal. It is a young dog she desires, so that he may love her.

For the seventh Impressionist show in 1882, not even Pissarro could support Degas's insistence on introducing two new members to the show, painters whose work the others found impossible.

Degas reminded them of his contributions to the group: hadn't he brought Mademoiselle Cassatt into their ranks, hadn't he discovered Gauguin?

Yes, but they were truly representative of the collective, in style and spirit; all agreed they were excellent painters, they belonged.

"Belong to what?" Degas was outraged, and began one of his harangues. "We none of us paint alike. Art is deceit, an artist is only an artist at certain hours through an effort of will. Objects possess the same appearance to everyone. Rafaelli is a far more vital painter than Monet, whose studies of nature are mere convention."

Rafaelli was one of Degas's current protégés, unacceptable to the others, though Mary Cassatt approved of him—but she kept out of the discussion, and deplored Degas's mulish insistence, which ended in a final fierce argument with Degas, his face a choleric scarlet, stamping out of the gallery. He cut off further communication, even with the diplomat Pissarro, and adamantly refused to participate in the 1882 exhibit. When Pissarro came to Mary Cassatt with the news of Degas's defection, she weighed her loyalties to the group and to the individual, then took a stand in defense of her friend.

"I refuse to show as well," she informed Pissarro.

ix

Mame was a horsewoman born, as her father said of her, and the trotting lanes that wound through the Bois de Boulogne were an escape from the strain of constant studio work and worry over her invalid family. Her letters to her brother Aleck were about family sicknesses, travel to health spas, and particularly about horses. Robert Cassatt had lately sold the pony Bichette and carriage, a gift from Aleck, and the subject of one of Mary's finest paintings, *Woman and Child Driving,* in which only Bichette's flank and tail showed against the impressionist blue-greens of the Bois. She now owned a horse named Deauville with a contraction of the foot that, alas, required an operation severing the nerve, a dangerous animal to mount even when the foot healed.

Mademoiselle Cassatt *would* take risks, according to Degas. He loved horses too, but he painted or sketched the animals; he did not mount, or go riding with her in the bois. After her accident he wrote to a friend: "Mademoiselle Cassatt took a fall from her horse, broke the tibia of her right leg and dislocated her left shoulder. . . . She is getting along well enough, but immobilized in casts for these long summer weeks and then deprived of her active life and possibly cured of her horsewoman's passion."

Dr. Raspail treated her with camphor for her broken leg. Mary was convinced of the efficacy of the treatment, writing to her friend Louisine Elder: "Camphor! Nothing but Camphor! Compresses of Camphor! Spirits of Camphor! Pomade of Camphor! It is wonderful."

Degas knew that his friend loved flowers, though he himself despised cut flowers (and once snatched up a vase from a friend's table and threw both vase and flowers out the window), and he brought her bouquets regularly. He was a devoted bedside companion during her recovery; the period of convalescence was a mellow time of rapport for the two defectors from the Impressionist ranks. In the four years between the seventh and eighth Impressionist exhibits, 1882 to 1886, Mary Cassatt and Edgar Degas were as close as they had ever been, and for a time collaborated on Degas's art journal, *Le Jour et La Nuit,* an excellent chance for Mary to return to the metier of printmaking. The journal had aborted for lack of money or, as Mary's mother believed, because of Degas's carelessness. Nevertheless, during the collaboration with Degas Mary had perfected her technique of printmaking, an art that did not require daylight illumination: she could work at etching long after the daylight failed, a laborious second love and satisfying alternate discipline.

Degas was right about Mademoiselle Cassatt being obliged to give up riding, but her family believed, along with her doctor, that Mary's dislocated shoulder would prevent her from ever painting again. On this point Mary Cassatt knew better than Dr. Raspail. It was her left shoulder that had been injured; she painted with her right hand.

Not until the eighth Impressionist exhibit of 1886 did the group realign with any sense of solidarity, and even that fragile unity was challenged by a radical new force introduced by the inclusion of the Pointillists Signac and Seurat, championed by Pissarro (who had shifted to Pointillism himself), but ridiculed by Gauguin as "little green chemists who pile up tiny dots." Mary Cassatt cared nothing for the Pointillists, but she would participate in the exhibit if Degas agreed to show. Degas's condition was that the exhibit take place from May 15 to June 15 when the official Salon was open; the others opposed him, but eventually relented. Among the works Degas exhibited was his masterful portrait of Mary Cassatt, *At the Milliner's,* but the old guard Impressionists received little notice; the exhibit was dominated by the new and troubling element of Pointillism, especially by Georges Seurat's startlingly innovative *La Grande Jatte.* It was the final exhibit of the original Impressionists; they would never show together again.

Degas jotted the note in his agenda: "Dinner at the Fleurys with Mlle Cassatt," then added, "Japanese exhibition at the Beaux-Arts." This was the 1890 show of seven hundred Japanese prints and objets d'art that overwhelmed the Parisian art world, as if the Orient had anticipated vital Impressionist elements centuries before. For Mary Cassatt—who went again and again to the show, more than once in the company of Degas—seduced by the Japanese techniques in color prints, the revelation was so affecting that a radical shift in her style of painting was immediately noticeable. For a time she would see the world with altered vision, as if through Eastern eyes. Degas was amused in his superior way by Mary's enthusiasm: he predicted her reaction and felt the influence would be good for her; he himself had already been exposed to Japanese art, and had absorbed as much of the style as he cared to make use of.

Mary began her own private collection of Hiroshige and Hokusai prints, then did studies from the Japanese, reverting to the student copying she had done in those early years at the Louvre. Instead of the traditional Japanese woodblock, she adapted the Japanese style to drypoint on copper plate. At first she worked long hours with a commercial printer to perfect her practical technique in the art of etching; she made twenty-five prints, then destroyed the plates. She had always been a demon for work. Now, with the Japanese influence to inspire her own laboriously acquired mastery of engraving, she entered one of her richest creative periods, producing works like *Maternal Caress* and *The Letter* in which the figures became Japanese, even to the almond-shaped eyes, yet with her own sense of design, use of color, and juxtaposition of light and shade. She adapted several of these paintings for printmaking, most notably the collective series *In the Tramway, In the Omnibus, In the Boat.*

Absorbed as Mary Cassatt was in her Japanese phase, the vibrant Parisian scene ceased to penetrate the narrow world of her atelier. She was therefore appalled to learn that in her absence the Impressionists, who still considered themselves allied, had formed a group they called Société des Peintres-Gravures Français. They were planning a show sponsored by Durand-Ruel that would exclude, because of the restrictive term "Français" to their society, both Cassatt and Pissarro. Mary was bitter about their so-called Société, with implications of a chauvinism not even the Salon had been guilty of.

In splendid defiance, she and Pissarro mounted their own exhibit on the Durand-Ruel premises immediately beside the 1891 show given by the Société des Peintres-Graveurs Français. Pissarro, who had taken up printmaking with the same enthusiasms as Mary Cassatt (she would be showing her recent Japanese-inspired drypoints), wrote to his son: "The others—the *patriots*—will be furious when they discover just next door will be a show of rare and exquisite work."

Neither show generated much notice, since public interest and current controversy had shifted to the latest outrage, Pointillism, or neo-Impressionism. Possibly because of their frustration at the failure of the enterprise, the Impressionists did not quickly forget Mademoiselle Cassatt's obvious provocation. Pissarro had shrewdly predicted the reaction of the "patriots," but he escaped their hostility, probably because it was assumed that Mademoiselle Cassatt had made the arrangements with Durand-Ruel and had paid for the show herself. She was to be invited to the Société's official dinner, and in all innocence attended.

To the end of her life, Mary would remember that invitation—apparently to show that she was still warmly regarded in their circle, but actually an occasion for retaliation—as the closest she had been brought to tears by men. When she remarked to Renoir with genuine interest on the colors in one of his garden scenes, especially the use of brown, he replied, "When Mademoiselle learns to speak our language, I will teach her how to paint with the color *brun.*" This was a completely inappropriate sarcasm, a blunt French disparagement of American pronunciation of the difficult "r," and she was hurt that Renoir would direct this snide comment at her.

Degas spoke up for her, insisting that Mademoiselle Cassatt spoke French perfectly well, Renoir's remark was a piece of insolence (Degas did not know the teasing was deliberate) and he should show more respect. Degas's defense only increased the attention paid Mary Cassatt, initially meant as vengeful fun—but at her expense, and cutting deep.

"I respect the lady for all she does. I especially respect her for the way she carries her easel. Have you noted, my friends, that Mademoiselle carries her easel like a man?"

At this, Degas stood up, pounding the table with his fat round fist until the wine glasses rattled: "*Ça suffit!*"

They had of course been drinking, but alcohol was not truly responsible for the baiting of Mademoiselle Cassatt. She had always kept her distance from their society, avoided the cafés and common rooms filled with their cigar smoke and cognac glasses, stood apart from their ill-bred horseplay and vulgar shouting matches over art. While Degas continued to pound the table, Mary Cassatt folded her napkin and quietly left the raucous banquet hall just as someone called out to Degas, "Edgar, have you read what Goncourt calls Mademoiselle Cassatt?"

"Your choirboy," shouted another.

Yes, she would always remember that dinner and Degas's defense of her. They did not know him as she did, a man of refinement and old-fashioned gallantry, capable of the most unexpected acts of affection. He often wrote her notes. She would never forget the flowers he brought to her after her fall. At that very moment curled upon her lap, a warm second heartbeat, was the little Belgian griffon he had found for her, and once he wrote a tender poem to her parrot, Coco—a *poem,* of all things! Let the others mock and be spiteful, let them carp; she had his little scrap of verse, she had this little dog because of him.

X

When she had painted the portrait of her sister, *Femme à la tapisserie,* Mary was all too aware of the symptoms of Bright's disease: she painted these grim indications into the portrait—the thickening of Lydia's face and the fingers swollen where they touched the loom. It was the final portrait of Lydia; in less than a month after the happy occasion of their brother Gardner's marriage, Lydia was dead.

Though her stationery was bordered in black for the next two years, Mary kept her grief to herself; her letters rambled on about horses and money and "Mother not so well." Lydia's death was the second traumatic family loss since the death of her little brother Robbie so many years before. Lydia had been more than a sister: she had shared Mary's atelier life as a model and best friend. Next to the demands of art, blood kinship meant the most to Mary; a death in the family took away a part of herself.

Despite the ruptures with her young women companions Eliza Haldeman and Emily Sartain, Mary wanted and needed long-term loyal relationships with women. Women friends had to be likeminded culturally, or susceptible to culture like Louisine Elder, now Havemeyer: Mary had no time to devote to idle acquaintances in the calling-card set. And there was Berthe Morisot. To be a serious painter *and* of good family (the combination was so rare) opened the way at least to a friendly exchange.

Berthe Morisot had been Manet's protégé, just as Mary Cassatt had chosen Degas as her mentor: the course of *la vie sentimentale* remained obscure. Mary Cassatt's liaison with Degas was maintained more and more on her terms rather than by Degas's autocratic demands (when he became impossible, Mary simply refused to see him for months at a time and at one point she burned his letters to her); Berthe Morisot, the lovely passive Parisienne, was heartbreakingly devoted to Manet to the end, and hopelessly so. The tentative friends maneuvered as diplomatically as possible with one another, using the formal *vous,* taking tea together, paying and repaying obligatory social calls almost as if they were of the faubourg social set and not reputable (and controversial) painters.

When Manet's reputation was at its peak in 1883—he had won the Légion d'Honneur for his *Bar aux Folies-Bergère,* to Degas's infinite disgust with acceptance of official honors—Mary Cassatt took her one close American friend, Louisine Havemeyer, to Manet's atelier with the idea that Louisine might be amenable to the purchase of one of his paintings. They were met at the door by Berthe Morisot, her face drawn, her voice strained.

"He is ill. He can see no one."

Mary Cassatt was surprised to see Berthe Morisot at Manet's atelier door, but not completely surprised. She had known of Berthe's devotion to Manet all these years and that Manet had long been married to Suzanne (though unmarried until their son reached the age of eleven). Berthe Morisot would never have entered the sort of casual sexual liaison that was so traditional in that artistic-bohemian circle, for her background and social standards were equivalent to those of Mademoiselle Cassatt—yet here was Berthe, not Suzanne Manet, greeting her at Manet's door.

The visitors went away not realizing the gravity of Manet's condition. With Berthe Morisot hovering at his bedside, he was being treated by shifting teams of incompetent doctors for the degenerative stages of locomotor ataxia. Degas wrote to a friend: "Manet is done for. The word is that Dr. Hureau de Villeneuve has poisoned him with doses of ergotized rye. The newspapers have gone out of their way to inform him of his approaching death." Homeopathy and herbalism were much in fashion, and Manet was subjected to these remedies, along with treatment by hydropathology. As a last resort his gangrenous foot was amputated, but Manet died shortly thereafter of tertiary syphilis.

Berthe Morisot married Manet's brother, Eugène, who had often posed for figures in Eduoard's paintings. Mary Cassatt kept in formal-friendly touch with Berthe—often considered her "rival" in the art world, but never so considered by either woman—until 1895 when "We lost Mme. Manet [Berthe Morisot] this winter carried off in five days by grippe."

By 1891 Paris had become a death-haunted city for Mary, even as she was preparing her first one-woman show at Galerie Durand-Ruel: color prints, pastels, paintings—among them a pastel of her father astride Deauville, a wooden view of Robert Cassatt's slumped back and a not very successful rendering of the horse beneath him. Before Christmas of that year, her father would be dead. In a black-bordered letter to Aleck, Mary wrote in her bland straightforward way, which gave no hint of the depth of her feeling, "It was the cold he caught on coming back to town that made him so ill, he got up one morning at four o'clock & opened all the windows to give air & that after sitting over the heater." Her first figure of authority and sometime adversary, then, in his later years, the foremost enthusiast of all the Cassatts for Mame's work, the unbending model for her own tough-minded, determined way, was gone.

With the death of her father, Mary Cassatt would devote herself to her mother, whose troubled heart required countryside quiet. (Mary could not forget her father, at the last, gasping for air in their Paris apartment.) The two women traveled together to health resorts and to the South of France, *en famille* as the Cassatts had always traveled, hoping to ingest cures but tiring themselves in travel, drinking the mineral waters of spas and inhaling the fumes of sulphur.

There was money from Mary's paintings now, from Aleck and from her father's legacy. Mary purchased the large and impressive summer estate at Mesnil-Théribus, Beaufresne, a spacious château (not the turreted fairy-tale castle the term implies, but a large distinctive French manor house) with extensive grounds for the two women alone: Mary unmarried and Katherine Cassatt a widow. A corps of hired servants lived on the third floor to see to their well-being. This move was in no way a retirement or withdrawal (as Degas withdrew more and more into his atelier shell), but a second and grandiose country establishment where Mary could paint in tranquility and her mother regain her health: "My Mother . . . says to tell you that the woman you knew as my Mother is no more, that only a poor creature is left! Which proves that her head is not quite so affected as she thinks."

Mary kept the apartment on the rue Marignan in Paris as a pied-à-terre, for Paris was the first place of harmonious inspiration and permanent nerve center of her art.

When Emile Zola's *L'Oeuvre* appeared in 1886, Mary Cassatt turned from it to Tolstoy's *War and Peace*, available in a French edition for the first time, a novel that helped her overcome the bitter after taste of reading Zola's depressing fiction of the Impressionist movement. Cézanne, Zola's old friend, could not fail to recognize himself as the distraught protagonist, frustrated by circumstances Zola had obviously observed at first hand. *L'Oeuvre* took as its theme the crisis and breakdown of a contemporary artist in a hopeless search for an aesthetic to live by: the central character, in pursuit of an impossible goal, was the metaphor for artistic failure and tragic waste. The Impressionists saw their joint endeavors mocked as dead end, their lives portrayed under the harsh light of the mighty Zola himself—Zola, their former defender and promoter! Cézanne was so personally offended by the novel that he and Zola—boyhood friends from Aix, breaching the ramparts of Paris together—were never to meet or correspond again. Not only did Cézanne read his fate in Zola's pages, but each of the Impressionists discovered some part of himself in the doomed protagonist, except for Degas, who ignored the novel, and Mary Cassatt, who dismissed it.

Mary was next reading another book that appeared that year, a curious volume "which has already occasioned two duels," she wrote to her brother Aleck, "& will probably give rise to a good many suits for slander etc." Edouard Drumont's *La France Juive* would give rise to much more, verifying the anti-Semitic mood in France that would make possible *l'Affaire Dreyfus* about to poison even the ranks of the Impressionists while it tore France apart.

Mary Cassatt and Edgar Degas were from the same social mold and shared the approximate prejudices of their class and time. Jews, to Mary Cassatt, were a breed apart. Pissarro was a Jew, but Mary considered him a painter first, and therefore not really a Jew at all—besides, Pissarro was a *friend.* Jews did not become soldiers; they were art dealers perhaps, or merchants, so what was this Dreyfus doing in the French Army in the first place? The man himself, a captain in the army, had been caught spying. It was disgraceful and sordid, a vast remove from what was important—that is, art—but everyone in Paris was concerned with *l'Affaire* and Degas apparently concerned with nothing else.

Eventually it came to Mary's notice that Captain Dreyfus might have been falsely accused, stripped of rank and insignia in a degrading military ceremony, then shipped off to the horrible French prison in the Guianas, for life, or whatever life was left to him. There were serious questions concerning the closed military trial (she would have to ask Clemenceau, a family friend of the Cassatts, about that). It was coming out in the liberal journals that evidence had been distorted, fabricated, or covered up to protect persons unknown. Since Dreyfus was after all a Jew, it was possible he was being made a scapegoat for some streak of corruption in the French Army itself.

You could not visit an exhibit or take tea or attend a dinner without hearing the name Dreyfus. In this affair, Degas was in a permanent state of agitation, at his worst, as if a demon had possessed him: he had instantly allied himself with the anti-Dreyfusards, and vehemintly condemned *all* Jews. To Degas, Dreyfus was the Jew incarnate and not a Frenchman at all, a Jew who would sell France to the enemy for a piece of silver, as any Jew would do. His choler was such that he would no longer speak with Dreyfusards and he carried his vindictive attitude to his usual extremes: even poor Pissarro was banished from Degas's narrow world.

Mary Cassatt dreaded the social occasions where Degas might be present and on the attack, for he had broken with so many lifetime friends she did not know how he would behave with her. She confided her misgivings to Louisine Havemeyer, who, as a young friend of Mary's in Paris had spent her allowance on a Degas pastel, her first purchase in what was to become the brilliant Havemeyer Collection. Louisine advised her by all means to accept the very next invitation.

"But this Dreyfus affair," Mary objected. "I know he will anger me."

"Don't hesitate. Go and silence him once and for all."

"You don't know what a dreadful man he is, he can say anything."

But she did attend the very next dinner to which both were invited. In her presence Degas was perfectly civilized and correct: "He has aged, dear, aged so very much," she reported to Louisine. "It made me sad, but I was glad to see him and he was very nice and did not say a disagreeable word."

Soon Emile Zola himself became entangled in *l'Affaire,* unwillingly at first, and then with the French spirit of a crusader. Clemenceau's liberal newspaper *L'Aurore* gave Zola the opportunity in 1898 to publish his incendiary manifesto, *J'Accuse!* The reaction to this was so violent that Zola, by defending the innocence of Captain Dreyfus, was prosecuted for libel and obliged to flee from France. The anti-Dreyfusards were in power, with the added strength of the French Army behind them, along with the Catholic Church; but a growing number of notables such as Clemenceau, Jean Jaurès, and Anatole France were saying "I accuse!" in turn. Evidence of forgeries manufactured by an army officer, Captain Henry, indicated that the army intended to keep Captain Dreyfus confined to Devil's Island until he died there, innocent or not.

The reasoning of the anti-Dreyfusards Mary Cassatt could not understand and could not tolerate. Reason, if reason there were, did not support polemic; there was only a blind insistence that the pristine glory of France had been polluted by the Jewish element, the tricolor desecrated, the army betrayed. The innocent captain who languished in that inhuman confinement had become a mere political symbol, forgotten as a man by both Dreyfusards and anti-Dreyfusards. In her long residence in Paris, Mary Cassatt had not been inculcated with the pieties of French nationalism; she was American still, and could not abide injustice in the name of *la gloire de la patrie.* In this instance Degas's vile attitude filled her at first with dismay, then disgust. She now opposed him with all the strength of her considerable will. Here was a necessary turning point, the final break with her first and most important mentor, her old ally and a once dear friend.

As for Pissarro, Degas's latest object of virulence, an impairment of vision forced him to abandon *plein air* painting and confine himself to studies of Parisian boulevards from the windows of one unsuccessful apartment after the other. For six years he had attempted to follow the divisionism, or Pointillism, of Seurat and Signac, a period of pure waste, he confessed when he was past sixty.

"Poor Pissarro," Mary wrote to her friend Theodate Pope, "has just fallen victim to a mistaken diagnosis of his disease." By this time Cassatt shared with Theodate Pope a growing interest in psychic phenomena, and had come to believe that "diagnosis is after all Psychical & few possess it."

Indeed, Pissarro was such a convert to homeopathy he abided by his doctor's decision to treat his abscessed prostate with pills. Here, in 1904, was something of a repetition of the medical bungling that hastened Manet's death. An operation was performed, but too late to save poor Pissarro. His son Lucien complained of the doctor in a letter: "He has never even raised the blanket to inspect the condition of his patient, the fool!"

The grand old man of Impressionism—the humble and colossal Pissarro, as Cézanne called him—was laid to rest at Père Lachaise Cemetery in his seventy-third year. Although his work was now recognized and even purchased by the Louvre, no mourner from the official art world attended his funeral. Pissarro was accompanied to his tomb by a host of friends and many of his early painter associates in the Impressionist movement he had virtually founded.

Degas had recently been reminded of how greatly he admired Pissarro's work in the early days of their friendship, but he shot back, "Yes, but that was before *l'Affaire!*" Augusto Jaccaci, a commentator and connoisseur of art, repeated the story of Mary Cassatt's meeting with Degas at Pissarro's graveside, where she was said to have rebuked him publicly: "You're mean to your brother. You're beastly to your sister. You're bad, you're bad!" If she said this—and she might well have done so, she was known to cover genuine grief with irritable snappishness—it was not at Pissarro's funeral. Degas did not attend the *pompes funèbres,* having already made his excuses, guiltily, to Pissarro's son Lucien.

xi

The local gossip around the village of Mesnil-Théribus was that a fine Mercedes-Benz, with chauffeur (not from the region), had driven through the gates where "Our Mademoiselle" was waiting in the shade of the ash trees to receive a distinguished-looking gentleman. He was without doubt American, though not as tall as Americans were supposed to be, a little past middle age but not quite *d'un certain age* of Our Mademoiselle herself—perhaps five years younger than she—but what difference was that, if two people were attracted by mutual interest and were of the same social position? *Un très chic type, distingué même.* And Mademoiselle Cassatt was a handsome woman of equally distinguished bearing: she had matured admirably, she was tall and wore her couturier garments and the plumed hats from Reboux with the natural grace one would associate with a born Parisienne. Those who remembered her when her mother, Madame Cassatt, was still alive and living at Beaufresne recalled Our Mademoiselle as not quite pretty, ever, and often bearing a haughty expression that earned for her the name *l'Impératrice,* the Empress. But she was surely a handsome woman now.

James Stillman, an associate of J. P. Morgan and of John D. Rockefeller, had at first come to Mary Cassatt in Paris as had many of his compatriates for advice on the purchase of paintings. Like her father, and her brother Aleck, Stillman had abruptly retired from business to live abroad, willing to let go—but not altogether let escape—the directorship of some forty companies and subsidiaries. At the beginning of their acquaintance Mary Cassatt asked him bluntly enough about this letting go: why had he given up his American life, his National City Bank, for Paris?

"I wanted to do something else."

She would learn that what Stillman really wanted was to move out from behind the massive desk on Wall Street where "little men" came to him seeking favors. He was of short stature himself, but not little in the way he referred to supplicants who appeared in his office. "Well, what do you want of me?" was his habitual greeting. He had destroyed many of those men come begging at his desk, or had abruptly broken their spirits, smiling what his colleagues called "that cold smile of a Japanese statesman." In business he had put together a substantial fortune almost as an afterthought. Money had an insidious warping effect on most men; it had made James Stillman powerful and independent, and irredeemably unloved.

Paris had changed his life altogether: he was discovering a contemplative serenity in this city of permanent beauty on a grand yet human scale. There was now something he wanted of another—in the company of Mary Cassatt the frozen smile eased into an expression of genuine warmth. Stillman's wife had left him: the man was impossible to live with—as cruelly demanding in marriage as he was in business. His wife had not been enough of a perfectionist to suit him. Mary Cassatt's perfectionism matched his own; her character easily accommodated his superior manner—had she not for years supported the *insupportable* misanthropy of Degas? She brought out the barely recognizable warmth behind Stillman's gelid countenance that not even Stillman knew he was capable of.

They were two equally independent spirits. Stillman knew immediately that he could not intimidate this woman or manipulate her, and with that realization he did not wish to try. With the money and status she had earned from her art she was a complete being and beyond his bullying. She took no proprietary interest in his excessive wealth except for that tithe she insisted he devote to paintings. He had, after all, come to her for advice about collecting European art.

Where his sudden passion for art came from, Stillman did not know. He was unprepared for the shock of recognition brought on by Paris and its aesthetic revelations—Mary recognized these symptoms as part of her own experience with Paris. Stillman's taste was naturally unformed: he had never really looked at paintings before coming to France. Paintings were artifacts of upper-class decor and, like company reports and stock averages, reflections of accumulated wealth. But for the shrewd guidance of Cassatt, he might have fallen into the patterns of indiscriminate pillage practiced by the robber barons now invading Europe.

Mary Cassatt, with her intercontinental connections, was the first to introduce American wealth to European art, a liaison that for some French artists made possible the practical continuation of modern art. A marketplace was created by Parisian dealers like Gimpel, Vollard, and Durand-Ruel, men with the flair and daring to stock and promote new and difficult works of art. When the Barbizon painters, then the Impressionists, were ignored in their own country, Mary Cassatt arranged for Louisine Havemeyer, then her brothers Alexander and Gardner, Mrs. Potter Palmer, the Gardiners, the Whittemores, Mrs. Montgomery Sears, and finally James Stillman to know and value and purchase these works just as these artists most needed support. It was through Cassatt that the great American collections were begun and the cultural vacuum she so deplored in her United States began to fill with works of art.

Stillman wanted to buy paintings for the wrong reasons; she wanted him to buy for the right reasons, and to teach him what the right reasons were. Only Mary Cassatt could impose her will on James Stillman in this way, and make him like it. She intended to separate him from the indiscriminate crowd of *arrivistes,* the robber barons who had discovered and were distorting the art market. George Vanderbilt threw away over a million and a half dollars for a plethora of third-rate acquisitions, often of doubtful authenticity, with only a single purchase worthy of the sum expended—a Delacroix. J. P. Morgan, one of Stillman's Wall Street cronies, lavished a small fortune on a Raphael that Mary Cassatt could have told him was a clumsy fake. At least the Havemeyers had the luck and good sense to be guided by Cassatt's discerning eye, and their private collection of modern and antique art was to become one of the glories of the Metropolitan Museum of Art.

Mary Cassatt did little to promote sales of her own works: James

Stillman became an avid collector of Cassatts, but not on the artist's advice.

"There was a painting of yours at the Wildensteins, and I truly wanted it. Not for sale, they said."

"They were quite right, and you were wrong for trying to buy it away from them."

"Some day," Stillman assured her, "Cassatts will sell for the same prices Degas gets for his—and be as much sought after."

Mary laughed aloud. Stillman's mouth turned down: he was not used to being laughed at. Mary took measured pride in her accomplishments but nurtured no illusions about the relative values of works of art. She was an *intimist,* a delineator of intimate life and a brilliant interpreter of character in portraiture. The Cassatt style did not attempt the risk and scale of a Manet or the multiple complications of a Degas; her paintings succeeded in nuance of coloring and a subtle aesthetic of composition—admirable attributes that would endure, but not necessarily by proclamation.

"Museums are not for me. My paintings belong on the walls of private homes," she insisted, and Stillman replied, "Then they belong on my walls."

He had chosen his walls well. The businessman's late-blooming love affair with art led him to settle into the finest *hôtel particulier* he could procure to house himself and his collection-in-progress. He chose the magnificent neo-classic gray stone edifice off the parc Monceau, in the fashionable 8th arrondissement. This flank of the park was a conmingling of streets named for painters (many of whose works he had acquired, one of the less practical reasons for choosing the quarter): Murillo, Velásquez, Ruysdael, Van Dyck. He installed himself and his paintings on the most graceful central spoke of these streets leading directly into the jewel-box of a park, at 19 rue Rembrandt. It was a short carriage drive from rue Rembrandt to Mary Cassatt's apartment on the rue de Marignan, in the same arrondissement and across the boulevard Haussmann, named for the baron who created this exclusive Parisian enclave where the well-to-do could live conveniently in the vicinity of the well-to-do.

By the time James Stillman had acquired twenty-four Cassatts, gossip would have it that he would like to have added the painter herself to his establishment on the parc Monceau. When word of this reached the ears of Mary's maid, the astonished Mathilde said to her: "Surely, Mademoiselle, you would not exchange the name Cassatt for Stillman?" No, she would not, but it was not pride of name that held her back. It was too late for marriage, too late for the promise of love and commitment to one person. Her devotion of that kind had been expended on her family, on her art. But Stillman was enchanted by the circumstance: never had he come upon a woman with as strong a will as his own; self-sufficient, shrewd, direct, and with a genius he was only just beginning to discover. His first marriage had been a conventional alliance. He thought at the time he was wise in the ways of social contracts, but the marriage was an inevitable failure. Now he knew what he wanted out of life—and he had come to wisdom not by success in the business of business, but by way of art.

It was now Stillman who accompanied Mary Cassatt to the grand couturier houses on the boulevard Haussmann, Rue La Boétie and the avenue Montaigne, the exceptional Parisian pleasure she had once shared with Degas; but Stillman—unlike Degas—was fascinated by the garments themselves. He would arrange private fashion shows at his mansion, an odd passion Stillman enjoyed in the company of Mary Cassatt where mannequins from Worth or Lanvin paraded through the grand salon as Stillman chose capes and evening dresses, with Mary's nod of approval, to send to his daughters in America.

In his maturity Stillman had become tame—often too tame and passive for Mary's tolerance: he had taken to retirement in a literal way while she remained a dynamo of nervous drive. The one concession to his chairman-of-the-board responsibilities was the private cable line, Paris–New York, he had installed in his library. The slack Latin routine Stillman had fallen into could be frustrating to someone like Mary Cassatt, and often, as she had done with Degas (for entirely different cause), she felt obliged to cut off relations with her torpid admirer. She was simply too annoyed to receive him, or even to accept his elaborate messages of apology. His plaintive yielding to her moods was significant of his feeling for her.

Her dogs were a sentimental indulgence, a way to her heart: how could she ignore the jeweled collars he offered the griffons?

"I will not have them spoiled."

She would have them spoiled, she spoiled them herself. En route to the rue de Marignan he would make a detour to the place Vendôme to pick up silver feeding bowls for the dogs at Cartier.

In pursuit of paintings instead of money—for Stillman was a fully committed collector now—he made the same journey Mary had taken to study European art. They traveled together, but with separate accommodations, the proprieties maintained, the understanding intact. Mary Cassatt and James Stillman thus spent many hours together, under what circumstances the world was never to know, for it was none of the world's business. Mary had drawn the same curtain of privacy over her relationship with Degas, and had even burned Degas's letters to make certain the curtain was drawn tight.

By stages in his burgeoning connoisseurship Stillman's taste was educated upward. At first Mary Cassatt discovered in him a natural attraction to the imitative or merely pretty. Those sentimental busts of angels, for example. They were dear sweet heads of seraphim a maid would sooner or later shatter when dusting; Jean-Baptiste Greuze was only a way station to the higher reaches of art.

"Then where should I start?"

"With Ingres."

She led her friend to the more substantial classicism of mid-nineteenth-century French art. She was not unsympathetic to the romantic settings portrayed by Fragonard—accomplished work of its kind and of its day—but she must see to it that Stillman recognized the greater worth of Titian and Rembrandt. Gently she would urge him in the direction of Corot ("I confess I have a sort of longing for you to own that picture [Corot's *Toilette*].") when he was much too impulsively taken with Chardin; step by step, through informed choice, she led him to accept the Impressionists. When he became dilatory, her advice was sharp, pertinent, and often remonstrative. In Spain, Stillman hesitated before an exquisite Velásquez.

"Buy it," she insisted. "It's shameful to be rich like you. Such a purchase will redeem you."

He did as he was told, brought forth his checkbook, and was redeemed.

"Dear Mr. Stillman" (for she addressed him formally, as she had always addressed Monsieur Degas): "I cannot bear to think of you worried and depressed and alone over here."

In 1910 Stillman was alone in Paris while Mary Cassatt was on tour in Germany, and then to Egypt, with her brother Gardner. She was concerned about Stillman: left to his own devices, he seemed unable to operate wholeheartedly. Stillman did feel lonely in her absence, but not worried or depressed. Mary Cassatt had advised him that art was a consolation and an escape from worry, and he found it so. He was now on intimate terms with the one true luxury he had ever known. Walking the streets of this incomparable city, a quiet evening's stroll down the radial streets of his quarter or through the parc Monceau, he experienced an almost constant sense of uplift, a satisfying lightness of step he had never felt in the shadowed canyons of Wall Street. He studied the animated Parisians, graceful in gesture and excitedly articulate, realizing how much of her temperament Miss Cassatt had drawn from this source—though she remained quaintly and endearingly, to him, American in all else.

Their letters were signed "Sincerely yours," or "Very sincerely yours," and she would never address him other than "Dear Mr. Stillman," yet each of the correspondents wrote tender variations of the heartfelt phrase, "I have missed you dreadfully."

Mary tried to amuse him with lively details about her trip: a shame he would miss seeing Munich's 135-year-old man, a hearty creature and apparently in good health. Her thoughts at the age of sixty-seven turned often to mortality, while Stillman's outlook in his sixties was of renaissance. Also Mary had heard of two equally ancient Egyptians whose acquaintance she intended to make beside the Nile, where death might yet be kept at bay, or where apparently the mummified dead existed beyond perpetuity in a necropolis of art and artifact. The funerary art of Egypt, ritualistically stiff and inert, made no great impression on her at first.

"I fought against it," she wrote, "but it conquered. All strength, no room in that first empire for grace, for charm, for children, none."

In France, grace, charm, children had been the underpinnings of her art, but in Egypt she was touched briefly, fleetingly, with the unaccustomed impulse toward change. "If only I can paint something of what I've learnt—but I doubt it . . . how are my feeble hands ever to paint the effect on me?" The doubts were reinforced by an awareness of that her sight was beginning to fail.

The reason for the tour was the recurrent Cassatt faith in travel to Germany's spas, and now to the hot dry climate of Egypt, that her brother Gardner's frail health might be restored. The family had made the same pilgrimage in the case of little Robbie, of Lydia, of Mary's mother and father—and once again, the change of air and water wrought no miracle of healing. Her brother's health had so deteriorated on the trip, complicated by something Mary called Nile fever, that he died as soon as the travelers returned to Paris.

Mary permitted herself no tears at Gardner's funeral service, held at the Church of England in Paris. She could only express her inner turmoil in that odd way of hers, by the sharp chatter of complaint. How the rector did drone on. A mistake to rely on an Anglican service—why drag in a prayer for the king of England? The rector could as well and more to the point have prayed for the president of the United States.

Mary was truly stricken by Gardner's death, but James Stillman, a familiar of stoic masks, understood better than any of her friends that this was her only way to mourn. Her favorite brother Aleck, having left retirement to manage the Pennsylvania Railroad again, had died in the United States in 1905. Mary was the last surviving Cassatt of the seven Philadelphians who had embarked upon the Paris venture exactly sixty years before.

xii

"To poor Miss Cassatt the loss was irreparable," said Louisine Havemeyer, who had been at Beaufresne in 1895 when Mary's mother died quietly in her sleep. "[Mary] struggled bravely, like many another, and sought to see through the mysterious veil that hides our dear ones . . . she was deeply interested in psychic phenomena." Since her mother's death, Mary had been attracted to the shadow world of Parisian psychics, and when her brother Gard died and she was alone in total bereavement, she was all the more anxious for spiritual communication from *l'outre tombe.* With Theodate Pope and Mrs. Montgomery Sears, she attended séances in the hope of "piercing the mysterious veil" to the other side.

A popular book of the time, *Human Personality and Its Survival of Bodily Death,* fell into her hands, a gift from Theodate Pope: "What a book!" Mary wrote in gratitude, "I am simply overcome." Her sense of the ever-present spirits of her mother and father, of Robbie, Lydia, Aleck—and now Gardner—was confirmed. At 1, place de l'Alma, Mrs. Montgomery Sears arranged for weekly séances, having engaged a black-veiled medium who called herself Madame de Thèbes. The spiritualist meetings attracted a number of distinguished visitors, including William James, and at one séance Mary Cassatt told excitedly of "a table which rose four feet off the floor, *twice.*"

James Stillman found it difficult to believe that this sharp, straightforward woman, sensitive to the cleverest fraud in matters of art, could be so convinced by these rigged phenomena. Mary had spoken of an appointment to visit a Madame Ley Fontveille, at 26, avenue d'Eylau, where she had heard: "They had seen a table more than once rise above their heads and hang suspended for *more than a minute in the air,*" and she announced that she had recently become a member of the Society for Psychical Research, a believer, in fact. He knew better than to attempt to dissuade her.

She brought back the body of Robbie Cassatt, buried at Darmstadt, to be reinterred with the Cassatts in the village cemetery at Beaufresne so that she might assemble her departed kin beside the château. Beset as she might be by the spirits of the departed, she received no clairvoyant contact beyond a fading memory's rapport with her dearly beloved dead.

News of Degas's unhappy state came to her in snatches of gossip and recrimination, for he had hurt or outraged every friend and these former *convives* were ready to speak ill of him in turn. Mary Cassatt knew better than to believe every innuendo murmured over the Paris grapevine, and was inclined to discount Degas's "affair" with young Suzanne Valadon (at eighteen, the mother of an illegitimate son, Maurice Utrillo), but the old man, now approaching seventy, was seen regularly making the arduous climb with his cane to her atelier on the rue Cortot at the summit of the butte Montmartre. Mademoiselle Valadon was a beginning painter under Degas's encouragement—he had done the same for Mary Cassatt, and that was that as far as Mary was concerned. The Degas-Valadon relationship ended when Suzanne married a wealthy business man; Degas climbed the butte no more, and shut himself into the growing darkness at 37, rue Victor-Massé. He was growing blind.

Mary could understand the pain and frustration of Degas's affliction, since she too was beginning to lose her sight. She had tried to continue engraving, but the light from the surface of copper plates brought tears to her eyes—perhaps this glare had been responsible for the damage to her sight, but she had also contracted diabetes and knew that this must have affected her eyes. Poor Pisarro had suffered the same waning sight in old age, and at the end he had taken to painting cityscapes of Paris from open windows. Degas had put his oils and pastels aside and turned to sculpture, but Mary Cassatt would neither sculpt nor stand before windows seeking light in order to paint, like Pissarro, empty Parisian boulevards. By 1912 the cataracts in both her eyes had so eclipsed vision that she was forced to abandon engraving altogether.

She avoided Degas in the last years, but she kept track of his decline. Zoe, his housekeeper of many years, declared that her employer was not completely blind: "He sees," she said, "only what he wants to see." On the street he would pretend not to recognize a face he had come to detest or notice a hand outstretched in greeting. He suffered an embarrassing weakness of the bladder, and Mary Cassatt was spitefully informed that he sometimes went out of doors with his fly negligently agape. He drank only cherry-stem tea, prepared by Zoe, to treat his bladder trouble. When Mary Cassatt learned that Zoe was obliged to give up her employ with Degas, she privately contacted Degas's niece, Jeanne Fèvre, and arranged for her to care for the old man.

Then they were saying that the poor man's house had been sold over his head. Mary knew the torment he must be suffering, to lose his familiar atelier, the place most vital to him in all of Paris. A temporary and unsatisfactory apartment was found for him not far away, on the tumultuous boulevard Clichy. When the stacks of paintings were carted there, paintings of his own and those he had collected, Degas was seen trailing after the movers, complaining piteously, "But what will become of *me?*"

He continued to haunt the streets of Pigalle along the confluent stream of boulevards: Courcelles, Batignolles, Clichy, Rochechouart, with never a pause at the old Café Guerbois where the Impressionists had gathered long ago in tempestuous debate. Though his eyes had failed him, his sturdy legs had not. He wore an ancient Inverness cape even in the muggy heat of summer, and a *chapeau melon* of unknown vintage turning green with mold, for he walked in the wet as well as in mild weather. He had taken to following the flower-laden funeral chariots of every passing *pompe funèbre,* and so was most often seen in the vicinity of the cimetière de Montmartre or slogging through the wet leaves along the winding *allées* of Père Lachaise.

His deafness was another on-and-off affliction related to his mood. If there was talk of war, he would not hear it.

She would not let talk of war scare her to the States. Mary Cassatt felt mixed sentiments and confused allegiance to the country of her birth, but these were the same attitudes she had toward France. Each time she returned to America there was the dread *mal de mer* to endure, and then the hopeless cultural vacuum of a society dedicated primarily to material gain. Its politics were ridiculous, its ambitions shameful. Nevertheless, she was irrevocably attached to America—her memory of it, or to a dim sense of an abandoned sanctuary. Stillman would no doubt take the voyage with her: "Sea-sickness is nothing to be afraid of," he assured her. "Just strap your belt tight and take a teaspoon of whiskey." How like her father he was.

Neither the dread of seasickness nor the inquietude that vibrated in the rumors of war affected, finally, her decision to stand fast. She would remain in France come what may—and war did come that summer of 1914. Stillman stayed on as well, engaged in a restless stint of war work with the Paris-American Chamber of Commerce. They were never to marry. In Mary's odd way of thinking, she may have intended to alleviate a rejection by making a proposal of her own: she offered to paint Mr. Stillman's portrait. It was an unusual impulse on her part—she seldom painted men, and had not been satisfied with the result when she did. It was his turn to say no.

After four years of World War I, James Stillman was drawn back, as Mary Cassatt feared all along, to the United States where he felt he belonged. It was 1917, the year Degas died. Because of the war, the great painter's death passed almost unnoticed: the bodies of so many Frenchmen were piled in the trenches to the northeast of the city, and there would be many more before the year, and the war, ended. Mary Cassatt could only express her grief in a letter to her young friend George Biddle: "Degas died at midnight not knowing his state. His death is a deliverance but I am sad, he was my oldest friend here and is the last great artist of the nineteenth century. I see no one to replace him."

At the ceremony in the cimetière de Montmartre, Mary Cassatt encountered Claude Monet: they were the only two surviving members of the original band of Impressionists still in Paris. The other remaining survivor, Renoir, lived in Cagnes in the Midi, seeking a tolerable climate for his rheumatism, painting, in Mary's description, his "enormously fat red women with very small heads."

Monet, Mary Cassatt always maintained, was the only true "impressionist" of the Impressionists, but she had never cared for the man himself. Their meeting at this time, at the Degas family tomb, was chilly on her part. She was snappish as always on such an unbearable occasion, but spared Monet the acid comment on his massive panels entitled *Nenuphars:* she thought of his waterlilies as nothing but glorified wallpaper. (This was an ironic recall of critic Louis Leroy's remark about the group he originally dubbed "Impressionists": "Why, wallpaper in its earliest stages is more finished.") Later, in tender reflection, she wrote to Louisine that Degas was no more: "We buried him on Saturday a [day of] beautiful sunshine, a little crowd of friends and admirers, all very quiet and peaceful in the midst of this dreadful upheaval of which he was barely conscious."

In March 1918 the first auction of Degas's work—along with his collection of Impressionists and other works—was held at the Georges Petit Gallery in Paris. Mary Cassatt attended despite a hail of shells from the German assault on the city. Strips of paper had been pasted on the gallery windows to keep the panes from shattering as the building rocked from nearby explosions, a kind of makeshift collage the dealer René Gimpel called "war art." Even as the padded ceiling skylight trembled during the auction, the bidding was fierce and the bombardment only temporarily halted trading: this first of four Degas auctions was the signal art event of wartime Paris, bringing in 12 million gold francs.

That same month James Stillman died in America.

The Steins, Mary Cassatt had heard, and the dealer Vollard were behind this new art movement in Paris, with people and events shifting from Montmartre to Montparnasse: well, Vollard's judgment was not to be trusted since it was he who thought Renoir's fat red women with very small heads were fine. Durand-Ruel knew better. Alas, Mrs. Sears was also caught up and quite excited about this New Art Mary had only seen a sample of.

"I can't tell you how vital they are," said Mrs. Sears, and for a moment Mary believed she was proposing a séance, to be held at some studio near the Luxembourg Gardens instead of at the Montgomery Sears home on the place d'Alma.

Vital to what? wondered Mary, when she understood Mrs. Sears was referring to the couple named Stein. Mary Cassatt had no time for the Steins—she had got the impression they were husband and wife, not brother and sister—but they were Americans (Jewish Americans) and Mrs. Sears persisted, so she allowed herself to be persuaded to accept an invitation to tea. She learned that her collector friend now sought advice on art from this Gertrude Stein and her "husband," who had created a salon in their studio home at 27, rue de Fleurus. The salon had become familiar to artistic and intellectual circles—circles, however, unfamiliar to Mary Cassatt—and these Americans were said to be an influence, an influence she wondered, for better or worse. Both Cassatt and Stein were curious about one another, but neither was someone who allowed her curiosity to show.

So Mary crossed the Seine by horse cab, accompanied by Mrs. Sears, to the western flank of the Jardin du Luxembourg. At first there was at least the civilized formality of asking where each was from, and to Mary Cassatt's surprise and initial delight, she learned that Mrs. Stein was also from Allegheny, Pennsylvania.

"Why, I was born there," said Mary Cassatt.

"So was I."

"My father was once mayor of Allegheny."

"Mine was not."

The conversation took a downturn from there, for the subject naturally became art. The Cubists at that time were being recognized and promoted by Gertrude Stein and her brother Leo. It was as if Gertrude Stein was in Paris to speak for the Cubists and explain them to the world, but it was Mary Cassatt's experience that painters could very well speak for themselves, and did so. The Steins had invested in the Cubist movement, and many of the paintings they purchased were hanging chock-a-block on the studio walls.

Mary Cassatt was accustomed to talking about art, sometimes at length, for she was an artist, but she found on this occasion she was being upstaged by her passionately articulate hostess. One would think the guest, especially if the guest were an established painter, would be asked to discuss painting (at least about her own work) instead of the hostess running on in Mother Goose language about art. Mary Cassatt listened to none of it. Reduced to resentful silence, she attempted to study through a glaucous haze the circus of color on the atelier walls. Above Gertrude Stein's carved armchair, where she sat as if carved of something herself, was what Mary Cassatt considered a vulgar portrait of her, a crude rendering the sitter herself had told the painter did not resemble her. "It will," the painter had replied—a Monsieur Picasso Gertrude Stein spoke of with enthusiasm—as if his clever remark made up for lack of artistic gift.

Later, Mary would write to her niece and namesake, Mary Ellen Cassatt, about the odd couple on the rue de Fleurus, still believing they were man and wife though Mrs. Sears had told her Miss Stein was unmarried, like herself, and the gentleman was her brother:

> As to this Gertrude Stein, she is one of a family of California Jews who came to Paris poor and unknown; but they are not Jews for nothing. . . . Little by little people who want to be amused went to these receptions where Stein received in sandals and his wife in one garment fastened by a broach, which if it gave way might disclose the costume of Eve. Of course the curiosity was aroused and the anxiety as to whether it *would* give way; and the pose was, if you didn't admire these daubs I am sorry for you; you are not one of the chosen few. No sound artists ever looked with scorn at these cubists and Matisse.

The woman was still talking, and who cared if her garment gave way or not? It hurt her eyes to try to look at these Cubists and Matisse, but there was nothing Mary Cassatt could do but fix her expression, tighten her fists, and endure. After the briefest possible interval to accommodate whatever notion of politesse passed in such company, Mary whispered to Mrs. Sears: "Please take me home."

EDITH WARTON in 1897,
with one of her cherished lapdogs.
(Warder Collection)

II

Edith Wharton

1862–1937

Goodbye, goodbye.—Write or don't write,
as you feel the impulse—but hold me long and
close in your thoughts. I shall take up
so little room, & it's only there that I'm happy!

Edith Wharton was descending the stairwell of mirrored panels leading to the First-Class dining room aboard the *Philadelphia.* She carried Mitou, the survivor of their male-female Pekingese pair, and ordinarily Teddy Wharton—a step or two behind his wife—would be carrying the mate, but Miza had died just before the Whartons' departure from New York. Puss, as Teddy Wharton happily referred to his wife, was devastated by the little dog's death: she was a woman who loved little dogs more than . . . more than what he could not say, but knew that it was not himself.

By the captain's dispensation the Whartons were allowed to tuck the miniature Mitou beneath the dining-room table at their feet. Animals were not ordinarily permitted in the dining room; the captain's *noblesse oblige* was the kind of gesture Edith Wharton most appreciated, the social form she practiced herself.

The reflecting panels cast an image of a well-proportioned woman of middle years carrying the dog just under her breast, and clutching at a fold of gown to keep the long low garment from catching at her heel—Teddy Wharton enjoyed this glimpse of slim ankle as well as his wife's slender waist ("Look at that waist!" he once crowed to a friend. "No one would ever guess she had written a line of poetry in her life"). Though the hard-set mouth and long line of jaw were drawbacks to a conventional prettiness, Edith Wharton was indeed a well-made woman, handsome enough now, a beauty when he married her. She had perfect skin. From the way she glanced into mirrors, it was evident she did not think ill of herself or neglect her grooming because of intellectual reverie. She greatly cared about fashion, one of the reasons Paris excited her so, and she had always been proud of her figure, buxom in the style of the day, so she dressed in a way to emphasize her bosom. The neckline of her dress was cut low, but with a modest fringe of lace at the cleavage. She had bearing and poise: to those with whom she was not intimate, she appeared stern or disapproving; when her strongly pronounced jaw did relax into a crease of delight at the mouth, her face became truly attractive.

Her eyes were especially fine, quick and penetrating in the observant writer's way; and her hair piled high was carefully, even regally, coiffed. She wore this auburn abundance rolled into a crescent off her neck, and Teddy Wharton noted the graceful curve of that neck. Though he could not feel the pride of possession—since his wife had never acquiesced to the marital vow of obedience—he could take pleasure, as now, in the public display of such a well-bred creature at his side. Her name was his. Wharton appeared on the volumes she wrote: she was his lady, legally and in fact. He was comforted in the pride of being married to a member of his own genteel crowd of impeccable social connections: the Rhinelanders, Van Rensselaers, Astors, Vanderbilts, she of the New York Jones-Rhinelander dynasty. But sadly he reflected on the theme of his wife's incongruous literary gifts after the delighted observation of that well-made waist. "I'm no good," as he once confessed to Edith's close friend Sara Norton, "on Puss's high plane of thought."

Teddy Wharton was a sportsman and horse fancier, an outdoorsman bred to the confines of Boston establishments. He was amiably functional at pouring wine at dinner parties, and knowledgeable about the wines themselves—he had got that much out of previous trips to Paris—but he was far more comfortable in the brass and leather lounge-bar of a club where the assembled were exclusively male. Teddy would rather have lingered at the splendid Wharton estate in Lenox where his set would be drinking hot whiskies at the Club.

The change of scene was best for Puss. She had earned it: Paris was her special place, the city that brought her alive after a lengthy mental wringing out. Writing took too much out of her, drained her in unexpected ways—this he did not altogether understand, for she wrote in bed, and what was the strain of that? But he was familiar with her episodes of deep depression, and dreaded them for her; he was subject to melancholia himself. Nevertheless, she was chipper now, and aglow with the prospect of Paris.

That novel of hers was out, *The House of Mirth,* a really smashing success. It was selling to beat the band; everyone in Boston and New

York and probably all over the country was talking about Edith Wharton. He had struggled through the book himself: he recognized some of the types she wrote about. It was a good thing she had changed their names. A great breakthrough for Puss, this book with *Edith Wharton* on the cover—how odd to see the name *Wharton* attached to a book, and to appear in reviews, and to be talked about everywhere.

Henry James had put his friend Edith onto the subject of *The House of Mirth:* the superficiality of New York society and the tribal rituals of the idle rich. "Don't pass [the American theme] by—the immediate, the real, the only, the yours, the novelist's that it waits for. . . . All the same, *do New York!* The 1st-hand account is precious." This was wise counsel to a writer who had previously exhausted herself writing a two-volume historical novel set in Italy. James praised, or overpraised that novel, *The Valley of Decision,* but implicit in his praise was the suggestion that an Italian historical romance was not where her literary gifts lay. Edith Wharton did know every corner and detail of Lily Bart's house of mirth, and knew "that a frivolous society can acquire dramatic significance only through what its frivolity destroys." But Edith Wharton was no Lily Bart, who had violated the code of New York society and was destroyed by the 400 to which she belonged. Edith was fleeing New York society rather than being rejected by it.

Lily Bart had believed that a European cruise would help solve her difficulties: "If she was faintly aware of fresh difficulties ahead, she was sure of her ability to meet them." It was not the difficulties ahead but the familiar past that nagged at Edith's conscience and spoiled the prospects ahead; there was Teddy to consider, the man who shared her cabin and her life. Earlier, at tea in their stateroom, she had passed Teddy the book she was reading, and drew his attention to a marvelous passage from *Heredity and Variation.* Teddy read the paragraph with the frowning intensity he applied to any reading matter, then lifted his head to remark: "Does that sort of thing amuse you?"

I heard the key turn in the prison lock, was her exasperated thought, and the thought resounded in her mind throughout the evening. The note would find its way into her journal that night, along with the French expression "J'étouffe" ("I am smothering").

Teddy, too, had a sense of smothering, but he could not have expressed this in English or French. The New York–Cherbourg crossing was a long restless winter's passage. Since it was snowing at sea and the iced decks were treacherous, there was little chance of outdoor exercise except for a cautious walking of Mitou twice a day. The staterooms, however spacious and with the amenities of First Class, were confining, damnably overheated, and airless.

In fact, Teddy's French was not bad. Walter Berry, Edith's cousin in Paris, had complimented him on this, and on his connoisseurship of wines. Walter was a good fellow, he would be glad enough to see him in Paris. There had been talk that Walter Berry and Edith had been on the verge of engagement, but Teddy knew better: he knew Walter. Walter Berry loved the ladies, but he was too bookish for marriage, and a bachelor born.

Edith had been engaged to Harry Stevens for a little while: the Stevens family was pushy and had eased into society on the strength of new money and very little name. You would have thought Minnie Paran Stevens, a grocer's daughter, was delighted to crown her position in society with a Jones-Stevens liaison—but no. The young people had courted over tennis nets and at archery in the same background so useful to *The House of Mirth:* Newport during the season there, then at Bar Harbor. The romance with Harry surely helped Edith during one of her dread depressions, eased her through the long black night of her father's death that same year, 1882. But the *arriviste* Mrs. Paran Stevens had been badly snubbed by the Joneses, and did not easily forget a social slight; also there was a financial complication: his mother would lose control over her son's considerable trust fund upon his marriage. The Newport *Daily News* announced the death blow to the engagement in entirely different terms: "The only reason assigned for the breaking of the engagement existing between Harry Stevens and Miss Edith Jones is an alleged preponderance of intellectuality on the part of the intended bride. Miss Jones is an ambitious authoress, and it is said that, in the eyes of Mrs. Stevens, ambition is a grievous fault."

Except for her father, and Walter Berry, the only man Puss ever much cared about—and that was because of a "preponderance of intellectuality"—was Henry James. Formally, in the right circumstances, Teddy got on with the man. There was a superficial amiability between the two, but so often in James's overbred company at Lenox or in London, where James had settled, Teddy felt or was made to feel a bumptious clod. James had become more English than the English: you could not read one of his cerebral letters (often addressed to both Whartons, but clearly meant for Edith alone) without a dictionary in hand. In company the man was an exhausting talker, and as difficult to understand as his letters.

Teddy had no way with words except in the commonplace exchanges and repeated banalities of the society to which he had been bred. Edith came of the same stock; they had that much in common. Teddy knew how to elaborate on the gossip of the day without sounding vulgar, and after dinner the Whartons sat in the ship's lounge with a small circle of vague acquaintances—Edith had known New York friends of the Philadelphia couple, Teddy had been to school with the brother of the fellow from Boston—while a trio of strolling strings played a medley of Strauss waltzes. The postprandial conversation followed a well-defined pattern of social notes and New York theatre commentary, with stock-market insights traded among the gentlemen. Edith Wharton presented a most agreeable facade of cultivation and graciousness mixed with indefinable reserve, a certain distance from the present gathering as if some part of her were in the stateroom writing, or as if she were already in Paris.

Eventually the gentlemen retired to the card table, with brandies, and the ladies were left to complete the tapestry of social talk, each weaving her part in the weft and warp of announced engagements, accomplished marriages, summer homes acquired, and Christmas parties just past.

Edith acceptably held her own in the inventory of social items examined and compared. She was as informed and voluble as any woman in their small party, as animated and as perfectly in her element. It was 1906, and *The House of Mirth* had appeared only six months before, but the subject of Edith's novel did not come up.

The Whartons slept apart, in separate staterooms on the *Philadelphia*, and had done so at Lenox and in their Manhattan townhouse since the last night of their honeymoon, twenty years before. That night had been a disaster, and both Edith and Teddy would have given their souls to undo the damage. It was not Teddy's fault, and certainly not hers. Not even their mornings were shared, for Edith's mornings, in bed with a board across her knees and Mitou curled at her feet, were devoted to writing. Aboard the *Philadelphia* she maintained the same strict discipline of a morning's work despite the tilting cabin as the ship rolled with the North Atlantic swells, the breakfast tray rattling beside her.

It was not her fault. She had been given no warning from her married women friends, or from her mother. Only days before the wedding ceremony this Victorian dialogue took place:

"I would like to know, about the—"

"The what?" was the sharp reply of Lucretia Jones. The mother and daughter were not especially close, and their relationship on such a delicate occasion was predictably strained.

"Well, the physical, that side. Of marriage."

Lucretia Jones was genuinely annoyed, but her reaction conformed to the prevailing attitudes.

"Goodness, haven't you noticed? Don't you know that men are, well, made differently from women?"

"How—could I notice?"

"You've been to museums, you've seen paintings. And statues, naturally."

Of course she had, and so the answer was, "Yes."

"Then for heaven's sake don't ask such silly questions. You can't be as stupid as you pretend."

This was said in so final a manner, the mother's back turned to the daughter, that Edith could only conclude that the interview was over.

After the exchange of vows at Trinity Church, New York, Edith Newbold Jones accepted Edward Robbins Wharton as her lawfully wedded husband. The bride wore white satin with a diamond tiara in her upswept burnished hair; the tiara was made of gems her mother wore at her own wedding. The newspapers, especially in New York, detailed the Jones-Wharton nuptials as the social season's ultimate spectacle.

Three weeks would pass before the young couple consummated their marriage. Her museum education was insufficient to spare Edith the shock of male-female relations in the bedroom, "the physical side" of married love. She would never again respond to any such lovemaking overtures on the part of her husband; Teddy, in fact, had long ceased to make any such overtures.

ii

The Whartons arrived at Cherbourg with luggage and servants enough for a permanent move to Paris, though the trip was meant only as a holiday from Edith's long labor on *The House of Mirth.* It was snowing in Cherbourg, as it had been at sea, and a light snow fell upon Paris although by the calendar it was spring. The suite they had engaged at the Hôtel Dominici was large enough to accommodate their separate sleeping arrangements; with the servants installed in *chambres de bonnes* in the hotel's upper rooms, and an adequate sitting room where Edith could entertain. The Dominici was ideally situated on the rue Castiglione, just off the place Vendôme, in precisely the same block of elegant structures and chic boutiques where so many transient Americans made their initial transcontinental sojourn. The rue Castiglione was where the Cassatt family had first settled—temporarily, like the Whartons—half a century before. The changes Haussmann had wrought were now permanent landmarks, and the Vendôme column Courbet had been accused of demolishing during the Paris Commune was again in place, a comforting restoration to the new habitués of the place Vendôme.

The Dominici became Edith Wharton's social reception center, the scene of her launching into French society. On a previous visit to Paris, and at her home in Lenox, she had met the succesfully established novelist Paul Bourget, who invariably referred to Edith as "Le Velásquez"—the title a puzzle to Teddy, but he did not always catch on to the allusions made by Edith's writer friends.

Paul Bourget was a key figure in the faubourg St. Germain enclave of French society. As a literary lion, and member of le gratin de gratin, he had access to the most exclusive salons on the Left and Right banks of the Seine. On Edith's prior visits to Paris she had been a visiting American of good family but of no particular Old World distinction or traceable lineage out of the *Almanach de Gotha.* At that time Paul Bourget was under no compulsion or obligation to integrate his American acquaintance into the closed circle of his French friends—in fact, he could not have done so. But now, on the tide of success from *The House of Mirth* (translated into French by Charles du Bos as *Chez les heureux du Monde*), Bourget saw fit to serve as literary ambassador. Since the French took literary distinction with great seriousness and respect, this was the perfect occasion for Bourget to be the discriminating go-between from the sealed precincts of the faubourg to the sitting room at the Dominici where he so often enjoyed tea and talk with the eminent novelist from America.

As Edith Wharton was making that first tentative approach toward the French aristocracy, Mary Cassatt was reading *The House of Mirth* in English and finding it tedious. "Literally I could not read it, such an imitation of Bourget, a writer I cannot endure, by the way, so a copy [could not possibly] please me. She tries James, for the character. . . . Dear, dear. No Art!" For her part, Edith Wharton, strangely insensitive to the art of painting, was unaware of or disinterested in the presence of her fellow American artist in Paris. Thus the two women, early residents of the rue Castiglione and expatriates from America both, were never to meet.

It was Paul Bourget who first thought of bringing together Edith Wharton and Charles du Bos, an introduction meant to serve both social and literary ends. A happy pairing it turned out to be. Du Bos, whose mother was English, was perfectly bilingual, and Edith Wharton was fluent in French—the translation would be more of a collaboration between two keen minds.

Though du Bos had been part of the Marcel Proust entourage, he had yet to exercise a latent writing talent with any success. *The House of Mirth* was the first substantial literary work he had taken on. Bourget thought him a dilatory and indecisive young man—handicapped, as was his maître Proust, by hypochondria—and he believed the translation project was just the impetus he needed to launch his career. Bourget also surmised that Edith Wharton would instinctively take this literary tyro in hand.

As middle age settled upon her, Edith Wharton began to enjoy the company of younger men like du Bos if there was some spark to their intellect and blueblood in their veins. Percy Lubbock, her future biographer and another member of her young male entourage, spoke of Edith's "frigid impenetrable hauteur that absolutely dispelled any pretensions to intimacy," and another younger man, Hugh Smith, wrote Edith Wharton: "You alarm poor Percy, but his admiration of you is that of all sane men."

However, du Bos found that an unexpected intimacy could develop from their two heads bent together in such close collaboration. Du Bos became more than the "clever and agreeable young man" Edith first described in her journal, and he revised his initial assessment of Madame Wharton's character. Like Lubbock, he had been put off at first meeting by her apparent remove from the moment, the chilling distance she placed between them; to du Bos she appeared absolutely self-assured and not a little condescending, but he soon discovered the essential clue to her character. Edith Wharton was profoundly shy. The cold repose was a cover, and behind the assumed *froideur* was a personable warmth and affection waiting to be found out. The facade of dignified composure was the screen behind which the real Edith Wharton hid: the apparent disdain in her expression masked a miscellany of fears. Edith proved to be the most loyal of friends and there came to be, on du Bos's part, the kind of love for this older woman that Mary Cassatt had inspired in George Biddle.

The House of Mirth was Edith Wharton's largest success to date, her ninth book in eight years of authorship. The writing of it, she said, had turned her from "a drifting amateur into a professional" as she perfected the daily discipline that would serve her ever after. The novel originally ran as a serial in *Scribner's Magazine,* and when her editor, William Brownell, attempted to push the hardbound edition with the suggestive blurb: "for the first time the veil has been lifted from New York society," the author wrote him that she had assumed *The House of Mirth* would be safe at the House of Scribner's from such blatant *réclame.* The blurb was immediately removed from the jacket.

Edith Wharton's name was made, as far as the reading public was concerned, but reviews of the book were not as unanimously approving. There were attacks on her own attack of New York Society: the author had depicted a rigidly corrupt modern social class, but offered no hope of "betterment"; as soon as one critic declared the novel a masterpiece, another would say not-quite or not-at-all. "How good, how good! . . . the best thing you have done," declared her friend Charles Norton, but in the next breath advised that "no woman not spotlessly virtuous can be the heroine of a truly serious novel."

Henry James was equally hot and cold about the novel, suspicious of the sales appeal of "Mrs. Wharton's pleasantly palpable hit"; but as he had suggested the theme in the first place to her, he referred to the book as an "altogether superior thing."

The House of Mirth was Scribner's all-time bestseller, and the royalties made a comfortable addition to the Old Money in Edith's three trust funds, her sizable inheritances from both parents, and the legacy from her grandfather Joshua Jones. She had the characteristic distaste of the artist for legal and financial matters, so most of her affairs were in Teddy Wharton's hands. The Wharton fortune was considerably less than the holdings of the Jones dynasty, and Teddy would not come into a comfortable estate of his own until his mother died—thus Edith's fortune and earnings made up the bulk of their wealth.

The author managed effortlessly to spend up to her income, for her tastes were expensive: there was the suite at the Dominici, with a retinue of servants, and the diamond-shaped enclosure of the place Vendôme was her de luxe neighborhood shopping center. She loved to move about, so a motorcar was *de rigueur* (with chauffeur, when Teddy was not at the wheel). Edith's brother, and Teddy, were trustees for her estate, and Teddy was the adept and willing manager of her security transactions; he was her personal accountant for income, outlay, all principal and interest concerns. Teddy always carried a one-thousand-dollar bill in his wallet—and in Paris, the equivalent in francs—"in case Pussy wants something."

Because of her wealth and social position, Edith Wharton was never to escape the image of herself as moneyed dilettante with an artistic hobby, writing, to fill the idle hours between social engagements. Her dedication went far beyond that easy stereotype, but few persons knew of her tortured striving, as she described the daily ordeal in the oddly phrased "to order the beauty even of beauty is." Hers was an artistic commitment as complete as the taking of holy orders. There was no one but her little dog, Mitou, to witness the long morning hours devoted to the task of authorship with a taskmaster's writing board across her blanketed knees. At the Dominici, the Louis XV bed had been moved to face the French windows that gave onto the eastern light of the rue Castiglione, so that Edith could duplicate the writing position of her bedroom at the Mount in Lenox.

The relentless strain of her literary endeavors had already contributed to more than one nervous collapse, the most recent apparently caused by the concentrated effort on her first long novel, *The Valley of Decision.* Her frequent journeys, especially to Paris, were meant to vary the strict routine; but even when traveling, Edith kept up the ceaseless discipline of pen and page and writing board.

Her closest friends accepted her as the gifted professional she had made of herself. Walter Berry had watched her literary skills flower from the first seedling attempts and, as her literary counselor, was in on the cultivation from the beginning. Her other trusted friend in letters, Henry James, had early on recognized Edith Wharton's way with words in delineating the characters and milieu of Old New York. She had hit upon—been born to, in fact—an invaluable backdrop and cast of players only she could know so well. So many other social satirists were merely looking through the windows of the elite salons, attempting to understand what passed inside those gilded premises. This was James's very own material, and he was somewhat uncomfortable knowing how large an influence his work had been on Edith Wharton: she was in fact—with less mastery, yet with her own flair and insight—poaching on his preserves.

Both Edith Wharton and Henry James had fallen victim to *snobisme* in the French sense of the word: *snob* being an abbreviation of the French term *sans noblesse,* applied to those who nurtured an excessive admiration of the titled, with a desire to be assimilated into that exclusive society. The irony was that each recognized instantly anyone with such pretensions, and just as naturally discerned the *snobisme* in each other but not in themselves. They both wrote with trenchant wit and genuine insight about the ignoble weakness of snobbery in all its forms, except the personal. Edith Wharton had been born to what passed for a social aristocracy in America, but by European standards the silver spoon was plated tin. James had managed with infinite patience and frank admiration to penetrate the British upper-class milieu, and now felt himself a distinguished member of that society. He was the Anglophile counterpart of Edith Wharton's Francophile.

Edith was now embarked on the same conquest of an even more hermetic social caste: the faubourg St. Germain and its exclusive salons on the Left Bank of the Seine.

At one of the more intimately relaxed of Edith Wharton's teas at the Hôtel Dominici, she met the comtesse Anna de Noailles, a tiny vivacious French aristocrat, like a miniature piece of Sèvres come alive, poet and *romancière* like herself. The immediate spark to their friendship was the mutual love of letters; but there was another sphere in which they were drawn together—Edith the silent but captivated listener, the comtesse expressing naturally and openly the philosophy of a passionate sexual being. Anna de Noailles lived the loves Edith had only imagined in writing, or had buried in her heart. The two worlds of the Parisian poet and the American novelist barely touched where Edith might have wished they were one.

Edith Wharton was bewitched by so free-spirited a creature, who to all appearances lived exactly as she pleased, as Lily Bart longed to live but was trapped in the narrow passageways of a House of Mirth. The difference was that Paris could delightedly accommodate a comtesse de Noailles while New York must and would destroy a Lily Bart. The faubourg respected the comtesse for her style; she was as admired for her spirit as for her literary gifts, and she could never lose face or find doors of the faubourg closed to her.

Like Teddy, the comte Mathieu de Noailles put in a token appearance at the Noailles salon, a ghostly, ineffectual partner attending his wife's teas, a functionary to his wife's further purposes—but Teddy was even less at home, in his own home or here, cut off by disinterest from book talk and by nature from the subtler forms of wit.

Very soon Edith kept a volume of *Le Coeur Innombrable* on her bedstand at the Dominici; she was reading the poetry of Anna de Noailles, and the comtesse was reading *The House of Mirth.* The French verses contained something Edith called the white heat of a poet's work, a Whitmanesque passion for living. *Le Coeur Innombrable* had been honored by l'Académie Française, poems heavily redolent of the sadness and euphoria of romantic love; the novels were chronicles of the liberated female spirit, very much in the style of Edith's favorite, George Sand.

For her part, Anna de Noailles found Edith Wharton an intriguingly original *Américaine.* Madame Wharton's cultivation was exceptional, and she was articulate enough to be French. The woman's large sense of dignified restraint was admirable, but Anna and others of the faubourg discerned a repressed emotional life behind the mannered facade. While Edith Wharton was in the process of being initiated into faubourg circles and accepted by the first families of France, she was at the same time being studied as a national type: Old France observing through its blasé lorgnette a puritanical product of Old New York.

Edith could not fail to observe, in turn, the strange interplay of relationships among her new French friends. Considering herself a social observer, as any writer must be, Edith did not close her ears to sexual gossip, nor was she greatly put off by learning of deviant liaisons. Here in Paris she was not so much aware of a comfortable bisexuality in the comtesse as she was indifferent or indulgent to the forms of love expressed. What intrigued and inspired Edith was that a woman could be so passionately *engagée* as a lover both in act and idea.

The easy tolerance of the French for "the love that dare not speak its name" had made Paris the capital for such homosexual exiles as Oscar Wilde, who had been released from Reading Gaol at the turn of the century and had come immediately to Paris. Edith became obliquely acquainted with her fellow American expatriate Winnaretta Singer, the princesse de Polignac, whose salon in Passy, not many steps from the Noailles *hôtel particulier,* was a famous gathering place for the musical talent of the city. Edith Wharton had no more attraction to chamber music soirées than to painting—the musical offerings took annoying precedence over literary talk—but the salon of the princesse (where Edith did meet Diaghilev and his Ballets Russes ensemble) was a necessary call, just as Natalie Barney's salon on the Left Bank was a must-not. The Barney gatherings at her small back-garden Temple de l'Amitié were less literary lion hunts than an excuse for promiscuous exchange of partners and the formation of lesbian liaisons. Edith warned one new friend, Blandine de Prévaux: "You must never go near Miss Barney," and declared that *l'Amazone* of the Left Bank was "something appalling."

Marcel Proust had at one time frequented the salon of the comtesse de Noailles where he encountered many of his fictional prototypes, but the Dreyfus Affair had driven him into cork-lined seclusion on the boulevard Haussmann, relieved by midnight sorties to his favorite table at the Ritz. Edith was an early and avid reader of Proust's *A la recherche du temps perdu,* and introduced the first volume of that work to Henry James, who became an immediate admirer of Proust's convoluted search for time past. Since Proust had withdrawn from salon life before Edith became a member of the de

Noailles circle in Passy, the French and American novelists were never to meet. Edith did meet at the de Noailles dinner table the vociferous anti-Dreyfusard Gustave Schlumberger, who nearly choked on his wine in choleric outrage over the total vindication of Dreyfus when the shattered captain had been cleared of all charges and was awarded the Légion d'Honneur as recompense for his ordeal. The Whartons were just settling into the Paris scene in 1907 when the Dreyfus Affair came to its muted conclusion: the great issue was no longer an acceptable dinner-table subject, kept heatedly alive only by such insistent anti-Dreyfusards as Schlumberger, Edith's friend Paul Bourget, and Degas.

The company of young male admirers brought a tremor of pleasure to Edith Wharton, even if this pleasure was at one respectable remove—the admirers were often first and foremost friends of the comtesse. It occurred to her that some of these gentlemen might also be bisexual or homosexual, but such predilections were shadowy background only and of little consequence. For Edith was tremulously aware of some sea-change in her own nature, and had not yet determined what this subliminal sensation really meant.

The comtesse de Noailles had perceived a certain glow in the visage of her friend Edith, intuited a growing sense of possibilities in her emotional development, and would have been happy to contribute to its fulfillment. She was lavish in her introductions.

However much Paris infected the emotional state of Edith, Teddy was pressing for a return to Lenox. The Paris he was exposed to was a ceaseless round of musical chairs at one salon or another, and the game had taken its toll. The Whartons had always been reasonable enough about indulging one another's wishes, and in this case Edith reluctantly agreed to Teddy's request. A side trip to London and the countryside of England was a pleasant enough distraction en route, and the one satisfying interlude for Teddy. Though he disliked the company of Henry James, James loved to travel about by motorcar and did not have one of his own: Teddy was the experienced chauffeur on their excursions, and he delighted in his central role as pilot of the Panhard.

When Edith and Henry managed to be alone, Edith could speak of literary matters, and then suggest, in the oblique and never-quite-stated manner of Henry James himself, matters of emotional impasse. The frustrated state of Edith's heart and mind James had already predicted when he first learned of "this inconceivable thing," Edith's unlikely choice of Teddy Wharton as her lifetime partner. James was as understanding as his own unmarried state permitted.

In Paris, Edith had the ear of a priest confessor all of the *haut monde* turned to, the devout and charming Abbé Mugnier, benevolent comforter of the troubled and personal intercessor for the sins of the faubourg. As it turned out, Henry James—not the comtesse de Noailles or the Abbé Mugnier—would help resolve passion's stalemate and provide an interim figure of resolution. James too, from some youthful "obscure hurt," had known the banked fires of love denied, and was as familiar as Edith with all the artificial outlets of sublimation. Whether deliberately or by chance, James would be Edith's agent for change. Surely she would be delighted to meet his intelligent young journalist friend, American born, resident for the past ten years in Paris, and a most decided man of the world.

iii

When Edith Wharton met him in 1907, Morton Fullerton had just turned forty-two. Since the 1890s he had been a keen observer of the European scene for *The Times* in London, where he wrote a series of notable articles on the Dreyfus Affair, being perfectly bilingual in English and French, and something of an expert on French affairs. In London he met Henry James and succumbed to his particular charm—and James to his, for the master addressed him as "dear boy," reserved for his closest young male friends—to the point of adopting certain Jamesian gestures and mannerisms, especially in James's hesitant and convoluted manner of speech.

While associated with *The Times,* Morton Fullerton had been a member of the Oscar Wilde circle, a set of individuals Henry James, like Edith with Natalie Barney, considered too conspicuous to know. Fullerton's affair with the sculptor Ronald Sutherland, Lord Gower, lay in the past, and Fullerton escaped London just before the scandal of the Oscar Wilde trial broke. It was the time of the Dreyfus Affair, and because of his expertise in French affairs Fullerton was appointed to the Paris bureau of *The Times,* on the safe side of the Channel during a wave of homophobia set off by the accusations against Wilde. Ironically, the two trials occurring at the same time, of Captain Dreyfus in Paris and of Oscar Wilde in London, were significantly revealing social traumas for the two very different nations involved—and neither could have taken place in the other country. Fullerton was to document the French affair only, the one he could be most objective about. His past indiscretions during the Mauve Decade might have fallen into oblivion, but fell instead—by way of letters to him from Lord Gower—into the hands of a blackmailer.

From his outpost in Paris, Fullerton continued to receive warm and voluminous correspondence from James, who came less and less often to Paris, finding that lively city too wearing and distracting for such subtle analysis as he applied in his late period to place. Fullerton in turn kept James informed of his Paris activities in such warm and winning prose as to evoke this reply from his older friend: "My dearest Morton! My difficulty is that I love you too fantastically much to be able, in intercourse and relations with you, in such a matter as answering your celestial letter, to do anything *but* love you, whereby the essence of the whole thing is simply that you divinely write to me and I divinely feel it. . . ." Many of Fullerton's confidences concerned affairs of the heart, and he sought advice from James on these Byzantine affairs, including the damning Lord Gower letters held over his head by his blackmailing landlady-lover in Paris.

At the same time, Henry James was receiving letters from Edith Wharton in Lenox, one of which spoke of the New World in tones of gray: "It's back to business courses and skyscrapers." She was growing more and more dissatisfied with her native America, and felt herself a misfit there: "My first few weeks in America are always miserable because the tastes I am cursed with are all of a kind that cannot be gratified here . . . *we* are none of us Americans, we don't think or feel as Americans do, we are the wretched exotics produced in a European glass-house." To distract herself from the bleak horizon Massachusetts offered, she took up as a diversion a nightly scan of the heavens with the help of a booklet entitled *A Fieldbook of the Stars.* One lucky evening she found "a handsome new luminary" standing out against an old familiar constellation, a star she considered significant enough to point out to guests.

When Morton Fullerton acted on James's entreaty to "let Mrs. Wharton know of your American presence," Edith immediately invited him to the Mount. Morton's resemblance in manner and mind to Henry James was the first thing Edith noticed about her visitor: he was a clergyman's son, and had returned to Massachusetts to visit his family in Waltham, the town where he grew up—a short but leaner version of James, twenty years younger, and with the Master's clear blue eyes. He brushed his thick hair (James was quite bald) back from his thoughtful brow; a thick mustache hid his upper lip. He dressed in a way to distinguish himself as a gentleman, but with a certain self-consciously Continental dash—another "wretched exotic" like Henry James and Edith herself, produced in the glasshouse of Europe. Edith was completely taken with this younger reproduction of her great good friend.

Morton was his own man, as well, in intellectual matters and personal idiosyncrasies. He was romantically imaginative, excessively so: he kept records of his erotic dreams, transcribed with classical allusions rather than the use of currently fashionable Freudian terms. At the end of the Victorian age Fullerton's gift for lyric wordplay was a great attraction for women. Morton Fullerton had a way, without seeming foolish or excessive, of breathing the poetry of emotion into willing ears.

As a writer he was drawn to a multiplicity of interests, a useful trait in journalism, but he regularly took up more subject matter than he could write about with sustained application. He lacked the Master's exceptional power of concentration. Fullerton was one of those intelligences gifted with energy and motivated by ambition, always spoken of as up-and-coming and with infinite promise, but who never quite accomplished the successes expected of him—somewhat in the same mold as Edith's young friend Charles du Bos.

At the time, he was working on a critical study of Henry James that aspired to bring the greatness of James to the attention of the American public. Nothing could have appealed to Edith Wharton more; in her brief note of invitation she offered: "If I can, in any way, be of help . . ."

Finding myself—after so long!—with someone to talk to . . .

He was another Charles du Bos, Gaillard Lapsley—a younger

Henry James. No, he was Morton Fullerton. Younger than Edith by three years, this small, intense man, fastidious in manner and dress, was cultured, intelligent, extraordinarily self-aware . . . and something more.

He arrived at the Mount one October afternoon, and by that very evening was reading aloud to her from his work on Henry James. On the following afternoon the hostess and her guest took an excursion through the Berkshires in the Wharton Panhard—with Cook the chauffeur at the wheel. An early autumn snow began to fall. Cook thought it best to put on the snow chains, and while they were stopped, the passengers wandered away from the car in a swirl of snowflakes, smoking together, deep in one of their discussions of life and literature. They paused to examine the late-blooming witch hazel.

"The old woman's bloom," said Edith, watching Morton's face.

"But the shrub," he said, "that blossoms late."

"True. It flowers most graciously when other plant life has long faded."

By some preordained or intuitive gesture the two reached out simultaneously to pluck a blossoming sprig each.

That night Edith wrote in her long-neglected diary: *I take up this empty volume in which, long ago, I made one or two spasmodic attempts . . . but now I shall have the illusion I am talking to you.* For many idle moments in the days to come, Edith was to mull over her symbolic interlude with Morton Fullerton. She was all the more delighted to discover that Fullerton found equal significance in the episode: in his thank-you note for the pleasure of his visit to the Mount (more intimate a message, in his delicate phrasing, than was customary) he enclosed a portion of his sprig of the witch hazel.

From Lenox, Morton Fullerton returned directly to Paris, and from there initiated an elaborate correspondence with Edith Wharton that rivaled his fulsome exchange of letters with Henry James. Edith had planned to return to Paris soon after the New Year, 1908, but found herself searching for excuses to book earlier passage. She decided to sail in early December; the reason she offered Teddy was this early autumn snow: the servants quarters at the Mount had become too uncomfortable. Servants' quarters in Paris were invariably top-floor *chambres de bonnes,* separated from the centrally heated main floors, usually under the poorly insulated roof, the rooms served by a separate, unheated back staircase, and would in any case be less comfortable than accommodations in Lenox—though Teddy tendered no such suggestion, knowing Edith had made up her mind. They sailed on December 5, 1907, and were to settle into a rented apartment belonging to the George Vanderbilts at 58, rue de Varenne on Christmas Eve.

Paris was in fact blanketed with snow that chill January, but Edith bundled herself thoroughly in her furs and set out by carriage or motorcar to enjoy a subtler Paris in winter than she had known, or reacted to so euphorically, before. Her mood was romantic. On the German liner *Amerika* she had been reading Ronsard, and now beside her study window giving onto the rue de Varenne and facing the guarded gates of the Hôtel Matignon she was rereading *L'Ombre des Jours* by the comtesse de Noailles and, in the way of philosophical thought, Nietzsche's *Beyond Good and Evil,* which suggested to her a state of being outside moral considerations of the public at large—the state of being of the comtesse de Noailles, in fact. She was keeping a diary—partly in code, much of it written in German—with the ever frequent initials M.F. dotting its pages.

The writing of fiction was in temporary decline; the quality was off, and she knew this, but she did manage to write two short stories that Paris winter, one of which, "The Pretext," was close to the theme of Henry James's *Washington Square* and in fact had been suggested to her by James through a scrap of gossip in one of his letters. The gossip had nothing to do with Morton Fullerton, but Edith's version of the story had everything to do with him. The character in "The Pretext" courts an older woman in a small New England town, but only as a pretext for lingering in the vicinity in order to pursue and marry another woman. The author may have been working out a nagging frustration over the apparent lack of enthusiasm on Fullerton's part to follow up the attentions so lavishly expressed in Lenox and by mail. If Edith had only known a particle of Morton Fullerton's background and present situation, she would have realized that the conclusion to "The Pretext" had more application to the actual than to random fancy.

Fullerton's Paris life was far too complicated to allow for a continuance of his dalliance with Edith Wharton now that she had so suddenly appeared on his turf. His bachelor quarters were located near the busy hub of the place de l'Opéra, at the corner of rue de Chaussée d'Antin where the rue La Fayette and boulevard Haussmann intersected in a lively swirl of horse and motor traffic. The building was owned by a Madame Henrietta Mirecourt, a woman *d'un certain age* with whom Fullerton had been involved in a passionate affair for some years.

Mirecourt may have been part English, but her justifiable jealousy of her lover's derelictions was, in its extravagant possessiveness, characteristically French. When she took up with him, Madame Mirecourt had been aware of Morton's previous entanglement with Margaret Brooke, the Ranee of Sarawak, but the Ranee was out of sight, in London, thus out of mind. Other affairs with women "of a certain age" she had also tolerated, or managed to terminate. What had aroused Madame's fury beyond previous bounds was Morton's liaison with a music-hall performer, Victoria Camille Chabert. To resolve the Chabert difficulty—Camille had become pregnant, and a Victorian melodrama developed—Fullerton married her not long before he became the father of a daughter, Mireille.

At the same time Henrietta Mirecourt discovered that Morton had married Camille, Camille learned of Henrietta, and of several other simultaneous affairs, and she sued for divorce on the very personal grounds that her husband had taken up with mistresses, under the very French legal accusation of "his having, as a result, refused to grant her his caresses." The privilege of divorce, under the Napoleonic Code by which Fullerton had married, most accedes in the husband's favor, and in this case allowed for Fullerton's countersuit for defamation. The court ruled that the statement made by Monsieur Fullerton's wife was indeed injurious and he, instead, was granted a divorce from her, while she was to pay all court costs of the action.

But Morton was not to escape so gracefully or legally from Madame Mirecourt's caresses. She had found a way, she believed, to channel her lover's wayward passions exclusively to herself: she had gone through Fullerton's effects and discovered the damaging Lord Gower letters (she could, unfortunately, read English) and was holding them over Fullerton's head. Money was another issue in the Mirecourt threat, financial demands beyond Fullerton's means. His landlady wanted first, reasonably enough, rent for the apartment he occupied and which she owned—but also a further 200 francs a month. Fullerton was obliged to write to his clergyman father for funds, and the perplexed parents in America, having only just learned of his abrupt marriage to Camille, could not quite understand his pecuniary responsibilities to Henrietta.

And then there was Katherine, who considered herself engaged to Morton and expected to join him in France, soon, for a wedding in Paris.

Actually, when Morton Fullerton was visiting with Edith Wharton at Lenox, he had just come from Bryn Mawr College fresh from having declared his love to Katherine Fullerton, swearing, "without marriage, there is no life for you nor for me." Thus Edith's story "The Pretext" was being realized even at its conception in her imagination.

For years Katherine had believed herself Morton's sister, as the two grew up together to all forms and appearances siblings in the Fullerton household: what she felt for her brother, she assumed, was an overwhelming incestuous affection. Only recently, when she began her position as a reader in English at Bryn Mawr, did she learn that she was really the daughter of Morton's uncle, and therefore first cousin to the man she had always called brother. Soon after the revelations of her own disguised parentage, she felt free to reveal to Morton what she had always considered a sinful passion: "I love you so much that nothing matters or could matter. I should always love you. Does that do you any good, I wonder?"

Her love, and the love of many others, evidently did Morton Fullerton enormous good—for he sought love at every turn, and fairly existed for the affection lavished upon him by the women who crossed his path. No sooner had he and Katherine Fullerton become engaged than he was knocking on Edith Wharton's door at the Mount.

iv

For the past four years Teddy Wharton's health had been acceptably stable, but immediately upon the Whartons' return to Paris he drifted into the depression he had suffered on other such occasions—when the incompatibility of his wife and himself was made clear by events. Though Teddy had not been present for much of the time Edith spent with Morton Fullerton at the Mount, he could not have been unaware of the special glow to that sudden friendship. Meanwhile his wife had thrust herself, and him, back into the whirlpool of Parisian society. Edith seemed perplexed over her husband's nervous collapse as she confessed her worry—and her concern was genuine—to such friends as the comtesse de Noailles and newly met Rosa Fitz-James. Without knowing that Morton Fullerton personified the most recent stage in the Wharton dilemma, Edith's friends knew perfectly well what was troubling Teddy Wharton, but it would have been a breach of taste to lay out such cynical facts of life to their naive American friend.

Throughout 1908 Edith was still seeing much of the Bourgets, closest of acquaintances, and seeing just as much of Charles du Bos, though he had defected from Edith's entourage of young bachelor friends by marrying the delightful Zezette. The comtesse Melanie de Pourtales was a new addition, but an old friend, to Edith's appointments calendar: they had met many years before in Cannes. The teas, luncheons, and dinners followed one upon another in a profusion of faces and distinguished names, parties at which Edith encountered the very living images from Marcel Proust's fictional tableau of aristocrats: the duchesse de Rohan and her daughter Princesse Marie Murat, Comte Alexandre de Laborde, the princesse Henri de Ligne, the comtesse Greffuhle, and Count Etiènne de Beaumont. Edith Wharton could as well be dining with the comtesse de Guermantes, the baron de Charlus, Albertine, and Swann. Boni de Castellane (Proust's model for Saint-Loup) was often in attendance, but no longer with his wife beside him. He had just divorced the American heiress Anna Gould, for whose money the wag and bon vivant had been obliged to submit to "the penance of the marriage bed." These were truly the grand figures of the *ancien régime*, and however much she was aware of the imminent decline of the French aristocracy, Edith Wharton could not resist attending these last notes of pomp and circumstance being played beneath the glowing chandeliers of the faubourg.

This obsession for knowing and being known by the cream of French society took its toll in writing time and creative concentration. Unlike Proust, Edith Wharton could never fully realize literary bounty from this intense Parisian social milieu: her novelistic successes were staged primarily in her own backyard, "the American scene" Henry James had advised her to make her own.

Edith continued to be disturbed by her husband's dolorous condition, and at the same time she was anxious about her lack of private communication from Morton Fullerton. He too, through friendly cross-Channel references and his connection with *The Times*, had access to the salons of the faubourg, and Edith saw him often across a dining table or in the crowded company of mutual friends where they exchanged only polite social banalities. They had not yet had an occasion to be alone together. Was Morton purposely putting her off? She could only confide her dismay in code in her journal: "I thought after all I had been mistaken," secretly and silently addressed to M.F.

During this time, while Katherine Fullerton was pressing her fiancé for some word that would put an end to "the wretchedness of our fate," Morton Fullerton sought advice about the Mirecourt predicament from Henry James. James could offer little but the counsel to sit tight while arranging whatever possible in the way of blackmail payment. As to the letters themselves, James warned in a P.S.: "*Destroy* those things—when you've made them yours."

In the midst of these intrigues to which his wife was not yet a part, Teddy Wharton, restless and uneasy over he knew not what, sought a change of scene. Edith was hyperactively engaged in salon life to relieve her anxiety over Morton Fullerton's silence, so by the end of that disconcerting winter of 1908, Teddy fled to Beaulieu in the South of France. Meanwhile Edith waited for some turn in her own fate.

The turn came at the same moment Teddy was boarding the southbound train at the Gare de Lyon. Immediately Edith sent a *pneumatique* to Morton Fullerton: would he lunch with her, alone, at 58, rue de Varenne? He would. At last the code word appeared in her diary, *Wir warren zusammen:* "We were together." They were together for most of the afternoon, a private reunion that set Edith aglow once more. The tête-à-tête was not yet a signal of commitment other than to carry on toward future possibilities. The discussion was of literary matters, including Morton's long-delayed essay on Henry James that had first brought them together. The afternoon was summed up by Edith as *unvergessliche stunden,* unforgettable hours.

Always, Paris had been an escape, a perfect sanctuary for creation—and the suggestive setting to a dimly conceived and yet unwritten romance. Now the poetry and poetic personality of her friend Anna de Noailles cast a further spell over Edith Wharton's imagination: she was even working on an essay—like Fullerton's piece on James, never published—comparing the comtesse's life and work to the poetry of Walt Whitman. Her vagrant thoughts at this stage included the legend about her mother and that unnamed English tutor whom she was said to have loved. Had her mother truly given way to desire on that one adulterous occasion? (There were even those in the Wharton and Jones clans who whispered that Edith was the offspring of this union, on the far-fetched belief that neither a Wharton nor a Jones could have produced the intellectual Edith.) In Paris one could truly live out those ill-defined longings considered shameful elsewhere. Surrounded as she was by mysterious stone walls behind which secret loves took place, she yearned to share the ultimate romance of Paris the comtesse de Noailles had not only written about but known. Edith was her mother's daughter, she was a product of her caste and clan: she must endure the torment of a Victorian conscience, play off now against never, consider all.

The Parisian way of life and love known to Anna de Noailles inspired in Edith the same vague aspiration to rapture that had excited George Sand, that brilliant Frenchwoman of the century before. In the tremulous beginnings of this new attitude, Edith took on not only an admiration for, but a mystical identification with both women—and now came a third inspirational figure among the more daring spirits of France. Edith was reading an obscure writer named Hortense Allart whose published letters from the early nineteenth century she ventured to share with Henry James. James read these serial confessions with some exasperation, and complained to Edith that Allart's attempt to render, as poetic as candor allowed, repetitive copulations with such lovers as Bulwer-Lytton and Chateaubriand was more than a little tiring as literature. Despite James's tepid response to the letters, Edith Wharton remained deeply moved.

Nothing would do but that Morton Fullerton accompany her to the small village of Herblay north of Paris to seek out the home of her new idol. Fullerton was agreeable to this personally significant quest. The excursion would be something of a replay of Edith's earlier pilgrimage, in the company of Henry James, to Nohant and the home of George Sand. From the Allart letters and descriptions of the view from her window, Edith made out that the writer must have lived in a cottage opposite the church. She had Cook park nearby, while she and Morton inquired at the church for any vestiges remaining of the writer, Hortense Allart.

The curé had never heard mention of Mademoiselle Allart: "Are you certain she was one of my parishioners?"

"She lived here," Fullerton replied drily, "one hundred years ago."

Hélas, the curé knew nothing of Herblay's only celebrated figure. There was no plaque on the cottage opposite, nor any gravestone inscribed *Allart* in the small cemetery attached to the church. Despite the obliteration of every trace of the writer, Edith felt a spiritual closeness with the forgotten belletrist of Herblay. While making their inquiries at the church, Edith imagined a veiled figure sharing the narrow pew with her, and in her diary that night gave the apparition the name "Happiness."

Two evenings after the drive to Herblay, Fullerton was installed in Edith's candlelit dining room after a late supper and a long talk. He was reading aloud to her from André Chevrillon, a writer Edith had recently met at Madame Fitz-James's salon. The servants had retired, and no sound came from the street below except for an occasional passing carriage or the clatter of a shutter being drawn closed. It was a deliciously intimate moment. Edith, feeling uncharacteristically domestic, sat opposite Morton with a basket of sewing in her lap.

Edith was greatly taken with Morton's expressed insights on Chevrillon's essay on George Meredith, for he would elucidate Chevrillon's literary style between the sections he read to her. At what he felt were appropriate moments, Morton Fullerton's strategy was to make classical allusions to the intellectual topic at hand, allusions parallel to their own shared intimacy that were subtly but suggestively sensual. He held his place in the Chevrillon with one finger, and moved closer to Edith. She had been sewing, and was startled out of her reverie by his touch.

Morton had misjudged the moment or moved ahead of the mood. His remarks had got too far afield of the literary commentary, and then the actual *touch* had undone all. The evening ended in confusion and dismay.

Analyzing the travesty of their cross-purposes, Edith could only conclude that men *were* different from women, but in ways beyond her mother's foolish lecture to a completely innocent daughter on the eve of marriage. She could somehow, almost, understand Morton's rash desire to make their spiritual union a physical one. Hortense Allart's ghostly presence as "Happiness" still lingered at Edith's shoulder, and she confided to her diary that the attachment of M.F. was as strong as ever. They were soulmates, forever linked in bonds of love and "mental companionship," but she could not hold back the regret that disturbed all these reflections. When she wrote, "Why did you have to spoil it?" she still wondered if she were addressing M.F. or herself.

V

Teddy was back from Beaulieu, and now Edith's psychosomatic symptoms were apparent: husband and wife suffered these alternating bouts of depression, but another of Edith's reactions of malaise—occurring especially when Teddy arrived on her doorstep, or was due home—was recurrent asthma attacks. In the United States she attributed this sense of smothering to a form of hay fever, and in Paris where no pollen other than that of cut flowers could penetrate the draped and tapestried interiors of these hermetic apartments, she blamed her indisposition on an excess of *poussière,* French dust.

The private meetings between Edith and Morton Fullerton were off for the moment while *la ronde* of making calls and taking tea spun on. An outlet for Edith's troubled state of mind was the local movement to raise funds for Abbé Mugnier, who was in disgrace with the Church for attempting to reconvert a rogue priest who had been excommunicated. (The good abbé was known for his slack orthodoxy: he once answered Edith's inquiry about the existence of hell: "*Bien sûr,* I believe, because hell is a dogma of the Church, but I don't believe anyone is in it.") For his presumption and naïveté in the rogue priest affair, Abbé Mugnier was banished from his beloved Ste. Clothilde, the miniature Gothic cathedral nestled quietly among the embassies, ministries, and *maisons particulières* of Edith's quarter, considered the most fashionable parish in all of France. He was sent to the 14th arrondissement, just the other side of the boulevard Montparnasse; but to the *beau monde* of the exclusive seventh, their abbé may as well have been banished from Paris itself. Edith had a particular gift for fundraising and was one of the leading sponsors of the faubourg movement to "buy back" their favorite priest and her personal confessor.

Another distracting endeavor was to try to lure Henry James to Paris, someone she could trust to offer consolation and advice in her hour of emotional turmoil. But James considered himself "on the shelf" as far as crossing the Channel was concerned, and he would observe Edith's unfolding drama from that shelf. "The truth is," he explained, "I shall never, never, never cross the channel again."

In truth, he crossed the Channel within a few weeks. He had genuinely not wanted to plunge again into Edith Wharton's maelstrom of socializing; he intended and hoped for a quiet visit as consulting authority in the slippery Fullerton affair. James stayed with Edith at her apartment, and despite his genuine protests, his hostess managed to inveigle him into half a dozen more social encounters than James felt up to, and even persuaded him to sit for what he called a "brainy and awful" portrait by the faubourg's favored portrait painter, Jacques-Emile Blanche.

Meanwhile, Edith Wharton and Morton Fullerton communicated by letter, an almost daily ritual: Fullerton's office notes were delivered to Edith with her breakfast tray. To one such note she replied: "Oh, mon cher ami. I don't think you can know what that little word of yours means to me today." Morton's messages blended beautifully into her morning's devotion to writing: she would begin the day reading the lyric passages of a lover before setting down her own heartfelt responses, then on to her daily quota of fiction. Unable to concentrate steadily on a novel-length project, she did rework an old poem, *Artemis to Acteon,* a reconsideration of the mythical Artemis' fierce need to preserve her hallowed virginity at all costs.

That March of 1908, not long after his sojourn in the South of France, Teddy Wharton decided to return to Lenox, sailing to New York on the *Philadelphia,* unrelievedly depressed in a way that was now considered clinical. There was no doubt that he understood the situation between Morton Fullerton and his wife, at least in part, and that understanding was in some measure responsible for his persistent melancholy. Apparently, however, no one else in the large cast of faubourg friends and acquaintances had deciphered the looks exchanged between Edith Wharton and Morton Fullerton, or guessed the sense of the cryptic remarks they made to one another in public. Edith and Morton were cool players in this extended game, and since neither felt any guilt about their relations so far—the commitment was to declaration only, never act—they played their roles with an ease of manner that gave nothing away.

The elaborately slow stages of their "loving out of total love" (*aimer d'amour,* a catch phrase Morton had picked up, ironically, from his fiancée Katherine) suggested the progression of a love affair conceived by Stendhal. Each party to this lingering mode of love—even the sexually precipitate Morton Fullerton—appeared to enjoy the game for the sake of the game, with its exquisitely delayed consummation. Since he had originally brought the lovers together, Henry James now played their doting old-maidish fellow conspirator, a happily observant audience of one. "I am kept here in golden chains," sighed James, "in gorgeous bondage, in breathless attendance. . . ." When they were not being received by the first families of the 7th arrondissement, Cook drove them—a trio now, James's bald dome in the front of the Panhard, the lovers together in the back seat—on excursions to bosky picnic sites, poetic ruins, and the cathedral towns on the periphery of Paris. Henry James stayed in Paris for only two weeks of this: no final act in sight, no one—certainly not James—pressed toward dénouement.

Edith did eventually succumb to flashes of guilt that broke into her euphoria. From America the doctors' reports were vaguely reassuring: little was known of the pattern of excessively spirited behavior followed by deep depression, the manic-depressive symptoms apparent in Teddy's case. The medical profession on both sides of the Atlantic attributed his symptoms to the side effects of gout. For the sake of form—form and duty were the two compelling demands of her character—Edith felt she must be at her husband's side in his time of need.

On May 23 Morton Fullerton accompanied her to the Gare du

Nord for her boat-train to Le Havre; he escorted her to her compartment and the two sat together until the conductor began slamming shut the train doors. Then Fullerton, a dashing hatless Byron, was on the quai waving, and Edith was leaning from the open window waving au revoir—or was it, she asked herself at that poignant moment as the train slowly pulled away, adieu?

Once the *voiture* was out from under the soot-stained glass roofing she could for long loving moments see the receding figure on the platform, and beyond, the larger frame of Paris a fainter and fainter vision, the exotic white bulbous towers of the Sacré-Coeur diminishing in the distance—a last alabaster impression of the city of love.

At sea, Edith Wharton took up her morning routine of tea and lapboard writing, facing the light through the stateroom portholes, composing journal entries to do with M.F., fragments of romantic verse, and finally—not many days out, at one inspired creative sitting—she completed a short story called "The Choice." The title was apt in a nakedly personal way.

A married woman, whose husband is the trustee of his wife's estate, discovers her holdings are being finagled with flagrant irresponsibility. Isabel Stilling is not so much shocked at these misadventures with her money, for her loathing of Cobham goes deeper than that, an unbearable frustration with her insensitive sports-minded spouse. Isabel has taken up with a lover, and a single obsessive thought about her husband resounds: "That he may die!"

The author of this tale, as she sailed on with ostensible intent of proving her solicitude at Teddy's bedside, was rather startled to see what she had written. In "The Choice," the husband is drowned in a lakeside struggle with the lover. Edith was assembling a collection of stories at the time, *The Hermit and the Wild Woman,* but she was made so uneasy by the blatant significance of "The Choice" she decided not to include this story in the collection.

In Paris, Morton Fullerton was again shifting and sidestepping the several simultaneous affairs of the heart he had neglected or postponed during the intense interlude with Edith Wharton. To complicate his life immeasurably, Katherine Fullerton, on sabbatical from Bryn Mawr, showed up, aching to resolve the impasse of her engagement to Morton. Her life had taken a sudden decisive turn: she had received another offer of marriage, while her youth was slipping by in passive attendance on letters from the artful dodging Morton. In the long ardent talks they had together, Morton could promise her nothing, for the moment. He even confessed—as was his custom, with whatever woman he was with at the moment—past indiscretions, and he particularly detailed the recent involvement with Edith Wharton. Along with these wounding revelations, Morton continued to interject reassurances of his abiding love for Katherine. He was adept and long-practiced at this style of articulate persuasion, using verbs in the future tense while his romantic declarations lingered in the present.

By this time even his former wife, Camille Chabert, urged Morton to release his *petite soeur* from this heartless dangling, and a current mistress known as Doll told him he played too much with fire, he must not trifle cruelly with the affections of this young thing.

Therefore "one bitter midnight hour," as Katherine expressed it, Morton was obliged to suggest that their engagement was in peril. Katherine cleared out of the Hôtel St. James and Albany early the next morning in confusion and despair: "I do not believe you have ever treated another woman so ill." She left Paris for Tours and there settled for a time at the Convent of the Sacred Heart, badly bruised but not yet resigned: "Oh, my own," she wrote him from the convent, "trust me and send me some word."

The sabbatical she had taken from Bryn Mawr was officially for the purpose of writing a novel, which Katherine Fullerton did complete. *Vain Oblations* was its apt title, as if referring to her oblations to Morton.

"Ici j'étouffe." In Lenox, Edith was smothering again, and warbling (her term for writing poetry), in the intervals between letters from Morton Fullerton. She was reading from Nietzsche's *The Genealogy of Morals* and John Donne's "The Extasie" (" . . . But O alas, so long so far / Our bodies why do we forbear?") and from these works drawing spiritual and moral conclusions contrary to Abbé Mugnier's

Christian belief in a split between body and soul: "Love's mysteries in souls do grow, / But yet the body is his book . . . "

Teddy was feeling well enough to consider her suggestion that she return to Paris and he would soon follow. Fullerton's letters had begun to trail off, their contents written in that vague style he employed when putting off Margaret Fullerton. This setback in their relationship—passionate at least in its epistolary form—triggered the panic in her journal note: "Let me face at once the fact that *it is over,*" and in confession to Henry James of her despair. James took her plight very much to heart, offering sympathy and the optimistic prediction that "some light will *still* absolutely come to you—I believe—though I can't pretend to say what it conceivably may be."

In search of that light, Edith decided once more to move up the date of her departure; she sailed for France in October 1908 instead of just after the New Year, long in advance of the sailing planned with Teddy. She was to visit Henry James in London, but first stayed a few days at the Hôtel Dominici in Paris. Her suite included a neutral sitting room, like the one Katherine Fullerton engaged for her tête-à-tête with Morton Fullerton; but Edith's talks with Morton are not recorded in her journal.

When Teddy joined her in Paris, he was *insupportable* as he shifted from nerve-edge high to despairing low, then manic again. Edith was genuinely caring as she saw to his needs, and made an effort to indulge his moods, but Teddy had developed a childishness that was now fixed, and he had become virtually helpless. By spring it was decided by all, including Teddy, that he must return to the United States.

"I would have sailed with him," Edith explained to Henry James, "I *wanted* to be with him, but I couldn't. I was worn out with him, I was simply *too tired* to travel."

Morton Fullerton had also booked a sailing for the United States in June 1909, a month later than Teddy's departure; Morton planned a visit with Henry James first, and then would sail from Southampton. James would have had the Fullerton version of the affair-so-far, but he urged Edith to send him the real, the *intime* story: "But the things, the things, the things—i.e. the details—I yearn for—!" Edith was sailing soon, as well. There was a little time before the lovers would again be driven apart—and they would not likely meet in America, might possibly never meet again.

With Teddy absent, seductive Paris became, ironically, a hindrance to further intimacy: "Voisin, Durand, etc!—No!" said Edith, knowing that these two fashionable settings to their romance were exactly where the lovers would be most remarked upon. They could "meet at the Louvre at one o'c, in the shadow of Jean Cougon's Diana," as if by coincidence, or in a small out-of-the-way restaurant "somewhere at the end of the earth (rive gauche) where there is bad food & no chance of meeting acquaintances."

Henry James would not join them in Paris: " 'Tired' you must be, even you, indeed, and Paris, as I look at it from here, figures to me a great blur of intense white light in which, attached to the hub of a revolving wheel, you are all whirled around by the finest silver strings." But why in heaven's name not lure Edith to London, with Morton, a safe haven on the eve of Morton's departure? Then let fate or nature or whatever was meant to be take its inevitable course. "You'll rest with me here then, but don't wait for that to rest somehow—somewhere *en attendant.* I am afraid you won't rest much in a retreat on the place de la Concorde. However, so does a poor old croaking barnyard fowl advise a golden eagle!"

There was no more time to consider and reconsider the invitation James extended than Edith and Morton took the Channel train to Boulogne and crossed the same day to London together. James had booked them into that Victorian pile, the Charing Cross Hotel, convenient to Morton's boat-train next morning. They would have but that one evening.

Henry James dined with the two excited travelers at the Charing Cross, a festive dinner, a reunion on the eve of departure that lasted late. James beamed over his outlaw lovers as if he had created them—in a sense, he believed he had—in a fiction. The ambiance was perfect, and the Charing Cross for all its overwrought commercial-hotel grandeur *was* romantic: the two were to share a two-bedroom/sitting-room suite of Edwardian charm. In no such hotel in Paris could they have felt so private and safe. By midnight, affections pledged liberally with champagne, James had discreetly withdrawn.

When Henry James returned next morning to the suite, he found Morton up and about, bustling, packed, ready to sail. Through the open doorway to one bedroom he saw Edith, ever the writer at this morning hour, propped up in bed with her lapboard in place, busily writing the lines to a poem later entitled "Terminus," meant not for publication but to be shared by Morton and herself only. Henry James did not have to read the revealing lines: "Wonderful was the long secret night you gave me, my Lover, / Palm to palm, breast to breast in the gloom . . . " to know that Edith Wharton and Morton Fullerton had at last consummated their long-enduring courtly love.

vi

While Morton Fullerton was away, Edith feverishly filled her days by joining the heady social scene in London, the season revolving around King Edward, then returned to Paris for more fireball socializing among familiars. The Wharton energy had taken on the dimension of myth: Percy Lubbock dubbed her *l'oiseau de feu* from the title of Stravinsky's controversial ballet then playing in Paris, and Henry James seemed now to shrink from his hyperactive friend he called at first "a golden eagle" and now "the Angel of Devastation."

She could not resist the crowded public calendar, but privately had come to the conclusion that society was a vain diversion, that she cared "less and less about 'general society,' and more and more for just a few friends." While she nervously awaited the return of Morton Fullerton to Paris, and paused to consider her situation, she was beset by her recurrent sense of smothering:

"It is impossible," she wrote Morton,

> in the nature of things, that our lives should run parallel much longer. I have faced the fact, & accepted it, & I am not afraid, except when I think of the pain & pity you may feel for me. . . .
>
> That I long to spare you; & so I want to tell you now, Dear, that I know how unequal the exchange is between us, how little I have to give that a man like you can care for, & how ready I am, when the transition comes, to be again the good comrade you once found me.

The transition was under way that summer of 1909 when Fullerton was back in Paris and with Edith again. He had still to resolve the threat of blackmail by his paramour Henrietta Mirecourt. Edith knew the story (Morton could never resist romantically enhancing his past in the telling), and she probably knew as well that she still shared her lover with his landlady.

The Macmillan Company had invited her to write a book about Paris for their great-cities series; Henry James was to do the companion volume on London. For all Edith's knowledge of the city and her abiding love for Paris, she neither solicited nor wanted such an assignment. It then occurred to her that Morton Fullerton would be the ideal author of such a book, and he was of course desperate for the money to free himself from the Mirecourt entanglement. Fullerton's literary career was in limbo since his impulsive resignation as *Times* correspondent in Paris, with only an occasional free-lance assignment to sustain his excessive style of life. Macmillan agreed to allow Morton Fullerton to write the book in Edith's place, since he came so highly recommended by both Edith Wharton and Henry James. The advance was to be £100. It was a sizable advance at the time, but the sum did not nearly solve Fullerton's financial dilemma. Edith thought of doubling it to £200, providing the extra amount herself, but she would need a co-conspirator to cover her involvement in the scheme.

Henry James delighted in such baroque business dealing—he had in fact written Morton Fullerton into the novel *Wings of the Dove* in the personage of Merton Densher, an impecunious journalist involved in an affair to receive funds from wealthy Milly Theale. The Macmillan plot James and Edith contrived together: Edith wrote out a check for £100 to James; James presented the check to Macmillan as if he were the origin of the supplement. James explained to Macmillan that sudden expenses had put the author of their Paris book into a precarious financial bind, therefore he, as a personal friend of Morton Fullerton, would provide this emergency sum which would *appear* to come from the publishers. Edith Wharton's role was to be played entirely offstage.

Fullerton, of course, knew about the plot from the first. His experience with publishers did not lead him to believe they would ever double an already stipulated advance on royalties. But everyone involved—including himself—was tiptoeing past the ethical issue in consideration of Edith's situation and Fullerton's pride. As the funds were thus funneled to him, "poor tortured and tethered W.M.F," as James referred to him, could but graciously accept.

Henry James put the case so brilliantly before the publishers that *they* agreed to put up the extra advance (at the same time doing prized author Henry James a favor) with the proviso that James make good the £100 in case the Paris book was never written. Fullerton did embark on a chapter or two of the project, but he did not complete the work, ever. Macmillan did not call in the note of surety—after all, Henry James was Henry James. Henrietta Mirecourt, however, was quite eager to call in the settlement she had initiated: she collected her sums and did return the letters she had been holding over her erstwhile lover's head.

Considering how important letters were, especially when, as Edith put it, they "survive their uses," she tried on several occasions to retrieve the loving sentiments she had written Morton Fullerton:

> Cher ami—Can you arrange, some day next week,—before Wednesday—to bring or send me such fragments of correspondence as still exist? I have asked you this once or twice, as you know, & you have given the talk a turn which has made it impossible for me to insist without all sorts of tragic implications that I wished above all to avoid.

Once Fullerton had a conquest, his attentions diminished to the point of neglect. He made excuses, he restated his affection in the most florid terms, he became most strangely absent, he continued to dangle tokens of hope.

Brooding over the one thing she could not bear, "the thought that I represent to you *the woman who has to be lied to . . .* ", she continued to ask that he define their relationship in its waning ardor:

> Three or four times I have given you the opportunity to make, gaily and good-humoredly, the transition which seems to me inevitable; & you have not chosen to do it . . . what you wish, apparently, is to take of my life the inmost & uttermost that a woman—a woman like me—can give, for an hour, now & then, when it suits you; & when the hour is over, to leave me out of your mind & out of your life as a man leaves the companion who has accorded him a transient distraction. . . .

She concluded by proposing an easy transition to *amitié* from *aimer d'amour,* but Morton Fullerton could not quite release Edith to the state of affection and regard she requested—it was surely his experience that women making this plea were only deceiving themselves, thus the one-sided romance reached no satisfactory closure. Slowly—painfully, for Edith—the two lovers did extricate themselves by degrees, as indicated in the reduction of intensity to their declarations, until finally Edith wrote at length, ending with: "My life was better before I knew you. That is, for me, the sad conclusion of this sad year. And it is a bitter thing to say to the one being one has ever loved d'amour."

Before Morton Fullerton appeared in her life, Edith depended upon Teddy to *be* there even when she wished him away, when his presence was inconvenient or smothering. In her unfathomable way (Teddy receives barely a single autobiographer's glance in her muted *A Backward Glance*), and in spite of all, she loved her husband. Teddy was a permanent part of her American background, her New World psyche, the Yankee in her. He was that portion of her life she could not disclaim or discard.

As Morton Fullerton faded from her immediate concerns, Edith was once again aware of Teddy's spiritual and physical decline. She was genuinely disturbed over the failing health of this once robust sportsman and bon vivant. Far more divisive than the Fullerton affair, Paris had come between them; but for the irresistible allure of Paris, above all the attractions of the faubourg St. Germain, she might have attended Teddy in his illnesses, as she would have done—and sometimes did, however dutifully—in Lenox or New York.

The allure of Paris did not diminish with the trailing off of the Fullerton affair; in fact, Edith felt all the more *parisienne* for having experienced a secret adventure in the city so conducive to romance: the romance of place and ambiance remained to her. Furnishing her splendid pied-à-terre on the rue de Varenne (at number 53, when the lease on 58 ran out) was a passion that helped distract from the chagrin of Morton's indifference. She could traverse Paris seeking out the absolutely perfect Aubusson to cover the parquet in her drawing room; she replaced the gas-jet chandeliers with choices of her own, and she expended much energy and research on a porcelain bathtub to replace the narrow copper coffin in the *salle de bain.* Henry James had cried out to her to *continue making the moments of life,* and she was doing just that.

Ten years past the turn of the century Edith Wharton remained a product of her class and station and gender. Her gift for literature and her need to settle in Paris did however modify the archetype. The affair with Morton Fullerton ran contrary to every assumption ever made about her; the relationship with Teddy was equally misunderstood, and was as true to her complex nature as was the passion for Morton Fullerton.

Poor Teddy, as Henry James so often referred to him, was as miserable at home as he was in Paris. His shrewd family doctor began to discern a pattern in the shifts from euphoria to melancholia, and he warned that Teddy's apparent good spirits (strangely, just at the time of his mother's death), were symptomatic only, and could swing back like a pendulum. Teddy also suffered a facial neuralgia and unrelieved periods of insomnia, irritability, and childlike impulsiveness. No one in the Wharton family except Edith was willing to accept Dr. Kinnicutt's dread diagnosis of "nervous disorder." Teddy's sister Nannie would allow for no inference that her brother might benefit from treatment in a sanatorium, or even that he required close supervision during his mood swings. When he was suddenly exuberant, he was simply "his old self again." No one attributed his exuberance to the inheritance he was about to receive, the most important money of his own aside from the funds he managed for his wife.

Not long after his mother's funeral in November 1909, Teddy—in the manic phase of his disability—came to the Hôtel Crillon to seek out Edith. While her apartment was being refurbished, Edith had taken rooms at the Crillon, and very soon had set off on an excursion to Germany in the company of art critic Bernard Berenson. Teddy learned that she was due back from Germany that afternoon, so he lingered uncertainly in the Tuileries, then crossed the place de la Concorde to pace the hotel lobby. The Crillon was furnished in Louis XV style, sofas and settees that appeared never to have been sat upon, a decor that might have been chosen by his austere but elegant and fastidious wife: and the hotel seemed alive with her accusing presence, though she had not yet arrived.

Teddy went up to the suite to await his wife, his eyes fixed on the vibrant expanse beyond the window panes, horse and pedestrian traffic circling ceaselessly around the vast intersection between the hotel and the pont de la Concorde. He was rehearsing his statement. When Edith did appear, still in traveling costume, she was prepared for and dreading a confrontation over the issue, obscure until now and never mentioned between them, of Morton Fullerton. At first Teddy's circumlocutions were like the nervous traffic spinning around the obelisque; he stared out the window instead of looking at his wife, then in great nervous clots of speech, poured out his confession:

"Last summer," he began, "I saw the opportunity to make large sums of profit with a little daring and courage." And the use of Edith's trust fund.

Edith sank into an armchair with an odd mixture of relief and outrage. Teddy, lacking sufficient cash for this rare opportunity, had been obliged to convert his wife's conservative holdings for speculative reinvestment. Through his troubled monologue, Edith could hear the narrative of her short story "The Choice" unfolding. With the first profits, which soon turned to losses, Teddy had purchased for himself an apartment in Boston.

"Did you occupy this apartment?"

"For part of the summer. Yes."

"Alone?"

"With a woman friend."

For all the surge of emotion Edith felt, she reined in her feelings and behaved with the admirable restraint of a Lily Bart. She had no more questions, but Teddy was unable to stop. Further, and unbelievably, he had let out the extra bedrooms to . . . chorus girls. And Boston actresses. There had been parties, there was now talk . . . and he had lost a portion of Pussy's money on the stock exchange.

Teddy had earlier confessed all of this to his sister. When Edith got in touch with Nannie, all was confirmed in a letter of apology: Nannie insisted that she did not at first realize the extent of her brother's unfortunate behavior, or that he had played fast and loose with his wife's money (he had none of his own), but that, at least, their dear mother was no longer alive to suffer the disgrace of Teddy's fall.

"It would have killed her," she wrote. Teddy must, and would, settle everything.

Edith did not hesitate to write of Teddy's fall from grace to Henry James. Even in her muted and condensed version of events, James found outlet for a longstanding grudge against Teddy. "Poor Teddy" now became in letters to James's friends "the unspeakable Teddy." James considered Edith's position a dreadful trial that called for the utmost sympathy from all who knew her. His name for her changed, too: from the Angel of Devastation she became the Angel of Paris, while James poured out his solicitude in his correspondence with her. James was of course aware of Edith's affair with Morton Fullerton, but this betrayal did not weight as heavily on the Jamesian scale.

Teddy and his family discovered that Edith could be forgiving—even noble, and completely understanding—in the face of this obloquy, and were now judging Edith in this light. The Boston Whartons had always thought Teddy had married down (a New York socialite instead of someone Boston-bred), especially after his wife became a writer and a "best seller." Teddy returned to the United States where brother and sister stood staunchly by him: his brother saw to it that $50,000, the major part of Teddy's legacy from his mother, would be transferred to Edith's trust funds in total restitution of the sum lost. Thus Edith suffered no financial loss, only temporary loss of face—no minor consideration in the circles she frequented.

As the perceptive author-observer of society's splendid ironies, Edith Wharton reflected long and hard upon her own role in this debacle. Teddy would have been involved in his amatory adventure, as well as the financial dealings, at about the same time she was engaged with Fullerton. Traditionally the adulteress, not the man, would be held up to public censure; but her affair was closeted while Teddy's, because of the accompanying financial scandal, was made known. These anomalies may in part explain the magnamity Edith displayed, but only in part. She was truly grieved. She realized that this scenario indicated Teddy's desperation (to which her own actions had contributed) and represented a mental deterioration to a degree she had not yet imagined.

Dr. Kinnicutt confirmed to Edith that Teddy's "confession," while true in the essentials, was an aberrant account of the actual situation. Yes, Teddy had engaged in a quiet affair with a woman in her early thirties; there were no chorines in the building; Teddy had never installed them in his Boston apartment or in any other "love nest." Only the financial speculation was true in every respect. Considering the mental condition of his patient, Dr. Kinnicutt found Teddy's inflated version of the affair highly significant.

Restitution of Edith's money had been made; Teddy was shamed and guilt-ridden by the episode—the situation was, as far as the Whartons were concerned, restored to normal. But Edith had placed herself outside the family council in this conclusion, and had known from the first what the doctors were convinced of now, that Teddy Wharton was emotionally unbalanced. A doctor friend of the family, passing through Paris, sent Edith a hand-delivered letter assessing Teddy's condition as he saw it: " . . . Ted's melancholy and exhilaration are not the only trouble with him, but that his mind itself—his consciousness and reasoning power—are not connected nor consecutive." Dr. Bigelow was all but offering a diagnosis not yet named: manic depression.

Since Teddy could not be left alone—or at least Edith believed he should not be left alone—he was temporarily cared for in a clinic at Neuilly, a fashionable Parisian suburb where the American Hospital would later be established. Eventually he agreed to be admitted to a psychiatric institution in Switzerland, near Konstanz: the Kuranstalt Bellevue. After a few days of treatment in the most advanced hospital of its kind, Teddy was begging to return to his wife in Paris.

vii

Edith and her neighbors in the Palais-Bourbon quarter were growing concerned over the winter rains of 1910 that had kept up for weeks, causing the Seine to rise from its tranquil passageway through the heart of Paris. The torrential overflow from the feeder-streams north of Paris—the Marne, the Essonne, and the Yonne—had brought the Seine past the level of the boot tops of the carved stone soldiers on the side of the pont d'Alma. Of the four figures in the stone relief, the uppermost Zouave was the marker for flood-crisis stage. At first the waters rose as high as the Zouave's ballooned pants, then to his chest, and finally the beard was engulfed. Eventually the Zouave and the pont d'Alma itself were submerged in the worst city flood since 1176. In that year, with most of the city under water, the bishop of Paris had marched to the river's edge holding aloft a nail from the true Cross, and intoned: "That thy dread waters return to their banks and spare these unhappy people further misery . . . "—at which point the waters did recede.

Of all the bridges along the Seine, only the pont Neuf and the pont Royal remained passable during the great flood of 1910. Edith's apartment was spared, but transport along many of the streets of the faubourg adjoining the Seine was by rowboat only. Plank walkways spanned the intersection at rue de Varenne and rue de Bellechasse only a few meters from Edith's building; the next cross street, the rue de Bac, was completely under water and Abbé Mugnier's beloved Ste. Clothilde was flooded as well. A measure of Edith's first loyalty was the note she wrote to a friend: "If it could only have happened in *Omaha.*"

Many of the faubourg set were deprived of heat and lighting, but a surprising number of Edith's neighbors remained in their *hôtels particuliers* through the deluge. From her dry perch on the second floor, Edith could observe the boats on rue Constantine rowed by footmen transporting their employers the Fitz-Jameses and the d'Haussonvilles to and from their regal front doors as if from one Venetian palazzo to another. A number of her acquaintances appeared to be keeping engagements committed to before the flood: one's social obligations did not cease when the Seine overflowed its banks; if parties were on the agenda, then parties would be given and attended. This spectacle took place during Edith's spell of fading enthusiasm for the patrician society of the faubourg: while she did not abandon cause with the bluebloods of her quarter, she did reflect on the folly of their stubborn rituals in a time of crisis and reconsider the essential worth of salon life at any time.

A few of the distinguished residents of the 7th arrondissement did volunteer their services to the Red Cross and other agencies caring for the stranded populace of Paris. Edith Wharton was one of these. Until now her principal active charity had been the ASPCA, contributing to the cause of abused or abandoned animals. Now, in the makeshift refugee shelters, Edith was coming into contact with fellow Parisians who were formerly outside her experience and vision. She took their tragedy to heart. Just as Edith Wharton was beginning to organize her sentiments and energies to this cause, her humanitarian impulse was cut short: the flood waters subsided as if the bishop of Paris had again prayed the waters back into their banks. The crisis passed with few lives lost and no serious epidemic, a miracle nevertheless. Later, Edith would be called upon, in the hostilities of 1914–18, to enlist in a greater cause of far more tragic consequences.

During the long aftermath of the Fullerton affair, and with the stress of Teddy's decline, Edith's literary endeavors appeared to have languished—Henry James thought of her as being in "nervous and intimately personal . . . rags"—but actually she was writing still, and steadily, on a short novel that many, especially in Paris, considered her greatest work. *Ethan Frome* may have been partly inspired by her first contact with the *ouvriers* and poor of Paris (transposed to New England), for it was a startling departure from the familiar world of an Edith Wharton novel. Edith did know the backcountry of New England's rural districts, but her familiarity with those rustic byways was through the windows of her Panhard. This passionate tale of imminent disaster was conceived from an aesthetic and instinct deeper than the author's superficial contact with the underclass she chose to depict.

Strangely enough, the first few pages of the story were originally written in French, as if another language would give the tale a certain remove—but ostensibly Edith was writing the first draft in French as a student exercise, a way of perfecting her use of the language. The first tentative pages were put aside during her involvement with Morton Fullerton, and left in a desk drawer during the flood; but soon after the Seine returned to its banks, the starkly realistic tragedy of Ethan and Mattie's clandestine love reasserted itself in the author's consciousness.

When the book was not at first successful, Charles Scribner replied to Edith's complaints of meager sales by pointing out that "short novels" always sold poorly. Furthermore, many of Edith Wharton's faithful readers were put off by a work so removed from their expectations. She was their contemporary Jane Austen; they wanted another version of the drawing-room strategies of the idle rich, not another slice of Dreiser's grim realism or Jack London's tragic encounters in the natural world. The publisher did not necessarily handle the author's disappointment with diplomacy: Edith Wharton was after all Scribner's most valued author at the time. Charles Scribner was stunned to hear that her next book would go to Appleton Company, who made a "very high offer" for the novel, *The Reef.*

Ethan Frome, contrary to Scribner's expectations, did finally win its way to become the most read of all Edith Wharton's novels, but it took another thirty years for the book to be widely accepted and Edith's original assessment confirmed. The reviews had been good from the first. "They don't know *why* it's good," she wrote Fullerton, "but they are right: it *is.*"

Teddy Wharton insisted on "going home" from the French and Swiss sanatoria after each initial attempt at treatment. In Teddy's manic phase and seeming robust health, he appeared to be altogether fit and the doctors were inclined to agree that further confinement was unnecessary. "Home" was the Wharton estate, the Mount, in Lenox, but Teddy was too restless to remain there alone. The method of treatment now seemed to be a series of excursions and tours: a fishing trip to the Rockies, then to Southern California and from there a voyage to the Far East, always in the company of a watchful friend. Teddy's sister Nannie Wharton believed he was on the way to a complete cure, and a long trip would complete the therapy begun in Switzerland. But the voyage to India, like the truncated rest cures, did nothing to break the insidious cycle of manic depression. By the time he reached Calcutta, he was in a state of "unusual nervous tension." When he returned from the trip, he and Edith immediately clashed over the arrangement for handling her trust funds.

Teddy's plea was understandable: "I want to feel still that I know about the funds and what to do with them and the Mount and that I can be of some *use* to you."

But Edith reminded him: "Your health unfortunately makes it

impossible for you to take any active part in the management of my affairs." She no longer said "our affairs."

"For twenty-five years I looked after those investments."

"And then?"

No sooner did Teddy appear to resign himself to Edith's wishes than, in a retrograde mood, he became truculent and insistent. Henry James was visiting during one of the running battles over the trust fund management: "The violent and scenic Teddy," James reported, "is negotiable in a measure—but the pleading, suffering, clinging, helpless Teddy is a very awful and irreducible quantity indeed." James had witnessed a scene in which it appeared to him, and to Edith, that Teddy had been provoked beyond control and was about to become violent; but suddenly Teddy reversed himself and begged Edith's forgiveness for calling her cruel and vindictive. Then Henry James watched this hearty sportsman deflate and collapse in tears.

On January 24, 1912, Edith Wharton turned fifty. Her attachment to Morton Fullerton had eased without tears into the nostalgic friendship she had anticipated in the twilight of their intimacy. She still turned to him with her emotional difficulties—the relationship with Teddy foremost—just as she still turned to Henry James, and to the men rather than the women of her entourage. To friend John Hugh Smith she confessed, rather mildly, "Things here were rather bad after my husband got back. He is much better physically, but very nervous & excitable." No one, as she knew, could properly advise her in this large dilemma. Should she sell the Mount and cut all ties with the United States and what she now considered the unhappiness of her American past? She wavered between possibilities and intentions, never coming to a decision about separation from her husband or compromised continuance. The old impositions of the past, and caste, weighed upon her still.

Dr. Kinnicutt advised her that the prognosis concerning Teddy's psychosis "is an unfavorable one," and suggested anew that he be hospitalized, not necessarily because confinement would bring about a cure, but in a sanatorium he might find some quiet relief from his unhappiness. The diagnosis only weakened Edith's determination to terminate her marriage and break completely with the past: to leave her husband at this time would be like abandoning a child.

Teddy wrote that he would come to her in Paris—then, in one of his unpredictable shifts of intent, went to Bermuda instead. Edith was beginning to suffer attacks of vertigo; when objects fell from her hand, she felt herself about to fall. She feared even to go walking in her own quarter: at the corner of the rue de Bac she saw a neighbor drop a book to the ground, her eye compulsively followed the falling object, and she felt dizzy and had to lean against the side of a building.

Her French doctor diagnosed a tension in the inner ear brought on by an anemic condition. She was advised to eat liver, *raisins sec*, and to seek fresh air.

The open air, for Edith, was best imbibed from a motorcar. Driving through a small French town with Mrs. Margaret Chanler, Edith remarked that this was a region she had never visited before, and she was charmed by the locale. It would be pleasant to stay the night at the quaint Hôtel de la Gare.

When the two women went to book a room, Edith was startled to see "Mr. and Mrs. Wharton" inscribed in the registry, written in Teddy's unmistakable hand and dated not many days before. He was in France, on one of his flings, and obviously he had escorted a woman from town to town.

"Evidently I *have* been here before," she murmured to Mrs. Chanler.

Their estate in Lenox was the one anchor of goodwill left to the Wharton marriage, and for Teddy the one place he could always return after an episode abroad. On one such return, driven by whim or agitation, Teddy abruptly sold the property. Some months before, Edith had agreed in principle that the Mount should eventually be sold and Teddy could manage the transaction; but now that he had done so, in her absence and apparently on impulse, Edith felt another wave of vertigo and was psychologically adrift. Paris was indeed her *résidence fixe,* but Lenox her last foothold in America. She had originally agreed to the sale when she decided that 52, rue de Varenne was now and forever her home; then, overcome by the nostalgia of a longtime attachment, she said no. But Teddy acted on the first expressed response, then sold the Mount without giving her formal notice. To Morton Fullerton she wrote: "Yes—he *promised* not to sell the Mount to any one, at any price, till after I reached Paris and he had communicated with me. . . ."

Following the sale, Teddy embarked on a manic rampage, traveling around Europe in the company of assorted women friends. The last attachment to her husband had been severed with the sale of their joint property in Lenox: Edith's mind was not set on divorce. "It's all settled!" she wrote Gaillard Lapsley. "But don't say a word to anyone, as the decree can't be pronounced till the courts sit again next week."

On the basis of her husband's adulteries—*le sieur Wharton s'est affiché tant à Londres qu'à Monte-Carlo avec différentes femmes et a eu avec elles des relations d'un caractère gravement injurieux pour la demanderesse* [the Sire Wharton has shown himself publicly in London as well as Monte-Carlo in the company of various women and has had relations with them of a kind gravely injurious to the plaintiff]—Edith was granted a divorce by the Tribunal de Grande Instance de Paris, April 16, 1913.

Despite the statutes of the Napoleonic Code which had served Morton Fullerton so admirably in the divorce action by Camille Chabert, Edith Wharton was given the advantage against her spouse. The divorce was granted on the basis of Teddy Wharton's adulteries, and the petitioner, Edith Wharton, was declared the injured party in the case: Teddy was even obliged to pay all court costs of the proceedings. After a short wrangle over "dower rights" (the wife's claim to a portion of the husband's property), Edith conceded the claim in order to retain her right to the name Wharton. Teddy's name would continue to appear on the covers of the Wharton books to come, his last tenuous connection to the author.

viii

"Some big and terrible things are shortly to be feared," was Morton Fullerton's interpretation of the unstable political mood in Europe. Edith was still in touch with Fullerton, but almost entirely by way of letters to her *cher ami.* Her persistent efforts brought about publication of his *Problems of Power,* the only substantial and sustained work he had ever achieved. Scribner's had become deeply concerned over the danger of losing Edith Wharton permanently to Appleton (she had contracted with their rival for only one book, so far), and could now oblige their best-selling author by publishing her good friend Fullerton. The book was a perceptive assessment of the current European scene in disorder, and could be read as a dire hint of horrors to come. Here was the first important prediction of the Great War about to be unleashed on the world, though little note was taken of the warning or the book.

Also by correspondence, Edith offered her experienced criticism of Fullerton's manuscripts, but this help was less appreciated by her friend. A number of misunderstandings arose over Edith's attempts at editorial comment—the kind of help she had willingly sought and accepted from Henry James and Walter Berry—so she gave up on this unwelcome literary guidance of Fullerton's career, but not quite on Fullerton himself.

Meanwhile, in those last months of peace, Paris and environs were more attractive than ever to her: " 'Eyes, look your last'—in and about Paris all things seemed to utter the same cry: the smiling suburbs unmarred by hideous advertisements, the unravaged cornfields of Millet and Monet, still spreading in sunny opulence to the city's edge, the Champs-Elysées in their last expiring elegance, and the great buildings, statues and fountains withdrawn at dusk into silence and secrecy. . . ."

More and more she was drawing herself into a splendid cocoon, seeing only her dearest and longstanding friends; among those, especially, an active revival of close friendship with Walter Berry, head of the Paris-American Chamber of Commerce, bibliophile, and the one American *convive* Proust could tolerate. Less a distant cousin than a staunch and devoted friend, Berry was as confirmed an expatriate as she, and constantly available to her calls for solace and company. "I suppose," she said of Berry, "there is one friend in the life of each of us who seems not a separate person, however dear and beloved, but an expansion, an interpretation, of one's self, the very meaning of one's soul." When Edith ventured beyond Paris, it was now Walter Berry who accompanied her on these excursions she had once so much enjoyed in the company of Morton Fullerton or Henry James. The *mauvaises langues,* evil tongues, began to speak of the association as one of the classic sexual liaisons common to the local scene. The gossips of the faubourg did not hesitate to refer to Edith Wharton and Walter Berry as lovers. Even Henry James spoke of Edith traveling about with Walter "like another George Sand and another Chopin." Edith's relationship to Walter Berry was an intimate friendship perpetuated since childhood and had never been more—but in the Wharton scale of loving, that was immeasurable.

The novel Edith published in the latter part of 1913 was *The Custom of the Country,* combining aspects of the Old World from the author's accumulated impressions of the faubourg St. Germain in confrontation—very much in the Jamesian manner—with characters and backgrounds drawn from her American souvenirs. Following the long interval of desultory writing, and the "warblings" in verse inspired by her love affair with Morton Fullerton, Edith Wharton presented this substantial tour de force and immediately reestablished her solid reputation with the critics as well as with her vast readership. Events of the following year were not as propitious.

"I joined a party at one of the tables," Edith wrote of that June afternoon, 1914, "and as we sat there a cloud-shadow swept over us, abruptly darkening bright flowers and bright dresses. 'Haven't you heard? The Archduke Ferdinand assassinated . . . at Serajevo . . . where *is* Serajevo? His wife was with him. What was her name? Both shot dead.' A momentary shiver ran through the company. But to most of us the Archduke Ferdinand was no more than a name. . . ."

Decidedly more than a name to Parisians was Socialist Jean Juarès, last outspoken opponent of the war, assassinated outside a café on the rue de Rivoli by a deranged arch patriot. Three afternoons after the shooting, Edith crossed the pont de la Concorde on an errand to a shop near the café where Juarès was shot down. As she crossed the place de la Concorde on the Tuileries side, to avoid the dense traffic, not far from the Ministère de la Marine Edith paused before a startling poster in bold black print: MOBILISATION GÉNÉRALE.

"That evening, in a restaurant of the rue Royale, we sat at a table in one of the open windows, abreast with the street, and saw the strange new crowds stream by. . . ." The Parisians who poured past the open window were pedestrians, since all of Paris had been reduced to foot travel; taxis, omnibuses, private automobiles had been confiscated by the War Office to transport conscripts, with whole families accompanying recruits to the train stations, "cross-tides racing to a maelstrom." Edith Wharton's evening meal was disrupted by the restaurant band striking up at intervals the *Marseillaise,* which required a show of patriotism from the diners who were constantly standing up, napkins and forks in hand, to honor the occasion.

Next day all of Paris shut down during the mass transport of soldier-draftees, with the population still pouring into the streets despite the lack of transport. Edith Wharton fell back on social classification to describe the spectacle of this human tide: "from the scum of the Exterior Boulevards to the cream of the fashionable restaurants." Haussmann's dispersal of the poor sections from the center of the city had for the moment broken down. On the third day the summer tourists and short-term expatriates joined the scramble for exit visas, and for train and boat tickets.

As for Edith Wharton, she would have shared the sentiment expressed by fellow expatriate Mildred Aldrich, who was present at the battlefront in her home overlooking the Marne: "All the time my heart is out there in the northeast. It is not my country nor my war—yet I feel as if it were both." At the time that critical battle was fought, Edith was stranded in London, for she had taken Walter Berry's misguided advice that the threat of all-out war would quickly dissipate, and she was anxious to see Henry James, who was failing, even suicidal, depressed by the war and his deteriorating health and the death of his brother William. When the dreadful news broke that the Germans were in France after having swiftly devastated the tiny kingdom of Belgium, and were, unbelievably, marching on Paris, Edith was desperate to return to her adopted country. Only now did she realize how critical was the situation in France, and she *must* share its fate.

Transportation across the Channel appeared to be out of the question, except for the transport of British troop reinforcements for England's beleaguered ally. Civilians were fleeing France, not seeking a way back. Edith Wharton's characteristic drive and persistence did make the impossible possible: she got in touch with her old friend Paul Cambon, French ambassador to England; swiftly the French Embassy in London made priority arrangements for her return. The Germans had got within ten miles of Paris when the tide of battle turned and General Joffre launched his offensive with a raggletag army of rear-echelon troops ferried to the front in that highly unlikely but very Parisian idea of expedient, by taxicab. The Germans were obliged to retreat to their entrenched positions on the Aisne River. For the instant France was saved.

What impressed Edith when she got back to the rue de Varenne was the emptiness and slowed pace of Paris: an eerie calm had muted the city streets and her own dear quarter on the Left Bank had never been as silent. One early morning she was startled awake merely by an exchange of *bonjours* below her window, and another dawn she awakened to discover the existence of the *vidangeurs,* the nocturnal sanitation workers who vacuumed out the faubourg's septic tanks. These observations might find their way into some future novel, but Edith Wharton was not made for sitting in passive suspense as events unfolded elsewhere.

"Many women with whom I was in contact during the war had obviously found their vocation in nursing the wounded, or in other philanthropic activities. The call on their co-operation had developed unexpected aptitudes which, in some cases, turned them forever from a life of discontented idling." At first Edith joined the formerly discontented idle, the *grandes dames* of the faubourg who were now committed to the traditional knitting of sweaters and scarves, sewing garments for the soldiers at the front—but this home-front project was hardly adequate to her energies and her fund-raising and organizational flair. She was led to establish a full-scale operation to employ young women to sew garments in an *ouvroir,* a large workroom where the seamstresses were provided with meals as well as reasonable wages—a great boon to the local working women, many of whom had been put out of business by the charitable activities of the original faubourg sewing circle.

Seeking war-charity funds from the affluent neighbors she knew well, and ready to make large contributions of her own, Edith suddenly realized she was cut off from her considerable wealth in America. This unlikely state had never occurred to her: she was a woman of means, money had always been at her disposal—Teddy had forever carried that thousand-dollar bill in his pocket "in case Pussy wanted something." But the international banking system had broken down: Edith Wharton had no money at hand, and found herself in the strange surreal state of fiscal vacuum. She considered her servants, how to pay them—Edith retained three servants, all women, for the men were subject to mobilization. She turned to Walter Berry at first for a loan, and then Berry with his influential Chamber of Commerce connections saw to it that American dollars were at last funneled into her French bank account in the form of francs.

More and more money and support would be necessary, for Edith had discovered Paris was inundated with Belgian refugees, many of them discovered orphaned children found in the rubble of Louvain after the German *Blitzkrieg.* Edith had always been uneasy in the presence of children, and had once remarked to Teddy, "It is perhaps just as well we never had children of our own." If ever she did have children, she said she would "deprive them of every *pleasure,* in order to prepare them for the inevitable unhappiness of life." This chilly attiude changed when Edith was faced with the Louvain war orphans, some of them maimed and others shell-shocked during a greater "unhappiness of life" than she had ever imagined. Edith Wharton now gave over her time and energies to setting up shelters for the Belgian homeless on the model of the shelters for victims of the great 1910 flood. She agitated for state support, enlisted her fashionable friends to help feed and clothe and house the refugees: she was the founder and director of the Children of Flanders Rescue Committee. "All the Belgians in Paris," said Walter Berry, "are feeding out of Edith's hands."

There was ever in Edith Wharton's mixed temperament a concern beyond its expression in her fiction for life's victims, children and others. She was deeply attached to the servants in her household—her only family, really—and now in wartime a long-repressed compassion spilled forth as she was confronted with the hurt, abandoned and wretched of Europe. She had become the Angel of Paris, truly. For her steadfast devotion to the refugees in France, Edith Wharton ("*femme de lettres* in the news citation in *Le Figaro*) was made a Chevalier de la Légion d'Honneur, France's highest award, given only on this occasion to a foreigner during wartime.

Both Walter Berry and Edith Wharton were now made to know on the grimmest terms the extended tragedy the Great War was to be. The horror of modern warfare could not have been been imagined by the small insouciant band of expatriates in Paris—nor, for that matter, by the belligerents themselves—and the Americans were numbed by the onslaught. Edith hoped and prayed for American intervention, and instigated a letter-writing campaign to that end, but the U.S. entry into World War I was slow to come about, and the delay only increased Edith's bitterness toward a president she had never liked, Woodrow Wilson.

Truly, the war had cut a sharp division between the slow graceful *Belle Epoque* Edith had known and the modern world to come: a poignant sense of loss overcame her in the rare moments she could spare in contemplation of the past. Edith's closest and dearest lights were being extinguished just as the wartime lights were being dimmed Class distinction held no sway, the privileged were cut down with the servants; thus, Edith lost her dear friend Robert d'Humières and her former footman Henri, both killed in action. Another young male admirer—an American art student in Paris, much like George Biddle when he knew Mary Cassatt—was Ronald Simmons, chubby, near-sighted, but of keen intellect and large spirit, whom Edith recognized "through his jolly fatness, all the finer things vibrating in his heart and mind." Despite the age gap, the two became close friends in the little time Simmons had left. As soon as the United States entered the war, Simmons joined the intelligence corps in Paris and was stationed in Marselles, where he contracted Spanish influenza and died.

"So much of me is dead," Edith wrote—for her beloved Henry James would not survive the rude transition from the graceful *fin-de-siècle* Europe to a world gone completely mad. He died of a stroke not long after the first Battle of the Marne.

In many respects, wartime France was Edith Wharton's finest hour. Her directorship of the Flanders Committee and other organizations was the single consuming passion now: she wrote no books, she lived for others and was much alone. Had the prewar faubourg been mere theatre, a fictive Paris of Proustian time lost? In the new austerity of wartime, Paris was a living evocation still. Because of the ghostly zeppelins floating above the city on bombing missions, the rue de Varenne was no longer illuminated by the lamplighter's torch. Edith found her way home as a pedestrian now—private autos were banned, or confiscated by the army, or were converted to ambulances as was Gertrude Stein's imported American Ford. When crossing from the Right Bank Edith passed Ste. Clothilde and knew she was nearly home, sometimes touching a familiar doorpost or embassy facade to feel her way to 53, rue de Varenne. She grasped the fleeting pleasures that came her way. When the shops reopened after a period of shuttering and empty shelves, she was delighted with a sudden shopping splurge: "the voluptuousness of acquiring things one might do without."

She was seeing life in a harder light, even as the lights of the city dimmed. She encountered Walter Berry often, and though he too was engaged in the war effort, his self-centered way of life—it had been her way of life not long before—now appeared trivial and useless. The old rapport with so many of her aristocratic friends was gone, unless she worked beside them at the many shelters and *cantines* she supervised across Paris.

Morton Fullerton was missing from her world as well. For many months Edith had stored his collection of books in her circular library, and she now wished to make room for temporary storage of Walter Berry's books. The letter concerning this matter came not from Edith but from her friend and assistant: "Mrs. Wharton begs you to excuse her not writing herself, as she is up to her eyes in work . . . but she asks me to ask you if you could conveniently send for your books, as she has to find room for a lot of furniture. Of course she has been delighted to keep the books for you, but now she is herself pressed for room. If it were not for that she wouldn't think of asking you to take them away."

In one of her last letters to Henry James just before his death Edith expressed her *tristesse* shading into bitterness over Morton Fullerton, whom she had so dearly loved.

"Morton . . . has completely abandoned me. He will turn up again when I can be of use to him. *Enfin!*"

CARESSE CROSBY,
posing with Narcisse Noir.
*(Crosby Collection,
Southern Illinois University)*

III
Caresse Crosby
1892–1970

"Yes" and never "no" was our answer to the fabulous twenties.

Caresse read aloud from Janet Flanner's *Letter from Paris* in *The New Yorker:* "The ceremonies of death are precisely graded in France. . . ." Her husband Harry, who had been in charge of Walter Berry's funeral, listened in silence. "The plume-decked, broidered catafalque with its flowing curtains and silver insignia and its four plume-decked black horses with the somber caparisons and white reins, headed a procession in Mr. Berry's last honor. . . ."

"The master of ceremonies," Harry told Caresse, "wore the official chains of his office around his neck, like a sommelier." Caresse had not attended the cremation at Père Lachaise, and Harry told her about the crematory assistants and coffinmakers, like Shakespearean gravediggers joking and drinking cheap wine, enjoying their midday meal while Cousin Walter turned to ash in the plain pine box. "Dieu, it must have been hot inside."

Harry assumed a secret smile when the subject of death came up, and the subject came up often with Harry. Caresse shivered. She had been very fond of Harry's "Cousin Walter," whom she remembered as "enormously elongated, slim as a straw and as *sec;* his small head poised erect above a high wing collar [and was] birdlike in its sudden turnings and its bright quick glance . . . his fastidiousness was part of his general aullure. His speech was witty, and his knowledge wordly; his manner with women was most gallant and wicked." She had liked him because he accepted Harry as Harry was, and had been most gallant, though not wicked, with her.

When Caresse and Harry Crosby settled in Paris in 1922 they immediately formed a close liaison with Walter Berry: Harry became a kind of literary protégé, just as Edith Wharton had been as a young woman. It fell to Caresse, for her decorative surfaces only, to serve as hostess—displacing Edith Wharton—at the distinguished bachelor's tasteful soirées. Edith's resentment of the Crosbys' appearance on the Parisian scene was first expressed in her letter to a friend: "Walter's young cousin turns out to be a sort of half-crazy cad." Edith and Caresse might have found common interest in their abiding love of small dogs, but even there Edith Wharton, along with all of the Parisian socialites the Crosbys had called on so far, regarded with horror Caresse's pampered whippet, Narcisse Noir, with its jeweled collars and paw nails painted gold.

There was still the matter of Walter Berry's books to be settled, a division betwen Edith Wharton and Harry Crosby, but the ultimate insult to Edith's sensibilities had been the funeral itself.

"Whatever did she want the ashes *for?*" asked Caresse. She remembered Walter Berry had stipulated that his ashes be "chucked out anywhere," but Edith wanted them delivered to the Pavillon Colombe, her country house outside Paris.

"Wanted to scatter them on her famous white roses, I would imagine."

With the legacy of the Berry Library still to be resolved, Harry had decided to be diplomatic and oblige Edith Wharton. He drove out to Versailles with the ceramic urn containing Walter Berry's remains, and at Pavillon Colombe presented the ashes to a moist-eyed Mrs. Wharton.

"All of a sudden there was a great banging on the front door, and when the maid opened the door two *agents de police* were standing there demanding to know what we intended to do with those ashes. They had followed me all the way from Père Lachaise."

By French law, ashes of the deceased may not, as Walter Berry wished, be "chucked out anywhere," but must be placed in a mausoleum or officially buried as would a cadaver intact. Edith Wharton, in deep mourning, was outraged by the intrusion and humiliated by the scene. The gendarmes were sent away with assurances, but ever after, Edith believed that Harry Crosby, "the half-crazy cad," had been reponsible for the grotesque mockery of that encounter.

Caresse knew there would be no reconciliation after this, and assumed that Edith would take advantage of Walter Berry's muddled last will and testament. Edith Wharton was to select whichever books she wanted for herself, and the remainder would go to Harry, which meant Edith could take possession of the entire Berry collection, a highly valued library that both Edith and Harry coveted.

"She might not leave me one book," complained Harry. "I think it's disgraceful and she should damned well be ashamed of herself."

"We will just fight her Grab Act tooth and nail."

Actually Caresse and Harry had completely misjudged Edith Wharton in their anticipation of the worst she might do. Edith acted out of conditioned restraint and dignified distance in these instances, and would never have squabbled over a legacy of books with the Crosbys. She was retreating altogether from the disturbing new age, the twenties, just as she completed her novel of her own age, *The Age of Innocence.* In the end she selected fewer then eighty volumes out of Walter Berry's vast library of eight thousand, a gesture of *noblesse oblige* that ended any further intercourse with the crazies and cads of this new generation.

The Crosbys were overjoyed, especially Harry, who had been made into a genuine bibliophile by Cousin Walter. The books had been stored at Edith's apartment, and Caresse reported on the exuberant rite of transfer, thousands of volumes with the sets in crates and the rest stacked into wicker baskets and carried on the heads of Maple's movers, carted across the boulevard St. Germain to the opposite end of the faubourg. On foot, Caresse and Harry followed the procession of their ambulant library, Harry singing, "Books, books, books, books—crate after crate, crate after crate," until they reached their townhouse on the rue de Lille.

ii

After a turbulent courtship of lovers defying a clan of scowling Boston first families, where else could the romance—and turbulence—be perpetuated but in Paris? The unspeakable word "divorce" was whispered in their wake; the derelict Crosbys could live as social black sheep in the United States or refashion their lives against an unfamiliar but alluring backdrop abroad. The scandal fell particularly upon Caresse's head: she was the "older woman" by six years. As Polly Peabody, D.A.R. and daughter of the Jacob-Peabody clan, her credentials were impeccable: eminent cousins were the Van Vechtens and Schuylers. "My mother," declared Caresse, "mixed the driest martinis in Manhattan. She was a strain apart, a strain that is dying out. Despots, darlings, sorcerers, ladies of steel." Polly of course wanted to be just like her.

The link between the Jacob and Peabody dynasties appeared to be the most suitable connection imaginable, a marriage made in that nearest place to heaven, Boston's Back Bay. The bride was completely enamored of the groom: Dick Peabody was an insouciant charmer of the private school set, "beloved and bewildering, the handsomest man I have ever seen, then or since." Polly Jacob met Dick Peabody when the two were fourteen, at one of those Eastern seaboard summer camps of insulated exclusivity: they dined on terrapin Maryland and Maine lobster. The setting inspired Dick to request tenderly of Polly that she wait for him through the six years ahead, until he became a graduate of Harvard. The teenagers were too shy to seal their contract with a kiss, but Polly, who loved to say yes, said yes.

Fatefully enough, Polly and Dick Peabody met again on the eve of World War I, one year short of the promised span. In the nervous exhilaration of the Great War about to be waged, their romance moved at accelerated pace: "Ours was a boy-girl affair," she admitted, as if they were still the adolescent campers beside the lake. Dick's vague intentions were no more mature than Polly's: "I was," she said, "to remain the perfect playmate."

They were married in January 1915; their son, William Jacob Peabody, was born a year later, the first boy produced in their Boston circle. Dick thought himself a tiger to have performed so brilliantly on his first try, and much was made of the father and son, while the mother was left out of the fun. But Dick wanted no part of the nuisance of being a father: when the smells and sound effects disturbed him he simply walked out, and came back—when he did come back—inebriated.

Dick tired of his job with Johns Manville and set up in his own business, private shipping, investing Polly's family legacy to do so. When the business went bust, Dick, encouraged by the Peabodys, so proud of the family military tradition, ran off to be a soldier in the "border troubles" with Mexico's Pancho Villa, since the United States had thus far avoided the Great War in Europe. Polly's nest egg was gone and so was her husband: she was without resources and pregnant with their second child, reduced to the domestic capitulation of moving in with her in-laws. Dick returned from the failed expedition to flush out Pancho Villa, stayed only long enough to take one look at his new daughter Polleen (he was appalled at the sight of the baby's streaks and pustules from heat rash), and this time followed his hero General Pershing to the war raging in France "to take a crack at those Huns."

For the duration of the war, Polly Peabody was constrained to live the "strange muted life, uneventful and unjoyful," of her in-laws. The Paris Dick Peabody described in his letters—hinting that it was hard to live like a monk in France—was no comfort to his housebound wife, constrained to chastity, rolling bandages for the Red Cross on Mrs. Peabody's kitchen table. "Dick might never return, and then what? I saw no further than the walls of my prison, I was stuck fast like a mussel in a mudbank and a mussel without money. Pocket money was doled out to me like war rations, very, very charily."

Before her marriage Polly, preparing a ball gown one evening, discovered a substitute device to replace the ugly and restrictive corset-cover young women wore beneath their gowns and tea dresses. She pinned two handkerchiefs together on the bias, sewed them with ribbons beneath the points of the breast bone, and knotted the handkerchief ends at her waist; the supporting ribbons were then pulled taut. Polly obtained a patent for this "jewel case" she called the Backless Brassiere, which she successfully introduced to her debutante friends. She managed to sell the idea to a former admirer who worked for the Warner Brothers Corset Company in Bridgeport. For the design and patent she received $1,500, a considerable windfall at the time, and a suggestion that a rude challenge to the traditional could bear unexpected rewards.

Prohibition awaited the returning gladiators, in the brave new world announced by the Treaty of Versailles. The war years, and the introduction of the doughboys to the wines abroad, had produced a legion of the wordly with a mighty thirst. Despite the Volstead Act of 1919, alcoholic beverages, however crude the product, appeared to be in supply equal to the demand: lining up a reliable bootlegger was one of a man's first responsibilities after demobilization.

On his return, Dick Peabody, already the reckless college boozer when Polly married him, was now an alcoholic. The domestic scene Dick came home to in Boston only exacerbated his need of drink. He would never, Polly realized, adjust to a life of conjugal responsibility; and now with the excitement of war games behind him, Dick was a desperate man.

Dick became an aficionado of fire fighting—without of course becoming a fireman. He installed a fire gong in their little house, an alarm connected to the nearest fire station, so that he could instantly join in pursuit when a fire broke out. This playtime substitute for the missing thrill of the battlefront in France was unnerving for a wife and mother of two small children. Dick was having a brass firepole installed in their home, with an escape hatch through the floor of their bedroom, when the fire department put a stop to his amateur participation in their fire emergencies. Frustrated, Dick began to spend more and more of his time at Boston speakeasies, his hobbies reduced to one familiar standby. By this time, Polly had been to see Uncle Jack (John Pierpont Morgan, Jr.) about family help for Dick's increasing alcoholism and erratic behavior.

J. P. Morgan was just then engaged in delicate negotiations concerning the massive loan operation for France, made bankrupt by the war. It was characteristic of him to put aside this world-scale transaction in order to receive Polly: Dick Peabody was Morgan's nephew and godson; he would do whatever was necessary, and bear the expense himself—besides, he was the one member of the Boston clan who was quite fond of Polly. At first Dick was accompanied everywhere by a male nurse, under constant surveillance, but this tactic proved as ineffective as Prohibition was for the country at large. Uncle Jack was again called upon and Polly was forever grateful for his help and concern: "Soon Dick had to be treated in a sanatorium. It was that spring I met Harry."

Polly had first seen Harry Crosby with his mother, from a distance. Her initial impression was of a pale young man, tall and thin in his field service uniform, his tunic bemedaled but the soiled puttees coming unwound: "In his restless eye I caught a look so completely *right* that from that moment I sensed my destiny." She was aware that the eye did not rest upon her. Later, at a lawn party, Harry did notice the pretty young matron wheeling a baby carriage, but took her for a child, the baby borrowed. He soon discovered she was Dick Peabody's wife, and learned that Dick himself was in a drying-out clinic for alcoholics.

It occurred to Mrs. Crosby that Polly Peabody would be an ideal "chaperone" for a Nantasket Beach party planned by Harry and a group of his friends. It would be a pleasant distraction for the bereft and troubled wife, charitable and appropriate for her to keep company with a younger set. Harry was twenty-one at this time, returned from wartime ambulance duty in France to enroll as a Freshman at Harvard, while Polly at twenty-eight was a settled-married-older woman—at least in Mrs. Crosby's eyes. Again, Polly could ascribe this innocent misjudgment to the inexplicable workings of predestination.

From the moment Harry Crosby arrived at the River Street house to pick up Polly (he was wearing plus fours, "the most unbecoming garment a man can wear"), she was the object of his intense gaze, the exclusive center of his attention. He rudely ignored his date and everyone else in the crowd to direct his interest to their chaperone. After the beach party they went to a nearby amusement park, and in the shadowed drifting confines of a tunnel-of-love, Harry whispered in Polly's ear, "I love you." Polly believed him, for "to know Harry was a devastating experience," and no one doubted his devastating sincerity.

Not long after their secret affair began—their first night together, at the Belmont Hotel in New York—Harry wrote Polly one of his death-haunted letters: "I don't know what to do and I suppose it would be better if I were killed. You're my religion and everything I look up to."

Being everything to Harry Crosby meant everything to Polly Peabody: her euphoric state of being loved and in love obscured the chill of those recurring references to death in her lover's extravagant declarations. She accepted this swearing unto death as evidence of Harry's lyric expression of devotion—her lover was a poet, no less.

Her infatuation blinded her "like a sunrise," and she did not truly register the fateful import of the young man's morbid concerns: "Cambridge on a Sunday night is like a morgue. And I haven't seen you for so long, dearest. . . . You write me and tell me that I must be all happy and cheerful but God don't you see that this is impossible seeing that I can never hope to marry you whom I love and adore and who means life itself to me. . . ."

If marriage was out of the question there was still hope of a soul-mating in the afterlife: "I promise you that whenever you want we shall die together and what's more I am perfectly ready now or will be anytime. With the absolute faith that we shall be One in Heaven as soon as we die forever and ever it is a great temptation to forsake this life."

Polly Peabody, stranded alone with her in-laws and two small children, might have been blinded by Harry's sun, but she was neither ready to die with him nor live with him, unprepared to desert the only establishment she knew, the world she had grown up in, "a world where good smells existed," for the poetic promise of her lover's outlaw paradise.

At 37, River Street the good smells of upper-class life mingled with the raw smell of the nearby fishing pier. The Crosbys lived at the upper-crust end of Back Bay—95, Beacon Street, very near Polly's address but a world apart in neighborhood distinction—and Harry began taking the daily floral arrangements from his mother's private greenhouse to Polly's house instead. Once, when Mrs. Crosby was about to give a house party and the servants were asked to create the usual elaborate floral decor, Harry quickly dispatched the chauffeur to 37, River Street to borrow back Polly's gift flowers for his mother's soirée.

Notice of the affair (Harry bearing great bouquets of flowers to Polly was broadcast enough) was bound to seep into the running exchange of confidences on the Back Bay social circuit. The situation had become intolerable for the clandestine lovers: they were neither of them comfortable with or resigned to a back-street affair, and Harry was urging Polly to confess their love to Dick Peabody and ask him for a divorce. When Polly did unburden her conscience to her husband, it was a new Dick Peabody to whom she appealed for an end to their marriage. Dick was completely understanding and unexpectedly cooperative; he was on the way to a complete cure, to the point of becoming a counselor to other alcoholics. Yes, he agreed to a divorce—Polly was for an instant taken aback. An ironic reflection occurred to her: while Dick was an altogether changed man, Harry had lately succumbed to the same dependence on drink that had originally undone her husband. At twenty-eight, Polly had acquired some measure of self-knowledge—often obscured behind a veil of romantic illusion—and she considered briefly but finally denied the possibility of a new design for the old self-destructive love.

Now that the word of their love was out general condemnation fell upon the heads of the lovers, the onus particularly on Polly. Dick Peabody had agreed to a divorce, and Harry was begging Polly to take the chance at freedom within reach. But the lovers were not alone in determining their future; the clans had gathered, pressure was being applied, and Polly's mother insisted that her daughter agree at least to stop seeing Harry for a six-month period. Polly fled Boston for New York, but the courtship went forward by mail. On most counts Harry was considered the innocent youth entangled in the designs of an older woman, a wife and a *mother:* Harry's maturity-by-ordeal on the battlefields of France was ignored, he was a beginning *student* at Harvard.

Polly's behavior was far from that of a designing woman, either before or after the divorce. In *Peabody* v. *Peabody,* she astounded both divorce lawyers and the judge at Domestic Relations Court by asking for no alimony; she had to be prevailed upon to accept, finally, modest child support. (She did agree to restitution by the Peabodys of the money she lost in the ill-fated shipping enterprise.) When the divorce was granted, Polly began seeing Harry again—he commuted by night train from Boston to New York—but she now began to see other men, and thought she might make a career for herself in New York. She set out to be a writer; she even auditioned for small roles as a film actress in Manhattan's burgeoning silent-screen studios. At all costs, Polly determined to dodge Harry's passionate entreaties and refuse his offer of marriage: she was still a conforming member of New York–Boston society and did not to want to suffer the fate of Edith Wharton's Lily Bart. With chin high she accepted the contrived invitations of Peabody and Crosby family members who wanted to see "how she was taking it." These were but facade occasions for the gossip that followed each encounter, and Polly knew it, but she would brave or flatter her way back into society's respect, if not good graces. Harry knew better. "Bostonians hate her (the lost lady) so I hate Bostonians."

In the gossip columns of a society journal called *Town Topics* appeared the following item:

> It looks as if the much-rumored engagement of Harry Grew Crosby and winsome and coy Mrs. Dick Peabody, one-time Molly [sic] Jacob, will not materialize into anything tangible for the present. The youth's father Stephen Van R. Crosby, has just executed a neat *coup,* which, for the present at least, will put a stop to all possibilities revolving in the minds of this infatuated young pair by sending him off on the *Olympic* last Saturday.

It was the *Touraine* that Harry sailed on, and not Stephen Van R. Crosby who was responsible for sending Harry abroad, but John Pierpont Morgan, Jr., Uncle Jack. In the closely entangled bloodlines of one first family to another, Uncle Jack Morgan happened to be Harry Crosby's uncle as well as Dick Peabody's—and godfather to both. Once again, as Polly Peabody's latest crisis came to a head, Uncle Jack was not unsympathetic to her ordeal: he truly hoped to do the best for both parties by arranging for Harry to work at his bank, Morgan, Harjes et Cie., in Paris.

He was arranging for their separation, but both Harry and Polly oddly considered this a kind of blessing—if the distance between New York and Boston had failed to keep them apart, how could the romantic prospect of Paris come between lovers?—and Harry was delighted to accept exile from "Drearytown." Uncle Jack was, he told Polly, "damned nice about you and me." By some reverse logic the lovers were counting on the vast Atlantic to bring them together, which oddly enough it did.

To pay her passage to London, Polly sold a strand of pearls for a first brief clandestine reunion with Harry. Harry had arranged for the Channel crossing by air, on one of the early primitive passenger flights, but for all the sense of adventure to their secret meeting, Polly was shadowed by odd tokens of guilt: she thought the Daimler Harry had rented for the drive to the airport should have flaunted a scarlet "A" on the license plate. In Paris the lovers appeared to live chastely apart, Harry in his apartment on the rue Cambon and Polly at the Regina, on the place des Pyramids. Polly was thrilled with her view of the Tuileries, but the gilded statue of St. Joan below her window—symbol of righteousness and purity—was a constant reminder of her own unsaintly state.

From café to café across Paris, or in the constrained intimacy of a *calèche* (the horse taxis still clattering over cobblestone), Harry spread out his magic city for Polly's delectation. He stole time from the Morgan, Harjes bank so that they might leisurely tour Paris and environs under their assumed names: the vicomte and vicomtesse Myopia. The subtler prevalences of Paris gradually overcame Polly's intimations of guilt: the lovers' moments together crossing and recrossing the Seine confirmed every vow either had made to the other. Already enamored, Polly was now committed to the man and his Paris for all time. But then, in the way of the world, "Boston trespassed into our Paradise again."

A strident Boston matron had sniffed out the renegade couple despite their maneuvers of secrecy. She traced Polly to the Regina Hotel, and there confronted her with the transgression of "corrupting young Harry Crosby." As it turned out, the mother accused Polly of leading Harry astray because Harry had casually flirted with the woman's daughter the summer before, and the daughter had taken his offhand declarations with great seriousness. Polly was spoiling the daughter's chances at a proper Boston alliance. The idyll had ended; Boston had found them out. Polly sailed immediately for New York, leaving the desolate Harry to his prayers: "Why did I let her go why why why O Sun-God tell me why."

Harry at this time was directing his questions not to God but to Sun-God, for he was evolving a love–death–sun religion, himself the sole adherent for now but with the possibility of converting Polly to the cult.

ENOUGH OF THIS HELL. SAILING STEERAGE AQUITANIA. HAVE ENGAGED BRIDAL SUITE FOR RETURN TRIP. SAY YES. ALL MY LOVE. YOUR HARRY.

YES.

iii

In Paris, Polly became Caresse. It was Harry's idea that the name of Polly reborn should suggest softness, and "Why not the French for caresse, with an e?" It was exactly the sound the poet in Harry responded to, the perfect acrostic for the Crosby Cross:

C
A
H A R R Y
E
S
S
E

The Boston Crosbys, with residual bitterness, had barely adjusted to Harry's marriage to Polly Peabody when the news came from Paris of her "tarted up" pseudonym, "Caresse." Immediately Harry's cousin Betty Beal wrote a sarcastic note to the newlyweds in Paris, signing herself "Baiser Beal." The joke was on her: *baiser* was indeed the word for kiss in standard French, but in the slang of the day had taken on a crude sexual connotation. To the Jacobses and Peabodys, Polly was still Polly—or Pollykins to her mother—and forever would be. Harry's cousin Walter Berry reacted to the name change with mild good humor at first mention, then called Polly "Caresse" without a smile from that moment on.

Caresse and Harry were in need of names and terms and touchstones to underpin their shaky Paris establishment which, without these whimsical embellishments and ritual tags, might be taken for a house of cards. Now that Polly had become Caresse, she was also Harry's Cramoisy Queen, for he liked her in crimson cloth and was in love with the word "cramoisy." Besides the caprice of inventing names, impulse ruled their lives as it had so romantically triggered their marriage. The rash voyage of Harry Crosby to America had bedazzled Polly for its flair and daring, and confirmed the heartfelt "yesses" she had whispered in Paris. Harry had fled France with less than a month's salary in hand, bribed his way out of steerage on the *Aquitania* with money he won at cards, then bluffed his way into First Class where he subsisted on hors d'oeuvres of caviar and *saumon fumé*, swam alone and naked in the ship's inboard pool, won more money at cards, and spent his winnings on champagne for the losers, a gesture that rendered him penniless again.

It was a fascinating adventure to relate to Polly through the grillwork barrier at Customs: a daring caper in the name of romance. The giving away of easy winnings in the form of champagne was the moral to the tale: "You can only keep," he assured Polly, "those things which you give away"—a maxim Polly was meant to subscribe to if she agreed to pledge herself to this wild youth with the restless eyes. Marry him she did, as soon as he cleared Customs—which took no time at all, for Harry carried only a pipe and matches, and he was wearing his entire wardrobe.

They were swiftly wed at New York's City Hall, then went to the Belmont Hotel where Polly had made reservations in sentimental evocation of the first night they spent together, in the very same room. On a wave of euphoria they knew the world must surely share, Harry took Polly off to reconcile his family to the glorious news. His sister met the new-married couple on the doorstep with a frozen greeting and a frown; Mrs. Crosby never once looked at the bride or addressed a single syllable to her.

"We left on the three-o'clock," Polly remembered—their spirits considerably lowered, the spell temporarily broken—"Our glorious adventure had lost its shine."

The shine would surely be restored in Paris; Polly could not fail to note Harry's mixed feelings now that the party balloons had burst. He had suffered the same letdown when the Great War was over; for Harry could not tolerate the monotony of the flat aftermath. Polly's children arrived, having been sent for from their separate private schools, but when Harry saw the children—he knew there *were* children, and had forgotten about them in his earlier excitement—his mood fell further. The *Aquitania* was making the return voyage to France within forty-eight hours of the City Hall marriage ceremony: Harry suddenly absented himself, and did not reappear until just before time to sail.

Polly's chin was high, her determination fixed. "I became a rebel when I married Harry," she told family, friends, and repeated to herself for reassurance. As she prepared to board, she was offered scraps of well-meant marriage counseling.

"You absolutely *must* whip Harry into shape," advised one cousin.

"I wouldn't think of it," she replied.

On the pier just before sailing, one of Harry's Harvard classmates took the groom aside and piously offered, on Polly's account, "Pray God you will be able to lift her up!"

Whatever else Paris offered Caresse and Harry, the city cast the spell of art-in-the-making, and fed their inchoate need to create. The honeymooners would be Rudolfo and Mimi living a twentieth-century *vie de bohème,* but with money. Caresse was first to act on artistic impulse by taking up easel painting and sculpture to satisfy her aesthetic energies. In the 1920s commercial art-teaching ateliers were still in vogue and increasing in number; Left Bank art galleries were opening to compete with the established prewar showrooms on the Right Bank, the stimulus of the New Art was in the air of Paris. Caresse intended to be part of all of this, and took up palette and brush at the Julian Academy, just off the Champs-Elysées.

The establishment had been recommended by Harry's banking colleagues at Morgan, Harjes et Cie. Soon enough Caresse discovered that there were two branches of the Academy, and she had been relegated to the Right Bank division reserved for women, no nude models allowed. It was as if the Seine divided a prevailing double standard, and Caresse, operating by the new freedom of movement and choice, immediately transferred to a long-established institute in Montparnasse, l'Académie de la Grande Chaumière, with its imbued spirit of bohemia and association with Toulouse-Lautrec and Amedeo Modigliani of the turn of the century—without the restrictions and reservations of that period. Caresse shared instruction and studio space with such notable pupils as Isamu Noguchi and Alberto Giacometti, and studied under the modernist painter Fernand Léger.

Her innate sense of design and a certain manual facility were not qualities to inspire Caresse to a life devoted to painting. Her interest in art was from a certain appreciative remove: she loved the studio ambiance, and enjoyed the company of artists. Soon she switched to sculpting, and studied with the aging sculptor of classic monuments, Emile-Antoine Bourdelle. Ironically, Bourdelle thought she was more of a painter than a sculptor—her touch "très fine et très fraiche"—and advised her: "il faut chercher la vérité." Bourdelle was more charmed by his attractive pupil than interested in her potential as a sculptor; the older man played the same admiring avuncular role as J. P. Morgan and Walter Berry, delighting in the decorative company of this vivacious young student of art. The training at la Grande Chaumière came to no fruition except to sharpen Caresse's selective eye and enhance her aesthetic appreciation. Her one significant artistic accomplishment was a lifelike bust of Harry.

For the first months the young couple conformed in their fashion to the workaday routine of Paris. Harry had little enough enthusiasm for banking, but as J. P. Morgan's newphew he was guaranteed a desk and title at Morgan, Harjes et Cie. His exasperated supervisor at the prestigious Franco-American bank could think of no other term to apply to Monsieur Crosby in his periodic evaluation except "fantaisiste distingué." Despite lapses, lateness, absences, and indifference, Harry was promoted to "financial researcher" at no extra pay, but with a larger desk (where he could read Rimbaud and Baudelaire, his latest favorites), a secretary of his own, and a better view of the Ritz directly across the place, only the Vendôme column and the massive banker's desk between him and champagne afternoons with Caresse at the Ritz bar. "If only I could summon up enough courage to resign, only my family would strenuously object with sound, practical, commonsense New England arguments."

Meanwhile Caresse, with her two children, lived in the antiquated private world of the Ile St.-Louis, a city island at the dividing point of the Seine. The airy upper-level apartment on the quai d'Orléans was smaller than their first residence on the rue des Belles Feuilles, and had the disadvantage of exposing Harry to Polleen and Billy—for Harry could not abide close proximity to the children's world, or the encroachment of their lives upon his. Caresse had the help of "petite mère" Madame Dorsenaud, or "Doosenooze," to see to the children, and to keep them as much as possible out of their stepfather's sight and hearing.

Harry had been the one to choose the river island in the heart of Paris, a choice as much to do with its prior resident, Charles Baudelaire (an interest that was becoming an obsession), as for its picturesque antiquity. Of mystic significance to the pagan in Harry's psyche was their neighborhood cathedral, Notre Dame de Paris, erected on the former altar for pagan worship. While Harry relished these obscure associations with the past—both Baudelaire and Harry had settled on the Ile St.-Louis at the age of twenty-one—the island was for Caresse a private kingdom where she inhabited a tower (her princess-in-a-tower look Harry delighted in) overlooking a city in miniature with its hushed and removed ambiance. Even the island mentality was a source of amused pleasure: the vegetables and fruit was marketed at slightly higher prices than produce sold just across the Seine because, according to her greengrocer, "they are imported from the mainland."

The Crosbys lived not only in the geographic center of Paris—Notre Dame being *kilomètre zéro* for cartographers, the point from which all other distances in France were measured—but at their own *zéro-kilomètre* point of a new life. In the foreground, another form of timelessness in the truncated ruin of St. Julien-le-Pauvre just across the Seine; beyond, the infinitely shaded gray *quartiers* sloped gradually upward to Montparnasse. Downriver lay the massive grandeur of flying buttresses and graceful Gothic placement in stone, the cathedral centerpiece and spirit of Paris itself, Notre Dame.

But not much farther downriver from their island ivory tower was a workplace Harry dreaded worse than death.

They would commute to Morgan, Harjes by canoe; it was summer, and Caresse could wear her bathing suit as she accompanied her husband to work. Mornings they climbed into the jaunty red craft tied to its iron ring at the bottom of the quai d'Orléans. If Harry decided to be at work on time, by eight-fifteen they were paddling downstream to the quai des Tuileries at the level of the pont Solférino, where Harry would debark for the short trek across the Tuileries to the place Vendôme, and to his despised desk.

Then Caresse would paddle back to *kilomètre zéro* alone. The upstream pull was strenuous, but great, she remarked, for the breasts. As she passed beneath the pont Royal, the pont du Carrousel, the pont des Arts, Caresse was delighted to be noticed by the pedestrians overhead, the men on their way to work applauding the spectacle, whistling, calling out to the bathing beauty paddling home in her canoe.

All-women events put her off, and Caresse would not have attended the luncheon at Larue's if she had known it was a gathering of women only: she was through with the social chatter-parties of Boston and New York, the talk a polite cover for catty asides. But in the stylish restaurant of white and gold panels, banquettes upholstered in rose-colored velvet, Caresse was to meet the fascinating Constance Crowningshield Coolidge, niece of the editor of *Vanity Fair,* who was recently divorced from Ray Atherton. Her former husband's embassy position in Peking had allowed Constance to dwell in a Chinese temple, learn the exotic sport of racing Mongolian ponies, and indulge a taste for opium. Each woman wondered what the other was doing at Larue's at lunchtime, no men present, dining on quail *à la* Souvaroff, neither in her element. This dark beauty, known as CCC, Caresse thought perfection itself.

"Whether luckily or unluckily, I am not a jealous woman," Caresse often repeated to herself. As luck or misfortune would have it, Caresse felt compelled to introduce Constance to Harry at a luncheon before next day's races at Auteuil. When Harry learned that Constance was as reckless a gambler as himself, there evolved a dangerous rapport and mutual attraction that Caresse could not ignore. The bestowing of names was a significant indication of Harry's affection: he began calling Constance the Lady of the Golden Horse.

Caresse recalled the confrontation with the mother from Boston whose daughter had been the object of Harry's attentions: that juvenile flirtation had been but a small part of the pattern of Harry's interest in other women. This had truly not disturbed Caresse until now. The affair between Constance and Harry was a serious involvement: Caresse had not seen Harry turn his attention so intently to another woman since she had met him. This time Caresse was jealous, and afraid—yet she still thought of her rival as the most beautiful and engaging creature she had ever met. "The Lady of the Golden Horse was tangled in my hair," declared Caresse, who was strangely attached to CCC even at the passionate height of the affair with Harry.

Constance herself broke the spell, abruptly declaring her love for another man. Actually she had received a distressed letter from Caresse admitting her heartsick misery, a letter suggesting that the three could somehow be friends. Constance did want to remain on affectionate terms with Caresse, and her love for Harry was evidently less intense than his for her. Unaccustomed to being the rejected party in an affair, Harry was shaken by the breakup with Constance, and wrote her, "You may say that [Caresse] & I can be happy now. It is impossible as I told you. I wouldn't leave her under any circumstances nor as you say would you ever marry me—all that isn't the point."

It was the point, but not the point Harry wanted to make. Although the Crosbys were very much a loving couple, in many respects ideally matched, Harry had established an idiosyncratic code of marital behavior that Caresse, "not a jealous woman," apparently condoned. He had already drifted into casual sexual relations with other women in Paris, for the pure thrill of voluptuous experiment, and in keeping with Oscar Wilde's dictum: "The only way to get rid of temptation is to yield to it." The aphorism may not have immediately appealed to Caresse, but Harry assured her the code applied to her temptations as well—though fewer such occasions arose—and she said yes to it. Paris seemed a paradise where their free-form marriage contract might best be fulfilled, an Eden of temptation with the flaming sword removed.

After the three-way exchange of letters, the love affair ended, and the correspondence did help create a triangular friendship short of the *ménage à trois* Harry intended, Caresse dreaded, and Constance wanted no part of. When CCC became the comtesse de Jumilhac, the de Jumilhacs and the Crosbys spent considerable time together at the Paris hippodromes. Once the fever had subsided, its dangerous potential spent, Caresse could again safely admire the beauty and recklessness of her exotic friend. And Harry could, almost, relax in her presence.

Not long after the affair with Constance ended, Harry innocently asked Caresse: "Would you rather be married to a banker—or a poet?"

"A poet, of course," said Caresse.

She knew that her husband, impulsive about almost every other venture, was tortured and hesitant about Morgan, Harjes. Harry was working for a token salary only, the job little more than ceremonial—a patronage position that served neither Morgan, Harjes nor its wayward employee. Harry and Caresse, with the two children and the servants, actually lived on the income from family trusts, about $12,000 a year, a large income for the time at the favorable rate of exchange. Harry Crosby, banker, was but a face-saving pretense, and something of a joke.

But Harry was tired of the joke, and Caresse—as winter came on, and the canoe became impractical in the late autumn rains—was indifferent to it. It was Walter Berry who had first introduced Harry to the "doomed poets" with whom he now so fervently associated himself: the *poètes maudits* Rimbaud, Verlaine, and Baudelaire. The inchoate character Harry hoped to forge for himself was directly inspired by the spirit of Baudelaire.

"There exist but three respectable beings," Harry read to Caresse, from Baudelaire, "the priest, the warrior, the poet." Harry had been a soldier, he was becoming the rogue priest of a new and personal religion; what remained to him, he reasoned, was to be a poet. All others, according to Baudelaire, were beasts of forced labor, fit only for the stables.

Caresse agreed that Harry should leave the stables.

The reaction from Boston was muted—anything could be expected of Harry Crosby by now—but an after-the-fact note from his father wounded Harry where only Caresse could see him bleed: "The idea of you writing poetry as your life work is a joke and makes everybody laugh."

On the final day of the year 1923—such precisely decided moments meant much to Harry's theory of significant numbers and dates—he left his desk at Morgan, Harjes et Cie. for the last time. He crossed the place Vendôme with an unburdened heart to the Ritz bar where Caresse was waiting for him to join her in a champagne toast to Poetry.

iv

When they left the Ile St.-Louis for the faubourg St. Honoré, Harry and Caresse failed to see the irony of taking on two new maids, a chauffeur, and a cook, in addition to the children's "little mother" Doosenooze, to be poets in the lavish establishment sublet to them by the princesse Bibesco. They had been introduced to the princesse, a woman of letters, by Walter Berry, and now were living in the Bibesco style. Caresse felt her life admirably simplified. The chauffeur could drive Louise the cook to les Halles for fresh vegetables and fruit, and to "Necessary Luxuries" for real American-style milk, the bottles with cream on the top, for the children. Hors d'oeuvres were delivered from Prunier, or Fauchon on the place de la Madeleine, and pastries from Rumplemayer's or Gateaux Penny.

Louise was Cordon bleu trained, but Caresse supplemented her accomplishments by teaching her to cream codfish New England style and to fry chicken *à l'Américaine,* with cornpone, as well as to create such homestyle desserts as prune whip and Brown Betty. Both children, Caresse noticed, were prone to overindulge when Beluga caviar appeared on the table, but never, she was happy to report, to the point of illness.

No longer the princess in a tower, Caresse was installed in a genuine princess's bedroom (the princesse Bibesco was born to the Hungarian aristocracy) with rose-colored wallpaper, pale green drapes, and one entire wall of mirrors. Harry could write (three hours in the morning, two in the afternoons when there were no races) in an office apart. There was a private garden where Caresse sequestered the children on fair days, or in foul weather Doosenooze could take them to the matinées at the Cirque d'Hiver.

Despite the heightened style of life, both Harry and Caresse turned to poetry with determination and discipline. As Harry launched his own poetic endeavors, Caresse was quick to follow—she was, in fact, quicker in completing her first volume of self-published verse, *Crosses of Gold.* Her first eager intent to paint and sculpt faded and became a drive to write sonnets. Harry approved, and encouraged her to be a poet like himself. Cozily they encouraged one another's efforts. Caresse read her sonnets to Harry in bed; Harry, in the white heat of accomplishment, declaimed his verses from the top of the stairwell or through the open French window to Caresse playing with the children in the garden below:

The château sleeping in its riverbed,
The waters like the gurgling of the dead,
The forest overarching overhead,
While I sun-dreaming at your feet, Caresse,
Unqueen the past for present loveliness.

Caresse's reply was also a quote from her lines of verse:

Yours is the music for no instrument
Yours the preposterous color unbeheld

They were inspired narcissists, obsessed and infinitely productive in the beginner's overflowing flush of inspiration. Caresse's party approach to art brought on bursts of happy insight at any time, but Harry established for himself a suffering five-hour stint of solitary morning composition, hellish hangover or no. In their determined way they coaxed the Muse to their new residence as if inviting Calliope to a party.

For all their hedonistic way of life and art, Harry and Caresse were never charter members of the Montparnasse café set, the current scene of aspiring American littérateurs, many of them mere poseurs. The Crosbys did cross paths with the more serious writers in Paris: Harry knew Hemingway from racetrack encounters and they had met the Fitzgeralds at a dinner party. Their only meeting with Gertrude Stein was an at home at the studio on the rue de Fleurus where the talk between Caresse and Alice Toklas had more to do with pets than poetry, and Harry failed to be inspired by Gertrude's conversation—so they did not return. Caresse enjoyed good talk, but Harry was proud of his taciturnity in public. Robert McAlmon, writer, publisher, and patron of the arts in Paris, declared: "It was passionately the fashion to be an artist or a genius," and Harry, McAlmon noticed, intended to be both. Caresse had fewer illusions, especially about her own gifts. But she also believed that "chance is such a busy servant to destiny," and that by chance Harry was destined to be a genius.

The salon society of the faubourg St. Germain had been open to the Crosbys through the introduction of Walter Berry (most Americans in Paris had no entrée at all, nor did they know such an anachronism existed), but neither Harry nor Caresse wished to join, and the *ancien régime* was too suspicious of these social outlaws to extend further invitation. However, the comtesse de Noailles—as unconventional in her way as the Crosbys, but her way was French—was happy to receive Caresse, and Caresse intrigued enough to respond. Harry was delighted with the report that the comtesse sat regally propped against lace pillows in a great bed, for he was fascinated with the stylish eccentricity of receiving in bed; a telephone on the nightstand did not stop ringing, but the comtesse made no move to answer. "I will tell you frankly," she confessed to Caresse, "I adore my poems," and she presented Caresse with a volume of her verse. Caresse was charmed by the poet and her setting, remarking on, and perhaps exaggerating, the line of limousines parked in the street, and the men she passed in the foyer with stick and gloves across their knees awaiting word with the poet. The advice the comtesse offered to Caresse was that to be a truly great writer one must, like Victor Hugo, "be understood by everybody"—a useless piece of counsel to carry home to Harry, but Harry was nevertheless impressed by the mise-en-scène Caresse described.

Caresse managed to glean what pleasure and part-time fulfillment her insouciant writing allowed, but in Harry's case the flame burned higher and he was in a great hurry to set the world ablaze with his verses. He shared with Gertrude Stein a fixation for publication in the *Atlantic Monthly,* as if the *Atlantic* granted a seal of literary recognition. Boston had first rejected Polly Peabody, and now the *Atlantic Monthly,* a Boston publication, added to Harry's frustration by continually rejecting his poems. He could only take out his resentment in verse:

Unclean City
(with your atlantic monthlies
and your approaching change
of life)
I curse you

When the world ignored his poetic worth and the rejections became too depressing, Harry sought more immediate gratification, Baudelaire's way, through alcohol, drugs, and sensual abandon. Caresse took a more pragmatic attitude toward the worldly reward of publication: "The simplest way to get a poem into a book was to print the book!" As soon as *Crosses of Gold* was ready, she went looking for a printer for her book of sonnets.

Printing costs in Paris at the time were minimal and manuscripts were plentiful—an ideal condition for the establishment of an independent press. "Little" magazines appeared and disappeared at the whim of a backer or the birth of a manifesto. On the quai d'Anjou, in one ancient wine cellar alone, three such enterprises thrived. At Three Mountains Press, Ernest Hemingway set type for his own first efforts on Bill Bird's eighteenth-century handpress. Robert McAlmon established his Contact Editions here, and Ford Madox Ford, assisted by Hemingway, edited the expatriate magazine *The Transatlantic Review.*

On the Left Bank, off the miniature place de Furstemberg, Caresse discovered an obscure printshop at 2, rue Cardinale. There was a man with the face of a plump fowl peering anxiously through the window—and so she went in to meet Roger Lescaret, who bowed, laughed, squinted cross-eyed through ink-smeared glasses, and agreed immediately to print her volume of poems. Though he had never before printed an entire book on his ancient handpress, Lescaret was ready to say yes to anything. He was excited and jovial, almost childlike in his enthusiasm to print something more challenging than For Sale notices and funeral announcements. Eccentric and energetic, the printer was the perfect partner to the eccentric, energetic Crosbys: the three established an unlikely but enduring enterprise, at first called Editions Narcisse.

Caresse knew the design she wanted for her poems, and provided her printer with a Bodley Head edition of John Donne as a model for *Crosses of Gold.* Lescaret followed her instructions scrupulously, not only in typography but for paper quality and choice of ink. "Beautiful, beautiful," he commented, "but it will be très cher the paper alone, and the Astrée italic, we must buy some special type, you know."

The clutter and chaos of Lescaret's upstairs printshop became a second home for Caresse: she devoted herself passionately to the Press. Lescaret knew little English; the editing of course was left to Caresse, and she worked alongside her printer doing typographic design, choosing paper and inks, spreading proofsheets across the table or hanging them from the rungs of a ladder when she ran out of space. Caresse designed a logo for Editions Narcisse of the mythical Narcissus gazing at his own reflection, though the name actually referred to their pet whippet, Narcisse, an ideal title for those first editions of vanity publishing. Harry was too fastidious to engage in any direct way with production work: he had an almost clinical horror of getting his hands dirty. But Caresse did not mind printer's ink on her fingers; she was caught up in everything to do with the printing and making of books, as if publishing had been her life's work all along, chance surely the busy servant to destiny when she happened on the Lescaret Imprimerie on the rue Cardinale.

V

When the princesse Bibesco returned abruptly to Paris and wanted to regain her apartment, the Crosbys were again obliged to pack up and move on. It was the spring of 1924; in less than two years in Paris they were looking for a fourth residence, an unsettled state that suited Harry's gypsy need for change, but Caresse yearned for a place of her own, a nest. They accepted temporary accommodations at 29, rue Boulard, just behind the Montparnasse cemetery, a small cottage called a pavillon. There were only two bedrooms, one of which Harry chose as a library-study, and so Polleen and Billy were dispossessed of their room during the day and installed in a leaky toolshed behind the house.

Montparnasse was by now the acknowledged artistic realm of

Paris, a shift from Montmartre after World War I, but neither Caresse nor Harry felt part of the self-conscious bohemian display of their new neighborhood. They did not join the American crowd on the café *terrasses* of the Dôme, the Coupole, the Rotonde, and the Sélect a short stroll from their pavillon at Denfert Rochereau. More conveniently for Harry was the nearby cemetery where his idol Baudelaire was buried beneath a brooding cenotaph. He was also drawn to the catacombs just across the place Denfert Rochereau, a subterranean necropolis of bones and skulls arranged in intricately grisly design, a region altogether appropriate to Harry's morbid concerns. To escape the limited dimensions of their dollhouse, he spent more and more time at Auteuil betting heavily on the races.

Caresse was often confined to the pavillon, which she attempted to furnish and decorate with the help of a maid named Céline, "Sea Lions," or strolling with the children along the strangely cheerful paths of the Cimetière Montparnasse, perhaps the tone set by the odd tomb of the Famille Pigeon, Monsieur beside Madame in the great marble double bed, a stone angel perched on the bedstead—a sculpture that amused Caresse as much as the children. Otherwise Polleen and Billy spent more time with their maids Doosenooze and Sea Lions than with either or both parents, and would remember their growing-up years in Paris—before they were shuffled off to private schools, England for Billy, Switzerland for Polleen—in flashback more bitter than sweet. Billy's acquaintanceship with his stepfather was tentative and formal, though Polleen did manage to establish a bond with Harry. In an amusing and offhand way he called her "Wretch," which delighted her.

Once Harry discovered Polleen carefully removing her shoes before passing through the house, and he asked her why.

"Well," explained the six-year old, "I'm not supposed to make any noise in case you hear me."

Harry immediately put her shoes back on and took her with him to the Ritz, where "I was given a glass of champagne and taken back absolutely blotto."

Harry generated that suave charm and careless generosity so attractive to children, and was unfairly favored when compared with Caresse. When Harry did condescend to enter their young lives, it was like a visit from Père Noël. He was spared the criticism of parental neglect leveled at Caresse, since Caresse was considered responsible. Polleen complained of being shunted aside to the toolshed and private schools—though it was Harry, not her mother, who ordered the sequestration—of being indifferently nourished and mostly ignored unless a servant saw to her care and grooming. She fell seriously ill, possibly from her chronic indulgence in coconut layer cake from Gateaux Penny and Beluga caviar, and "some specialists were called in and they blew up at my mother, and really told her a thing or two." Harry came along with a chilled bottle of Mumm's in hand, saying, "Oh, Wretch, I'm told you're going to die. You'd better have a glass of champagne."

Polleen later discerned a disturbed psyche behind the insouciant facade: "He was unbalanced, no doubt about it, in a sort of extravagant glorious way." How could she resist the magical unbalanced stepfather holding out to her a bubbling flute of champagne? Certainly her mother could not.

In one of their Parisian homes, Polleen spent most of her time behind the green baize door to the servants quarters, listening for the buzzes on the signal panel in the kitchen: one ring was for her mother's personal maid, two for the parlormaid, three for the chauffeur, and four for the children. "Four rings were seldom heard, but I never stopped listening for the extra buzz."

When Caresse skipped an afternoon at Auteuil or Longchamp with Harry, she would give over an interval to her children, alone. With Harry safely away for the afternoon, she brought Polleen and Billy out of exile and into the forbidden adult realm of the living room. The language became English and their mother wore a tatty bathrobe Polleen and Billy adored, for it was Caresse's playtime costume and represented their rare contact with Maman. On one such occasion—in the midst of their three-way amusement with cards and dolls, a private family circus on the floor of the salon—Harry suddenly appeared on the threshold with his racetrack cronies the comte and comtesse (the Lady of the Golden Horse) de Jumilhac. Games and giggles immediately ceased and the scene became a still life of scattered toys and frozen smiles. On an impulse—a generous one, to his mind—Harry had left Auteuil and brought along Constance and her husband to join them for the last few races of the day. Appalled at the sight of his wife in her worn-out bathrobe "being motherly with her brats," and humiliated that the de Jumilhacs had witnessed their sprawling domesticity, Harry turned away in cold fury and hustled the comte and comtesse out the door.

For three days Caresse had no news of him. When Harry did decide to rejoin his family, he came with expensive marionettes from Le Nain Bleu for the children and a suggestive un-maternal negligée for his wife.

It was time to leave Denfert Rochereau.

Caresse was no snob, and the chilly ambiance of the faubourg had originally put her off, but having a place of her own in that walled enclave of fading aristocracy resolved perfectly her nesting instinct and her love of the suggestively romantic. They leased at long term an entire wing—three floors—of the townhouse at 19, rue de Lille; more than a nest, a mansion. The austere facade denied the luxury within, where paneled levels of space, space, and more space were hung with crystal chandeliers and lined with French windows on the two streets and interior court. Caresse felt the sense of another age, an age of permanence and repose. The memorial plaque at the courtyard gate noting that Charles Floquet (Deputé de Paris, but otherwise unknown) "est mort dans cette maison—le 18 janvier 1896" led Harry to speculate on a plaque someday honoring his and Caresse's death *dans cette maison,* for he too had his notions of permanence and repose.

At the rate of exchange for a constantly rising dollar, Caresse was already calculating that they could manage quite reasonably in their new quarters on $10,000 a year, not including Harry's losses at the hippodrome. In French francs this was a lavish sum, and the Crosbys habitually exceeded the outer limits of Caresse's optimistic fiscal reckoning. She did not take into consideration Harry's attitude toward money: for example, his placing a gold coin at the foot of Baudelaire's cenotaph before quitting the neighborhood of his idol's final resting place.

Caresse made the rounds of the antique shops, Drouot's auction house, and even the Marché aux Puces (flea market) at the porte de Clignancourt in search of eighteenth-century furnishings to fill the eighteenth-century space. The principal necessity for her scavenger hunt was to find a suitably vast and luxurious bed to accommodate the custom the Crosbys had taken from the comtesse de Noailles of receiving, or lounging the evening away, in bed. Harry wrote his poems in bed, and the Crosbys often dined in the bedroom they called "the Enormous Room," after the e. e. cummings memoir. The host and hostess would loll in Persian splendor among the poufs and pillows, the guests assembled at half-moon tables set with offerings of caviar. *Invités* wore whatever evening attire occurred to them, knowing the Crosbys would be dressed for bed: Harry in red and gold Magyar kimono and Caresse in her cloth of gold robe and Scheherazade slippers.

The first mammoth bed discovered by Caresse was seen only in sections, buried beneath bric-à-brac and a coverlet of dust in an antique shop, but it seemed appropriately grandiose, odd-shaped, and original. When the parts were carted to the house, then assembled in the Enormous Room, Caresse groaned aloud. The bed was even more than Caresse's sense of humor or Harry's taste for the grotesque could abide: the gargoyle carvings on the bedstead were possibly designed for the Devil's Chamber of the brothel known as the House of All Nations. They dismembered the monstrosity and then, for several evenings after dark, played at assassin, carrying the separate sections of bed as if they were detached limbs of a corpse to be disposed of in the Seine at the quai Voltaire.

At the end of the rue de Lille were the enclosed school grounds of l'Académie des Beaux-Arts: when students spilled out of the gates after life-study classes, they often gathered for a cigarette and chat at the rue Allent beneath the Crosbys' windows. Once, Caresse was inspired to call down to a trio of students, inviting them in for a drink.

"Tous?" one student called back.

"Bien sûr."

She did not realize she had invited their entire class of thirty-two, but Caresse was all the more delighted that her invitation was taken up by the crowd. Harry ordered a cask of wine from the bistro at the corner of the rue des Saint-Pères and borrowed a trayload of their spare glasses. The students, en masse, turned out to be good-humored, extremely polite, with the trained reserve and repressed effervescence of lycée adolescents. The true nature of these lively young French art students was liberated at their annual orgiastic costume ball. The Quatz' Arts ball was still some months away, but Caresse—who, after all, had been an art student herself—and her husband, *le poète,* were invited to the closed event, as yet too far in the future for Caresse or Harry to anticipate with their usual zest for any new experience.

"Social rules are made by normal people for normal people, and the man of genius is fundamentally abnormal." In his eclectic reading, Harry had come across this phrase from Schopenhauer, and knew that it was meant for him, that he was exceptional in some as yet unrealized way. Caresse was as opposed to social rigidity as Harry, but she did not share his erratic and impulsive defiance of every norm nor court disaster in his same dashing manner. She went as far as an adventurous nature (and loyalty to Harry) demanded, testing some of the same dangerous limits without the life-and-death commitment of her mate.

Once their odd unwritten extramarital contract was established, both partners were permitted spontaneous gratification of desire. Caresse was now made aware of Harry's serial sexual adventures. His journal was open to her scrutiny; he wanted, even needed her to read: "Saw a young girl crossing the rue de Rivoli, the wind blowing up her skirts around her neck. Followed her across the Tuileries (a lean hungry greyhound walking after a heifer . . .)—" The young girl acquiesced to an invitation by her hungry pursuer to dine on oysters and Chablis in the black marble and silver decor chez Prunier, after which the heifer offered herself up to the wolf in a hotel room nearby. Time and again Harry carried out these irrestible but fleeting seductions, truly for that exciting moment in love with his anonymous partner—which was the secret of his success at seduction.

Caresse accustomed or steeled herself to sit at a restaurant or café while Harry stared fixidly at an attractive woman at another table. Inevitably he would leave her side and go to the other woman: *l'adorable inconnu des robes qu'on soulève* (the adorable unknown whose garments one removes). There was nothing coy or flirtatious in his approach, no "approach" that Caresse could discern or "line" that reached her ears. It was as if Harry had just remembered something lost or forgotten and needed this lovely new accomplice to help him recover it. Nothing in these episodes suggested the wild intensity of Harry's pursuit of Caresse, nor of his continued ardor for her. These two people were simply speaking casually together—as far as Caresse could observe, each time in her stunned and baffled isolation—or rather, Harry was speaking in an undertone, while the woman simply allowed her gaze to be locked in his. Caresse watched the playlet as if observing two strangers enact their "devastating experience." Then the woman would get up—she did not forget her gloves, her purse—completely unflustered. In a moment Harry was leaving with *l'adorable inconnu.* The woman herself may have abandoned a companion or a party, even her husband, to leave with this importunate gentleman whose name she neither knew nor cared to know. These were casual times, Caresse remembered, years of folly and fate in the city most appropriate to romantic impulse—yet nothing of the times or Paris quite explained this curious phenomenon.

Harry Crosby picked up women as casually as he would pluck a flower for his buttonhole—more casually than that, Caresse reminded herself, for Harry was compulsive about the ritual black carnation he wore on his lapel. Never to Caresse's recollection, nor to any other witness of Harry's public trysts, was he rebuffed or the woman's escort outraged, nor was there an ugly scene of any sort.

His stepdaughter Polleen commented on Harry's extraordinary magnetism as an experience of intense personal engagement: "When he would talk to someone he was so focused on them, and his dynamic charm would be turned on you like a great beam of light, as in hypnotism, I suppose. It wasn't fake; it was true; that's why it was so powerful." Like her mother, she would announce openly, "I was absolutely in love with him."

The café encounters were but the passing fancies of a man drawn to any woman who could accommodate the desire of that moment; Caresse accepted the fancies as such, or had been conditioned to shrug and swallow hard. For Caresse, Harry's plucked flowers from the garden of sexual delight were floral arrangements only: "décor," as she called them, or "Harry's girls."

Every impulse we try to strangle broods in the mind and poisons us, appeared in Harry's journal; the paradox tempted Caresse, and she would like to have operated, like Harry, on its daring premise. The "contract" granted her the same permissiveness as her husband, but she did not at first permit herself to yield, nor was it in her nature to initiate an affair purely for settling scores. The insidious influence of Boston still weighed heavily in the balance, and that code of puritanical restraint lingered in her psyche. In some masochistic fashion, she began to relish a stab of pleasure when her charming partner would so charm other women. While she sat alone and Harry wandered, she played with her pain. Beyond all else, Caresse still knew that she alone was the sun in Harry's universe—the sun, principal symbol and pagan obsession—that she was his "cunningest concubine"; with all other passion spent, she remained her husband's first and best and only girl.

But there were the not always so fleeting or superficial of Harry's attractions, the affairs that extended beyond café *terrasse* and nearby hotel. First had come the threat of the Constance Coolidge attachment, and now an unnerving affair with Josephine Rotch, of Boston, engaged to marry Albert Bigelow and in Paris to shop for her trousseau. Josephine and Caresse looked alike, their hair cut sharply in the helmet style of the twenties, Josephine the dark and mysterious side to the lighter coloring—and spirit—of Caresse. This parallel love affair was neither hidden from Caresse nor confessed to her: since Harry did not believe in guilt, he did not believe in confession. He lived these affairs openly, then noted every episode in his diaries and poems.

Josephine Rotch was the Fire Princess of his journal; she was also the Venus of his volume of poems *Transit of Venus,* a poem for every week of the year inspired, as he wrote his mother, by the charming Josephine: "She was mad and madness is very appealing especially to one who is mad." (Though Harry would never discuss his conquests in braggart's belt-notching terms, he did oddly enough flaunt these adventures in Freudian letters to his mother.) Caresse could not fail to recognize the importance of Harry's obsession with the Fire Princess, for he kept Josephine's photograph on his desk opposite the skull he had stolen from the catacombs. One of the poems inspired by Josephine in *Transit of Venus* bears the same death notice Harry frequently inserted in his early love letters to Caresse:

I wish tonight I were a cat
That I might slink
To where you sleep demurely
(Sleeping above the brink of dream)
And suck your breath
Slowly and surely
Into death

Caresse might draw what consolation there was in Harry's coded associations: Josephine paired with the stolen skull, while Caresse still represented the passionate life force of Harry's sun. With her trust in fateful turnings—turnings for the best, for her outlook was generally optimistic—she need not worry the foreshadowings in Harry's verse too closely, nor dwell despondently on his vagrant loves.

Their Roman-style bathroom with its vast sunken tub of pink marble (more indoor swimming pool than *baignoire*) was the first setting to the Crosby need for sensual display, with the dream, Harry's, that their amateur paganism might inspire further debauchery. He once invited a guest from Boston to watch through a peephole as Caresse disrobed, and observe her at her bath. Caresse would have been delighted to be seen in the nude, and was amused to learn that the man indignantly refused to peek. Soon enough the Crosbys assembled their kinds of guests to participate in ensemble bathing, a foursome or more, soaping one another and steaming together. This was but a tame preamble to the orgiastic circus of the Quatz' Arts Bal.

Like two children invited to a grownup party—instead of the only adults made welcome at a students' ball—the Crosbys had anticipated their roles for weeks before the gala. The very scale of the event was to make their own Roman bathtub parties no more than a rehearsal. The night of the ball Caresse rode bareback, and barebreasted, on a baby elephant rented from Helen Scott Can Get It For You, an agency catering to the American colony for unlikely items even Necessary Luxuries could not supply. Harry bought a brace of unplucked squab at les Halles and made a neckpiece of the dead pigeons to wear against his golden chest. He carried a canvas sack of live snakes in one hand, and in the other a paintbrush dipped in red ochre to touch up the unpainted breasts of student maidens.

The ball itself answered all of the Crosby expectations and more: reckless and raucous, a drunken moiling near-riot at the Salle Wagram. Caresse was overjoyed to win first prize in the costume-and-body contest, a badly needed reinforcement of self-image, winning in competition with all the young beauties of the Beaux-Arts. The prize was twenty-five bottles of champagne, so of course the Crosbys would transport the wine, drunken dancers, dragon porters (Caresse now encased in the gaping mouth-of-fangs of their papier-mâché dragon), baby elephant, live snakes, and dead pigeons to 19, rue de Lille to keep the orgy alive and the excitement still throbbing. Harry distributed his snakes to the students and as many naked guests as could coiled on the giant bed together, paint-smeared and doused in champagne, a writhing Laocoön tangle of naked bodies and snakes, with panting perplexed Narcisse Noir in the midst of it all.

In the thin Parisian dawn of a gray hungover morning, Caresse awoke as part of the entanglement of nude bodies, the bodies so deadly still she thought not so much of carnival's end but the aftermath of a mass execution. She struggled free, and against the odor of bodies and pigeon stink went to the open window for air. In the courtyard below she watched a nude and gilded maiden from l'Académie des Beaux-Arts, stoned, tenderly offer her breast to the snake Harry had given her the night before.

vi

There was something of Harry in the slim blond sailor—as tall, and with Harry's earnest look about the eyes—and Caresse was immediately attracted to him. He was carrying a seabag filled with red-waxed balls of Edam and Gouda, which he exchanged for francs, or for food at the rue de Buci open-air market. Assuming the Black Sun Press did commercial printing, he had stopped to peer through the window at 2, rue Cardinale—a printshop it was, and cheap enough from the ill-lighted cluttered look of the place. It would have to be cheap. Frans had no cash to speak of: there were the cheeses, or he could do quick-sketch caricatures of the *patronne* or the printer in exchange for an order of calling cards. The printer, Roger Lescaret, still did odd lots of local custom printing, but the shop was now devoted to the Crosby publications, books and folios for the Black Sun Press.

Caresse was too intrigued to allow the charmer to pass by, so Lescaret printed the cards for Frans and Mai de Geetere: *Artistes-peintres,* "aboard *Le Vert Galant*—out of Amsterdam." Their barge was tied up at the point of the Ile de la Cité, and the barge was named for the statue of Le Vert Galant that dominates the island-garden off the pont Neuf. The calling cards would help attract any trade or company that might come their way.

The Crosbys would come their way the next afternoon. When Harry first heard of this rare couple, he was eager to meet such intriguing marginals. As they came aboard the barge, Harry and Caresse were greeted with the sight of kittens tumbling about on the rusted metal deck; Frans was bare-chested, playing an accordion, and Mai passed around a basket of cherries, the de Geetere way of welcome. The one item of luxury was a cask of cider from Normandy, for the barge had just passed through the Norman canals; so Caresse and Harry drank cider from mugs and spat cherry stones into the Seine. Here was a fresh scene for the jaded Crosbys, an unexpected revelation of *la vie simple* lived at water level, in the shadow of Le Vert Galant.

Besides trading his sketches and cheeses for food, Frans painted shop signs or carted vegetables at les Halles, any odd job for a few francs and the couple's daily bread. Mai was a quiet, hardworking wife (the barge cabin and below decks were dutchmaid clean, with neat checkered curtains at the portholes), too shy and uncertain of her French to leave the barge except to wash laundry at the public *lavoir* at the opposite embankment. Frans was their roving contact to the excitement of Paris beyond the Right and Left Bank spans of the pont Neuf.

The Crosbys began visiting the de Geeteres daily, often paddling out to *Le Vert Galant* in their canoe. They once surprised the couple at their bath, a crude arrangement of tin basins and buckets of water: Caresse invited them to make use of the lavish bathing facilities at

19, rue de Lille. From that time, on Saturdays, Frans and Mai luxuriated in the Crosbys' marble sunken tub, steaming and soaking for as long as they liked, sipping Harry's Armagnac from pear-shaped snifters, but reluctant to use the perfumed soap and thick towels Caresse put out for them. There was at first a limit to the barge couple's adaptation to the ways of the well-to-do. They came each time with their own crude soap, a single towel for the two of them, and a change of underwear in the sailor's duffel bag.

Harry wrote to his mother of the strange new relationship: "If it is possible for two people to be in love with two people then we are in love with them." The Crosbys and de Geeteres were enjoying a four-sided attachment of remarkable affection, though Mai was somewhat lost in the overlap when Frans developed an adolescent love for Caresse. But a truly loving four-way partnership it was, threaded through with streaks of *amour de famille,* desire, perversity, envy, and great respect. In that hedonistic time of experiment in Paris, the Crosby–de Geetere romance lasted longer than most conventional affairs.

Caresse was enamored of Frans in return, with Harry watching over the pair with something like paternal pride and concern. There was no way to know of Mai's attitude in the matter, for she never referred to her husband's infatuation with Caresse. Each day Caresse accepted Frans's love token with the keenest delight, a single rose from the Halles flower market. Here was a triumphant conquest of her own for a change, with Harry in the unfamiliar role of passive observer from the sidelines—yet Harry appeared to approve. It would seem the Crosbys had adopted the de Geeteres, grown children not much younger than themselves, bred to other forms of innocence and now entangled in an incestuous connection.

The de Geeteres were ever subject to the disasters that befall the bohemian poor: "Then one terrible day," Caresse recorded, "after a wild night of tempest, water began to seep in along the seams of the *Vert Galant*—literally the bottom was about to drop out of their world! They might even find themselves and their hopes at the bottom of the Seine." The Crosbys arranged for the barge to be towed to drydock, and offered to house the de Geeteres during the overhaul. But Frans and Mai would not abandon their *bateau-mouche,* even though they would be in drydock outside Paris, far from the supply of food and Frans's marginal earnings. Before the barge was to be towed, Harry and Caresse threw a potluck party aboard the vessel, each guest to bring some form of nourishment: "wine, cakes, eggs, ham, cheese or fruit, and I remember the Dolly sisters, then dancing in Paris, brought a case of champagne which was consumed that same evening." Word of the party went round the expatriate colony and drew not only the Crosbys' acquaintances but counts and countesses, artists and models, even the Maharanee of Cooch Behar—for those were the party years in Paris and any word of fête attracted an eager gathering of the city's diverse mix.

The kittens, now grown, had scrambled safely to the cabin roof, eyeing the motley and mundane crew of guests dancing on deck to Frans's accordion, dancing until dawn when the towing tug arrived and the leaking water of the Seine had reached the dancers' ankles.

The de Geeteres were not as untouched by worldliness as first appeared. Harry was especially pleased to note that de Geetere art portfolios were filled with prints and drawings of the crudest sexual nature; he abjured pornography in the strictest sense of the term, but was highly receptive to erotica that conformed to his self-defined aesthetic principles. What made the erotic art of Frans and Mai acceptable to Harry was the same streak of decadence that informed the work of Oscar Wilde and Aubrey Beardsley, and a sexuality haunted by the gothic minutiae of death: "the defiled body of a young girl . . . (his art has the taste of death in it) . . . and there is the interesting study of legs (carbuncular legs) in the river scene where the suicide is stretched out upon the quais." As soon as Harry learned that Frans had been inspired in his work by the poems of Rimbaud and Baudelaire, he considered their meeting a soul-mating of the rarest kind, two distinct temperaments drawn inevitably to the *poètes maudits* and to one another. Yet, compared with Harry, Frans was still the primitive innocent, and his attentions to Caresse suggested the attachment of a smitten naif rather than the *liaison dangereuse* Harry might have wanted it to be. For games and vices beyond the de Geetere experience and purse, Harry would provide introduction.

"—there was drinking of absinthe and gin," wrote Harry, "and we all went to the Bal Nègre and Frans and Mai were there (how Mai could dance with those negresses!) and afterwards a mad party (censored) on the barge."

Harry and Caresse also invited the de Geeteres to join them for the next Quatz' Arts Bal, which was uninhibited fun that the Dutch couple could invest with their own energy and flair, a glorious romp they might have discovered for themselves. The races at Auteuil were another matter, given the de Geetere state of finance. Caresse at first wanted Harry to stake Frans and Mai to as many races as they cared to play, but she realized this would largely annul the sense of risk and mystique of chance. She watched over Frans and Mai like a bemused mother with her two entranced children at their first circus. Bright-eyed and fevered, the de Geeteres suffered agonies of suspense over every race, affected by every win or loss in the most vital way, since every centime was important in their narrow fiscal accounting. Watching them was a revelation, an enchanted reverse image of her own blasé disengaged afternoons at Auteuil.

There were other worlds worth introducing to these penniless outlaws, the subterranean pleasures of Paris, hallucinatory depths into which Harry had already led Caresse.

"We had smoked before," Caresse recalled, "but not at Drosso's." They were taken there by Caresse's nemesis and now friend, Constance Coolidge, comtesse de Jumilhac. "She was wrapped in a mysteriously dark cloak, and her eyes had a look of childish fear and anticipation that enticed one to follow her even against one's better sense." Harry of course was eager to follow the comtesse, even though the Crosbys had been about to retire for the night.

As the cab moved out of the faubourg through the chic 16th arrondissement, Caresse noted the golden horse that dangled from the bracelet Constance wore: obviously she relished the title Harry had bestowed upon her. Suddenly they were in a far more plebeian neighborhood than Caresse was familiar with, the outline of low buildings and the chimneys of the Citroën works just across the Seine. The Lady of the Golden Horse asked the coachman to draw up at the curb. It was a completely undistinguished street, empty at this hour. They walked a little distance past a series of brooding facades, the comtesse in the lead.

There was no light, but Caresse noted the house number by a street lamp facing the entrance: "We pushed the iron grille at No. 30 and entered the vestibule like thieves. After we had tapped on the glass as instructed, the door swung open and we followed the tiny Chinese servant down a blacked-out passage." They were met by another servant in slippers and silk kimono—Achille, Constance called him—who bowed them into a foyer where Caresse could smell a bitter yet sweetish odor, the pungent incense of the place. Achille presented each of them—serving the comtesse last—with a kimono like his own.

Pierre, an habitué of the den and Constance's friend, greeted them languidly from his divan of black cushions, his arm wrapped around a tiny Frenchwoman Caresse seemed to remember from somewhere, whose eyes were staring into nothingness, her head nodding against Pierre's chest. The Lady of the Golden Horse stretched herself out on the other side of Pierre, Caresse and Harry beside the drugged Frenchwoman.

Drosso arrived. Harry and Caresse called him "Monsieur Papillon" because of the kimono he wore, with huge red and gold butterfly across the back: "He looked like an insect with gaudy wings that were attached to a dry little body."

"We will prepare the next pipe for you," Drosso promised.

The servant who had met them at the door brought to their low Oriental table a black-lacquered tray with smoker's gear: long flutelike pipes, steel needles the length of stilettos with ivory handles, ceramic bonbonnières, and statuettes of Buddha, one entwined with black beads like rosary beads. The tiny lamp of perfumed oil was called a *keden,* over which the servant prepared the pipes: boulettes of opium base were melted and the trealy substance worked with a needle into glistening black droplets, then the molten black pellets placed in the bowl of the pipe ready for the smokers to "suck the bamboo." The servant, or *congais,* marked on a blackboard the number of pipes smoked: "Caresse smoked five pipes and I seven," Harry noted.

Caresse was drawn to the scene at Drosso's—the kimonos, the Oriental music from a *tourne-disque* behind the drapes. It was one illicit adventure she could share with Harry, a secret thrill to know that Drosso's was sometimes watched by the police, and she was not adverse to the comfort and blessings of her five pipes. She naively believed that opium was no more habit-forming than tobacco, "the handmaiden of dreamful ease, the unraveler of pain, the nemesis of passion and deceit," and that criminals used only the lower forms of the poppy, hashish and marijuana. Caresse would never have taken opium on her own, nor become addicted as Harry was, any more than she would have shared Dick Peabody's alcoholism. She admitted to only two sorties for the dream pleasure of a few pipes: to le Chauve-souris and to Drosso's one time each, though she had in fact visited Drosso's more times than that single venture. Harry often took opium pills at home, but the ambiance at Drosso's counted for much: the experience called for Caresse on the low divan beside his. In his journal it was always: "Went with C to Drosso's."

The Crosbys would at times share their opium dreams with friends known as the Crouchers, so called because of their constant crouching poses when taking photographs; or with their British friend, Lord Lymington, later to become Earl of Portsmouth, but at the time writing poetry in Paris. Lord Lymington was becoming another love interest for Caresse, like Frans de Geetere. Perhaps it was through the ceremony of the pipe at Drosso's (Harry would have devoutly wished it so) that Caresse first felt the old inhibitions pass away in smoke: she could begin to share Harry's mystic drift to experimental promiscuity.

"My pipe was ready now," she wrote in *The Passionate Years.* "It was handed to me and I crouched above the tray. I drew the sweet smoke deeply into my lungs, then very slowly exhaled and breathed in again. With each indrawn breath, the little pellet glowed; cooled by the long jade stem, the smoke creeped into the crannies of one's heart . . . smiling, one relaxed and drowsed, another's arms about one, it mattered little whose." It mattered only when the dream was done: Caresse then wanted the arms about her to be Harry's.

Eventually Frans and Mai were included in the ceremony of the pipe, and when the parlors at Drosso's or the Chauve-souris were closed, the Crosbys and the de Geeteres retired to the afterdeck of *Le Vert Galant* to smoke pipes they prepared themselves. Harry purchased the opium he called "black idol" from a retired sea captain living in a suburb of Paris. "C and I and Frans and Mai to Melun and on a little way to a small house where we smoked with a man who was on a French submarine during the war."

By the time of Drosso's and the Chauve-souris, Caresse was part of *la ronde* of outlaw loves Harry made his principal indulgence. Probabaly her first dereliction was with Manolo Ortiz, whom she met at the opening of the Salon d'Automne; at least Harry believed him to be the first. Ortiz was in the company of a Russian portrait painter, Polia Chentoff, with whom Harry became instantly enamored, so Caresse paired off with Polia's partner more by reflex action than inspired passion, a way finally of turning the perpetual triangle into a rectangular arrangement. Caresse's reticence about these first affairs had to do with a persistent guilt related by a friend: "It was one of the demands Harry made on her, one of the complete reversals of everything she had been trained as a child, and a young girl, and a young married woman to respect." Polleen referred to Ortiz as her mother's "gypsy lover" when the couple went off to Cannes together, but Caresse kept the details of the escapade to herself. In Paris, the separate couples—Harry with Polia, Caresse with Manolo—would unexpectedly meet at restaurants or at the theatre: the Crosbys were still living together, apparently as close as ever, yet going their separate ways. What jealousies were aroused might be indicated only by such incidents as Caresse burning the portrait Polia Chentoff painted of Harry, because it was "metaphysically disturbing."

As for Caresse's debut with adulterous partners, Harry was as tolerant as the unwritten contract implied. While he poeticized his loves—Polia had adorable feet "pitterpatting through my head"—Caresse's way was to write off her serial episodes as if jotting inconsequential items in a journal, along with the comings and goings of servants in the household, no more emphasis on one than the other. From Caresse's offhand inventory of love affairs outside marriage there is no way to judge which, if any, of her stray loves were genuinely passionate during the Passionate Years—except for her ever faithful love of Harry.

Only by Harry's occasional displays of jealousy is there any clue to the seriousness of some of Caresse's random attachments. From the original understanding between them of equal freedom to explore the maze of sexual possibility, Harry began to suggest that the contract was still valid for Caresse only if he initiated the carnal experiment, as with Manolo Ortiz, or approved the new partner in question, such as Lord Lymington. There was a period when Harry went out of character and control over his wife's rogue affairs, especially as she became acquainted with Armand de la Rochefoucauld, the handsome bon vivant and owner of the Château d'Ermenonville. Once Harry became so abusive over Caresse's choice of lover she threatened to throw herself from the window into the rue de Lille.

But such explosions were rare. On the surface, and in public, Harry coolly nodded his acquiescence or even appeared to take pride in the extramarital partners Caresse collected, insouciantly listing his wife's lovers, with the oddest possible vanity, in a letter to his mother: "The Comte Civry, The Tartar Prince, Ortiz, Frans de Geetere, Lord Lymington. . . ." Harry continued to remain on very close terms with each of these men, while Caresse seemed indifferent to them once the affair had burned out.

vii

While Harry dreamed on to the "bubbling sound of another pipe, and another and another and the round contour of a breast and the touch of delicate fingers delicately gently snow upon snow. . . ." Caresse was awake to the real: the Black Sun Press. The fine editions from the little printshop on the rue Cardinale were beginning to attract more than passing attention, and not only in Paris, now that the Press was introducing work other than the Crosbys' own. Caresse remained responsible for each book's conception from inks to paper to typographical and artistic design. When the Crosbys published a limited edition of Archibald MacLeish's long poem *Einstein,* the poet was so delighted with the result, he announced: "This was quite a book to make for a man. Somebody, and I rather suspect it was Caresse, had taste. Harry had it too, but somebody *really* had it."

Caresse engaged Frans de Geetere to illustrate Lautréamont's *Chants de Maldoror,* which was having a vogue with the new movement called *surréalisme,* and especially influenced the surrealist André Breton. Harry Crosby was attracted to the *Chants* by their Luciferian defiance of divinity and society, but also because the poet died "under mysterious circumstances" at age twenty-three. At first Harry's taste for the bizarre prevailed in the selection of the authors the Black Sun would publish; Caresse was concerned with producing hand-crafted volumes that were themselves works of art.

Naturally enough Harry sought works from the Mauve Decade, the School of Decadence, the French *poètes maudits*—poets whose bizarre temperaments addressed his own, or whose nightmares might have been conceived against his own gothic dreamscape. Frans de Geetere had been the ideal illustrator for such works, and then Caresse discovered another illustrator whose style was right for these publications, an artist who called himself Alastair.

> He lived in a sort of Fall of the House of Usher house, you know, with bleak, hideous trees drooping around the doors and windows—we always suspected him of having them trimmed to look that way—and he had several blackamoors for servants. On the night when we first came to see him, a blackamoor ushered us into a room where there was a black piano with a single candle burning on it. Soon Alastair himself appeared in the doorway in a white satin suit; he bowed, did a flying split and slid across the polished floor to stop at my feet where he looked up and said, "Ah, Mrs. Crosby!"

For a time the fascination with Alastair muted the Crosbys' friendship with the de Geeteres, though Harry and Caresse were capable of combining several such divertissements at once. Their new friend was either a Bavarian baron or a Hungarian count, depending on which pedigree Alastair (Hans Henning von Voight, or "Hanael") produced at the moment. He favored silver lamé costumes with black velvet capes; he played and looked the part of Count Dracula with his deepset hypnotist's eyes in an indented skull, blood red lips against his stark white face. He worked at his strange illustrations by candlelight, singing to himself in falsetto betweentimes at the piano. Harry called him "the *only* person I have ever seen that expresses my idea of genius."

Alastair produced suitably macabre drawings for Black Sun editions of Poe and Wilde and *Les Liaisons Dangereuses* by Choderlos de Laclos—and especially for the weird verses of Harry Crosby's *Red Skeletons.* For Oscar Wilde's *The Birthday of the Infanta,* Harry himself wrote the Foreword, proclaiming Alastair's illustrations as "Voluptial, Funebrial, Stabbed."

Whatever Alastair may have thought of his publisher's views on his art, he did consider himself stabbed, or certainly wounded in his dealings with Caresse. The Crosbys were rich, but their idea of an artist's stipend was far below Alastair's expectations: he began to follow up his contributions to the Black Sun Press with letters of recrimination over the low pay and personal hurts. The relationship dissolved over a misunderstanding with Caresse. She had insisted on the completion of a series of drawings in time for publication deadline: Alastair did produce the drawings by working nonstop through the night. (Night was his favorite time, but nonstop not his customary pace.) When the Crosby chauffeur failed to appear that morning to collect the drawings as Caresse had promised, Alastair dispatched a huffy note: "Please do not act like that—I do not accept it from my friends."

The Crosbys, however, were accepted on their terms or none at all.

On April Fool's Day, 1927, Harry decided to shift from the influence of the Decadents to the inspiration of the Moderns: the shift was a happy one, to Caresse's mind, for she was much more compatible with their contemporaries in Paris, expatriates who were making waves far more exciting than the receding tides Harry dipped into. Between the two Parisian cemeteries where his heroes Oscar Wilde and Baudelaire lay buried sprang up new creative life too vital for even Harry to ignore.

While Caresse was encouraged by Harry's dismissal of decadence for a contemporary trend she much preferred, she was disturbed by another element to Harry's sudden disillusionment with his idols of the past. He was gradually giving away their books, rare and valuable editions from the Walter Berry collection, and his own. After Caresse had worried through the crisis with Edith Wharton over those books, Harry was now reducing the library by several volumes a day, presenting the first editions to anyone he might meet, a stranger or acquaintance, as he strolled about the faubourg.

"I loved those books," Caresse admitted, "but he loved them more and had this idée fixe about reducing the things that surround him."

Harry would tour the bookstalls along both banks of the Seine, pretending to browse, then slip a priceless Rimbaud or Baudelaire among the bookseller's mundane stock. He could not of course dawdle forever waiting for these treasures to be discovered, but he could relate each clandestine giveaway to Caresse, allowing his imagination to create the dénouement. Ordinarily accepting of Harry's irrational or impulsive behavior, of these scattershot gestures Caresse finally asked, "Why?"

"My wealth I measure by the things I do without."

It was a maxim Caresse could respect, if Harry truly intended to live by it. Not only would he rid himself of valuable first editions, folios, and letters, but perhaps he was beginning to discard the attitudes of the doomed poets who had originally inspired him.

The principal reason for this shift in outlook was the discovery of James Joyce. Joyce, of course, was beginning to be discovered all over Paris—first by Ezra Pound, who convinced Joyce that he could best live his life of "silence, exile, and cunning" in Paris rather than Trieste, and more importantly by Sylvia Beach, who had the foresight and courage to publish Joyce's *Ulysses.* But the Crosbys were not too late to join in rendering homage to the great Irish writer. Caresse intended to offer James Joyce $2,000 for a book of excerpts from *Work in Progress* (*Finnegans Wake*), to be called *Tales Told of Shem and Shaun.* She was eager to crown this coup with another, a frontispiece portrait by a second acknowledged genius living in Paris, Pablo Picasso.

Harry had respectfully broken the ice by offering Joyce a rare copy of *The Book of the Dead* from the gradually decimated Walter Berry collection. To Joyce, penniless in Paris except for funds from Sylvia Beach and from alternating patrons secured for him by Ezra Pound, any gift, help, or homage was most welcome: "Is it not extraordinary," Joyce remarked on his good fortune in Paris, "the way I enter a city barefoot and end up in a luxurious flat." The $2,000 from Caresse was another windfall, since the excerpts the Black Sun would publish—"The Mookse and the Gripes" and "The Ondt and the Gracehoper"—had already appeared in *transition.* The Crosbys were invited to Joyce's "luxurious flat" at 5, boulevard Raspail, actually a cramped overfurnished apartment on that long, somber residential avenue.

Joyce's son Georgio was there, and his daughter Lucia (a withdrawn young woman, self-conscious about an eyelid defect that made her squint), speaking Italian together, perhaps so as not to have to speak to the guests. Nora Barnacle would not become Joyce's legal wife until the end of the twenties, but very much the middle-class wife she was, hovering in the background of the apartment she had made into a passable replica of a Dublin flat. Attempting to launch a literary conversation, Caresse admitted she "could not strike a spark," and even Harry, for once, was overawed in Joyce's presence and unable to create a spontaneous moment of consequence. There passed an interval of suspended animation till Caresse mentioned music (George Antheil's *Ballet Mécanique*), when Joyce came suddenly alive, sprang up, and put a record on the gramophone of the Irish tenor John McCormack, then sang along in his own sweet but strained tenor voice, a tender moment, and the evening was saved.

But Joyce remained for a time put off by Mrs. Crosby (Joyce did not use first names); Caresse was the managing partner and moving force behind the Black Sun Press, but he was used to lower-keyed women like Sylvia Beach, or women serving as background, like Nora. Also, Joyce was wary of dogs, and when he came to the Crosby townhouse, Narcisse Noir had to be shut in a broom closet before he would cross the threshold. Joyce was there to scan, through his one thick eyepiece, plus a magnifying glass, the proof sheets of "The Ondt and the Gracehoper," and after each correction he gave a laborious but learned discourse on the origins and usage of the Joycean language created for *Work in Progress.*

As Harry led Joyce down the staircase, he asked him: "Are you superstitious?"

"Very," replied Joyce.

They were passing beneath a medical-school skeleton Harry had hung in the stairwell. He wondered if Joyce had felt it was bad luck to pass under a skeleton, a condom dangling from its jaw like a tongue; Harry considered it good luck, and hoped at least to share this superstition with a genius—but Joyce had not even noticed the ghoulish mobile.

Joyce was particularly elated to hear that Picasso, at Caresse's urging, might do a frontispiece portrait for *Tales Told of Shem and Shaun,* but Picasso, Caresse discovered, "was as indifferent to Joyce as Joyce was not to Picasso." Caresse did not realize that Picasso was part of Gertrude Stein's entourage, and could not be seen to shift allegiances: such were the Byzantine relationships in the Paris world of arts and letters. Picasso was, however, charmed by Caresse and greatly entertained by her dog (who yawned enagingly—"Bored," said Picasso, as he showed his Dinard paintings to Caresse) and hoped he might obtain the offspring of Narcisse Noir, with the suggestion there might even be an exchange of one of the paintings he was showing Caresse for the puppy. Caresse was as unwilling to part with the puppy Fleur Noir as Picasso was to provide a frontispiece for Joyce's book.

Next, the frontispiece project was proposed to the thick-bearded Constantin Brancusi, and Caresse found the sculptor far more receptive than Picasso had been. She accepted with pleasure an invitation to lunch at Brancusi's garage-like studio beside the hôpital Necker. The gentle Romanian with his thick workman's hands impressed Caresse in the same way as had the de Geeteres and their primitive-rewarding style of life. Workbenches were strewn with chisels, saws hung from pegs, wood shavings and stone dust lay underfoot. The centerpiece of the working-and-living quarters was a white-tiled forge with sheet-metal hood, and in the coals potatoes were roasting.

"I attempt to simplify," said Brancusi as Caresse examined the smooth-polished metalwork surfaces and heavier stone effigies. Several upright wooden sculptures were decidedly phallic. "It is sculpture for the blind."

Brancusi's preliminary drawing of Joyce, a clever caricature, she thought might not be appropriate for the frontispiece to *Tales Told of Shem and Shaun.* She considered his sculpture-for-the-blind approach, and suggested something more abstract for the near-blind James Joyce. Brancusi played with a design impression of what he perceived as Joyce's inward-winding thought, a simple spiral plus three vertical lines—exactly what she wanted for the book's frontispiece.

They dined at one end of a workbench covered with the rough sheets of newsprint Brancusi used for preliminary sketches: her host carved the small chicken—also roasted on the forge—with a sculpting knife. Meanwhile Narcisse romped with Polaris, Brancusi's white spitz, in the wood chips and sawdust.

"I will go nowhere without my Polaris."

Caresse remembered seeing the dog with Brancusi the riotous night of George Antheil's debut concert, *Ballet Mécanique*, a composition for xylophone, player piano, and airplane propellor.

"Polaris enjoys Charlot also." When Brancusi went to the cinema to see Charlie Chaplain he reserved an extra seat for Polaris.

With the chicken and potatoes they drank rosé chilled on the windowsill while Brancusi spoke with hesitation but warmth of his early days in Paris. Throughout the refreshingly simple repast Caresse followed the milestones of Brancusi's life, knowing she could not have done so at Foyot's or Larue's—if one could possibly imagine the sculptor in those swank environs—with the rapt attention she paid to Brancusi here. Even the dogs had stopped playing and appeared to be listening, an ear cocked each.

"Shall we have little 'hearts of cream' for dessert?"

The loaf-shaped *petits suisses* were served with strawberry jam—and afterward, Caresse recalled, "We pulled the wishbone together."

How different was the life she and Harry had chosen—or had they chosen? To what degree did destiny control the direction they took? Was Paris truly home, a place of pleasurable limbo or a kind of purgatory?

The wishbone came apart with a snap: "I don't remember who got the wish."

viii

A country house outside Paris might counteract their jaded existence in the city; a house of their own was what Caresse had always wanted, and an occasion suddenly presented itself: a curious escapade of Harry's resulted in the unexpected purchase of a piece of real estate at Ermenonville.

The Crosbys had been invited to the château d'Ermenonville by Armand de la Rochefoucauld, one of Harry's racetrack acquaintances—and a current rival for the affections of Caresse. Harry was disturbed over the duke's evident interest in his wife, but he could not resist Armand's reckless high spirits and a character very much like his own. Ermenonville was forty kilometers north of Paris, and once the Crosbys arrived, Armand de la Rochefoucauld lavished his attentions on Caresse. He contrived to escort her over the grounds of the château while Harry seethed alone in the library pretending to read a bestseller of the day, *The Green Hat*.

Just before dinner, Harry announced to Armand, Armand's brother, and other members of the party that he was taking Caresse back to Paris immediately. When she saw the fixed expression on Harry's face and understood his black mood, Caresse did not protest. On the return drive, halfway to Paris, Harry realized that he had allowed jealousy to displace his habitual composure; he had lost his proud reticence and become *ordinary*. He turned the car and began driving back to Ermenonville. At a roadside bicycle shop, Harry purchased five pistols, as if he had achieved some strange enlightenment on the drive.

"What on earth are the pistols for?"

"One each, for every man at the château."

He drove Caresse back to the party where the guests were now at dinner: Harry offered his apologies around the dinner table, then presented each of the five men with a pistol.

"Shoot me, one of you, any of you. For my rudeness."

As Caresse knew, Harry was capable of uttering such a command in deadly earnest. The stunned guests looked away, or down at their gift pistols with painful embarrassment. Caresse was completely humiliated. She had been catalyst to the incident and responsible for this grotesque scene, as guilty as Harry meant her to feel: she felt as stricken as anyone at the table.

Only Armand de la Rochefoucauld, with his remarkable savoir faire—the composure Harry had for once ceded to someone else—turned the challenge into a pleasantry. "Then you must," he said to all, "shoot me in turn." He chuckled as if the scene were a staged entertainment, which in part it was. The tension was broken. Harry was able to laugh, which released a contagion of laughter all around, a catharsis. Harry had once again maneuvered the spotlight to himself, after his sun had earlier been eclipsed by Caresse.

While on the stroll with Armand, Caresse had been shown a parcel of the estate that enchanted her as much for its historical connection to the famous Diamond Necklace scandal as for the natural beauty of the place. Also, Jean-Jacques Rousseau had once lived on the property. Caresse was a romantic, and Harry a necromantic; the attraction of the Mill (as the property was called, later changed to Moulin du Soleil) was that mesmerist-alchemist Alessandro Cagliostro had lived there awaiting trial in the affair of Marie Antoinette's diamond necklace. The story of the notorious necklace, romanticized by Alexandre Dumas, could not have failed to impress both Crosbys with its historical connections to the pre-Revolutionary past. A few months after the episode with the pistols, perhaps in expiation for his jealousy and loss of face and very likely in reaction to Armand's story of the Diamond Necklace, Harry flew to London, where he purchased a $30,000 diamond necklace created by Cartier as a love offering to Sun Queen Caresse.

Caresse's belief in coincidental circumstance and Harry's mood of the moment led them to offer to buy the Mill. Armand was as reckless as Harry in his disregard of conventional transactions, and had the added attraction of bringing Caresse into his vicinity if he sold—but without knowing what the value of the property should be. According to Caresse, Harry then proposed a blind deal: he would write a blank check for his total bank balance at Morgan, Harjes—as ignorant of his bank balance as Armand was of real estate values—and that would be the price of the Mill. Armand agreed. Since Harry never carried a checkbook on his person, hated even to carry currency in his pocket, he tore off the linen cuff from Caresse's sleeve and wrote out a "check" to Armand de la Rochefoucauld on the strip of linen, signing over the current balance of his account.

(Morgan, Harjes was accustomed to Harry's spontaneous check writing on whatever unorthodox surface came to hand: a table napkin from Foyot's, a page torn from a telephone directory, and once on a plate at Zelli's nightclub. The bank invariably honored Harry's "checks," which left Caresse to conjecture about how they were filed.)

In this deal it would seem that each man was showing off for Caresse, challenging the other gambler's romantic limit, a financial dare instead of an actual duel with Harry's pistols. The transaction was resolved on Harry's bank balance of $4,000 paid over in twenty-dollar *pièces d'or,* one more theatrical gesture to enhance the extravagant spirit of the exchange.

Armand's mother, the duchesse de Doudeauville, was not, however, as open-spirited as her son. When she learned of the sale she went into a fit of weeping, begging that the Mill be offered as rental property only. Harry gallantly agreed to this, even though he had already paid the full purchase price. "In business affairs," he told Caresse, "you can't beat the French." Harry also agreed to double the rent being asked, as well as agreeing to pay all upkeep and improvements on the property—it was part of his philosophy to pay more for an item than it was worth, even for Caresse's necklace, and never to bargain for less.

As a property of value, the Moulin du Soleil turned out to be all the Crosbys had invested in it, and more. As a tranquil sanctuary, it turned out to be worthless.

Caresse and Harry simply transferred the perpetual party scene from 19, rue de Lille, to the Moulin du Soleil in Ermenonville. To compensate for evenings no longer spent "sucking the bamboo" at Drosso's, Harry stocked a considerable inventory of alcohol and narcotics at the Mill: champagne and scotch by the case, opium in capsule form, laudanum, hashish—and his own pipes. Chantilly was nearby, but to duplicate the Parisian hippodromes, the Crosbys built their own miniature replica of Auteuil, to entertain their "raft of royalty" with donkey races daily.

This entertainment of royalty was Caresse's new fetish, perhaps set off by her flirtatious assocation with Armand de la Rochefoucauld. Formerly she had been indifferent to the faubourg aristocrats, but now she began to cultivate, as much as her country garden, the noble names appearing in the *Almanach de Gotha.* The Maharanee of Cooch Behar, who had been at the barge-saving party for the de Geeteres, was now a *convive,* as was prince Jean d'Orléans, duc de Guise and pretender to the nonexistent French throne; along with

Princess Indiria, Prince George of England, and the newest reigning favorites, Mary Pickford and Douglas Fairbanks, whose titles as the "royal couple of the silver screen" were as relevant as those of duc de Doudeauville or duchesse la Salle. Salvador Dali summed up the visitors he met at the Mill as "a mixture of *surréalistes* and society people who came there because they sensed from afar that it was in this Moulin du Soleil that 'things were happening.' "

The happenings were a ceremony of surfeit and chaotic distraction. Life at the Mill took place on zebra-skin rugs and at the swimming pool the Crosbys had built, fed by the millstream, and on the donkey-polo field and in the vast stable converted to a dining room where Madame Henri served meals in relays at all hours, with magnums of champagne in tubs of ice, and outside a menagerie among the sunflowers, pigeons circling their open coop and pets at liberty including a cheetah and python, a variety of animals to match the mixture of guests who shared their domain. Harry saw to the champagne, and to his private supply of narcotics; Caresse helped Monsieur Henri, the caretaker, collect snails in the garden after a rain and was delighted with the abundance of mint she found growing beside the millstream. She began placing sprigs of mint in every corner of the Mill as a symbol of the simple life.

Of the literary crowd mixed with the titled guests, Caresse found Hart Crane "dynamite to handle." Her strategy was to install the poet in a tower room with a case of Cutty Sark so that he might complete his long and still unfinished *The Bridge,* a masterpiece she intended to publish in a Black Sun edition. The scotch sent Crane off on a mindless rampaging campaign to seduce any and all of the titled guests. When Harry confiscated his hobnailed boots and Caresse hid his clothes and confined him to his tower, he was, in Malcolm Cowley's words, "as morose as a chained bear." The Crosbys tried to keep the help out of his clutches: Auguste, the chauffeur, would drink Cutty Sark with him but resisted any other overtures; then Crane seduced the local chimney sweep, leaving sooty black handprints of the sweep's passage through the whitewashed tower, but no trace of the remaining stanzas of *The Bridge.*

The Black Sun Press was to publish a collection of short stories by Kay Boyle, a beautiful young woman Harry had discovered at Raymond Duncan's handicraft shop on the rue de faubourg St.-

Honoré. In Harry's romantically appraising eye, she was something of a maiden in distress, working for no wages, having joined the Duncan commune in Neuilly. Raymond Duncan was the brother of Isadora Duncan, the great dancer, and his commune was a Greek revival movement aspiring to the beauty and simplicity the Crosbys intended to fashion of their lives at the Moulin du Soleil. Kay Boyle had rashly "signed over" her daughter to Raymond Duncan's care, so Harry and Caresse—along with Robert McAlmon, co-author with Boyle of *Being Geniuses Together*, who thought the whole caper rather melodramatic—rescued Kay from the Duncan cult by kidnapping her child and bringing the mother and daughter to the Mill. However, the little girl was no better off there, for Harry was still resistant to the presence of children, having dispatched his own stepchildren to private schools far from Paris. The little girl's tears and whimpering disturbed him, so other arrangements would have to be made.

Caresse and Kay Boyle had become friends, although it was Harry who had shown interest in Kay at the beginning. She was a strikingly handsome woman whose nose had been broken as a child, a defect she felt ruined her face when in fact her nose was a distinctive and attractive feature that only added to her beauty. Caresse was drawn to her: they could share a number of confidences about the men in their lives. But Caresse could not accept Kay's blunt opinion that Harry, for all his worldly charm, was actually "a very cruel and heartlessly self-centered man." Kay Boyle had seen Harry at his worst, the ringmaster of the celebrity circus at the Mill; and she would certainly resent his attitude toward her child. Caresse could very much identify with her friend's history of exploitation, and both women had been victims of the male ego rampant, but Caresse still considered herself fortunate in her marriage to Harry, an opportune happiness that had never been Kay Boyle's lot.

When Kay left with her daughter for Paris, McAlmon left with her, summing up the experience at the Moulin du Soleil: "It's so depressing I can't even get drunk. They're wraiths, all of them."

Harry would awaken, "a little battered from the riot of last night," to leave bed—right foot, never left, must touch the floor first—for the daily servitude of his rituals. Letting Caresse sleep (she was his death-in-love partner from the dark hours), he arose to fondle the skull stolen from the catacombs, then twist upon his finger the gold ring said to have been stolen from King Tut's tomb—before climbing like a muezzin to his minaret in the Sun Tower for morning prayers chanted into the very face of the awakening sun.

D. H. Lawrence shared with Harry a pagan fascination with the sun, and through this odd affinity the two found grounds for friendship. At the Crosby's invitation, Lawrence and his wife Frieda joined the lively scene at the Moulin du Soleil. Caresse wanted to publish Lawrence's *The Escaped Cock* with the Black Sun Press and Harry hoped to inveigle Lawrence into writing an introduction to his own collection of poems, *Chariot of the Sun.* Lawrence obliged his host with an obscurely negative assessment, with such left-handed compliments as "What does it matter if half the time the poet fails in his effort at expression. . . . Failure is part of the living chaos." Harry was nevertheless pleased. Of Frieda and D. H. Lawrence, Caresse said, "I loved him and disliked her." There was room at the Mill for Caresse and Fried to avoid open conflict, but later Frieda wrote to Caresse over a question of payment for *The Escaped Cock:* "Are you only a business woman? With the usual tricks? No, my dear, Harry was different, he wasn't that kind. Yours in disgust, Frieda." While at the Mill, Frieda played over and over again the same jazz record on the gramophone until—to the sweet satisfaction of Caresse—Lawrence lost patience and smashed the record over Frieda's head; or so Caresse reported.

Caresse could not stop weeping. She hid this from Harry but in her solitary moments, rare as solitude had become, the tears sprang forth. The life they were to have lived at the Mill had as much to do with the philosophy of Jean-Jacques Rousseau (who had also lived there) as with the romantic assocation with the Diamond Necklace Affair, but the prevailing motif was no longer Rousseau's "noble savage" and more and more the corrupt disruptive spirit of Cagliostro.

It was not in Caresse's nature to cry, but an unfamiliar and persistent *tristesse* permeated her days at the Moulin du Soleil. There was the death of her beloved Narcisse Noir to account for tears, when the dog was killed by an automobile on the road to Ermenonville. And lately she had been disturbed by the ominous presence of

Harry's new bodyguard-companion, Goops, who seemed to Caresse an evil omen (he had gangland connections in the United States, and appeared to have been a petty Prohibition mobster himself), but not an omen she would have wept over. Harry was amused by him—he was ready to "rub out" anybody Harry cared to finger—but Harry's amusements were increasingly threatening.

She had never cried before about Harry's women, only now they were more evident than ever, more mysteriously involved with him. His "harem" became more than the passing decor Caresse had accepted and was accustomed to, and aberrant episodes multiplied. Commuting regularly to Paris, Harry would rendezvous with a woman he called the Sorceress at the Ritz. Caresse knew of the Sorceress from Harry's journal: "feline as a puma she is more feline and amorous by night and now we are together into sleep and . . . "The ellipses were more troubling than if Harry had been explicit about what followed. At thirty-five, the competition for Harry's amorous nights with a feline girl actress was all the more unsettling, and perhaps prophetic. Harry had proposed that the Sorceress vanish with him—vanish where?

ix

Caresse had been the loving partner to her husband's sybaritic indulgences, the foremost admirer of his flair and daring, but by the end of the 1920s his largest requirement of her love and loyalty was that she be willing to vanish with him, to die as he decreed in immolation to the sun. His intimate journal was dedicated to Caresse: "Queen of the Sun—if my lady should die, I will die with her." Harry's passionate intensity was to Caresse one of his most engaging traits, and his loving her "unto death" a flattering extravagance—but had she really signed that together-in-death contract Harry kept in his pocket with a *pièce d'or?*

Harry had ordered a tombstone for them both with the Caresse-Harry intercepting cross carved into stone, their birth dates and the date of their mutual death, fifteen years hence, 1942. He kept the gravestone on display at the Mill: it was destined to be placed in the cimetière de l'Abbaye de Longchamp, very near the racecourse where they had spent so many hours together. Yes, she had signed the contract—Harry's earnestness about it overcame any tendency to smile or put it off—but that was in 1927: Caresse had said yes, and their ashes were to be scattered over the English Channel. The monument with their agreed-upon death date was still on the premises, but Caresse no longer saw the tombstone or if she did, did not think about it: besides, 1942 was an eternity away. Meanwhile there had been, and still were, poems to write, loves to be known, Paris to discover to its very heart.

The isolation of the Mill did at times become intolerable, and Caresse and Harry could return to the city in less than an hour—though Harry went more and more to Paris alone. When the newest sensation could not surpass the last, Harry scoured the demimonde for new perversions: he prowled the *maisons closes* to watch the deformed make public love, attended a black mass and left his tribute, a gold coin, in the collection plate, paid to see a young girl beaten bloody with a whip.

They were becoming younger and younger, Harry's girls. In *Shadows of the Sun* he told of an afternoon "saved by seeing a young girl (15?) dressed in yellow with a yellow hat (yellow is the fashion this year) who had nice eyes and a slender body girlish and sunburnt and clean and I looked at her through my field glasses and forgot my losses but as she was with her mother I could not talk to her." He christened one fourteen-year-old beauty Nubile because of her maturely developed breasts, and about her he remarked, "To corrupt the young is a temptation." Caresse now feared that even Harry's stepfather-stepdaughter intimacy with the Wretch was suspect. Later Polleen confessed: "Even when I was very young, I understood that my stepfather's flirtations with me were very different from the normal love of father for daughter. I was passionately in love with Harry. He alone was allowed to kiss me on the mouth, which he did frequently, hiding under the rug at the back of our Voisin so the chauffeur could not see, or sometimes in the nursery when no one was about. It was a deep secret between us. . . ."

"I should like to have a harem," Harry wrote, "no girl to be over fifteen except Caresse."

Hero worship often inspired Harry to higher-minded pursuits than the obsessive gratification of the senses. He, who had been seduced by the Icarus dream of being one with the sun, would take flying lessons to defy the limitations of his earthbound life. This new aspiration was inspired by a self-effacing and intrepid young mail pilot who arrived in Paris by the most dramatic route imaginable.

That day in 1927 Caresse and Harry drove out to Le Bourget for the spectacular arrival of Harry's new hero. The plane, *The Spirit of St. Louis,* had been sighted off the coast of Ireland earlier in the day, but the landing would not take place until nightfall: "Then sharp swift in the gold glare of the searchlights a small white hawk of a plane swoops hawklike down and across the field." Harry began jotting notes while still at Le Bourget airfield: "C'est lui Lindberg, LINDBERG!" Despite his own fascination with the landing, Harry had the presence of mind to hold onto Caresse to keep her from being trampled by the crowd suddenly stampeded trying to get to Lindbergh, to touch him, to touch the plane: "to touch the new Christ and that the Cross is the Plane . . . hands everywhere tearing . . . it is freezing cold but what an event! Ce n'est pas un homme, c'est un Oiseau!"

Caresse was also suddenly in love with this man, this bird who had crossed the Atlantic alone in his fragile craft, whom she saw as "boyish and touseled and very much like Harry." Charles Lindbergh was three years younger than her husband, and except for the thatch of reddish hair looked like Harry's mirror image. From the moment *The Spirit of St. Louis* touched the runway, and the cry, "Il l'a fait! He's done it!" rose from the crowd, Harry was fired with new determination: "I definitely decided to learn how to fly. I *do* know how to fly in the *final* and *real sense* of the world that is the soul of Flights to the Sun but now I wanted to learn also in the Lindbergian sense of the word. . . ." His intention was to be "an Arrow Arrowing into the Sun."

Harry's sudden fever for flying was one endeavor Caresse could encourage with genuine enthusiasm: she preferred her husband airborne rather than earthbound in the embrace of the Sorceress. She bought him a book called *The Art of Flying,* and Harry did begin to take flying lessons: in time he became a competent, even prudent, pilot; he was a fresh new image to Caresse in his goggled flying cap and leather jacket. the profile and persona of Lindbergh, the Lone

Eagle. But Harry's flight to a rendezvous with the Black Sun was not fated to be solitary.

In the early part of 1929 Caresse became aware that Harry was receiving a constant stream of letters from Boston; an old affair—a dangerous one, like the Constance Coolidge attachment—was heating up again. The letters were from Josephine Rotch, who had been Harry's Fire Princess in a passionate entanglement during her prenuptial fling in Paris. No sooner had she married—she was now Josephine Rotch Bigelow—than the torrid love messages to Harry began. In his journal Harry waxed ecstatic over her wild endearments: the messages were as precious, he declared in his journal, as pure gold, and characteristically Harry did not care if Caresse knew of this renewed-by-mail love affair or not. Unlike the Constance Coolidge threat, Josephine Bigelow was far away in Boston, and besides, Caresse was having affairs of her own: she did not react to the danger she felt in this long-distance liaison.

"Lord L. all the way from England to dine with C.," Harry wrote, with some pride that Lord Lymington would go to such lengths to have dinner with his wife. Caresse had found a romantic pied-à-terre in Paris for Lymington at 1, Gît-le-Coeur, but she kept no record of their rendezvous except to comment on the charming but oblique view, through the narrow atelier window, to Notre Dame. Lord Lymington's slim likeness to Harry—they were the same age, from the same leisure-class origins, both desperate to be poets—explained much in Caresse's infatuation for him. Another part-time love interest was with Harry's pilot acquaintance, Cord Meir. She called him the Aviator "with keen eye and handsome foxy profile"—again, a duplicate of Harry in appearance and attitudes. But these episodes outside marriage seemed tepid or forced: Caresse would have been exclusively "Harry's girl," had Harry allowed her to be.

For all these adventures in promiscuity, the experiment of living in fevered delight, the crazy years of the Crosbys in Paris were moving toward a sober end. In less than three months after the Parisian fanfare for Charles Lindbergh, the mood of 1927 had turned ugly: the anarchists Sacco and Vanzetti had been executed in Dedham, Massachusetts, and the French reacted with a passion reminiscent of the emotions aroused by the Dreyfus Affair. The execution set off some of the most alarming riots of the decade in the streets of Paris; the anti-American feeling was so great that expatriate Americans were reviled or beaten up at the cafés where they were known to congregate.

The summer of 1929, Hart Crane, unable to bear further confinement at the Moulin du Soleil, caroused the streets of Montparnasse in search of cheap thrills in that now ragged and disordered spectacle. He got into a drunken quarrel with the vindictive Madame Sélect of the Café Sélect on the boulevard Montparnasse where the vogue and tolerance for visiting Americans, drunk or sober, had long passed. Madame Sélect ordered the waiters to subdue the poet, then called the police: Crane was carried off by officers of the local gendarmerie, his head banging brutally against the paving stones on the way to the police van. July was a bad time to be arrested in Paris: French officialdom was in suspended animation during that national vacation month. Word of the incident filtered back to the Crosbys at Ermenonville via Robert McAlmon and Kay Boyle, but not before Hart Crane had spent several days behind the grim cinder-colored walls of la Santé prison.

Harry and Caresse went to the magistrate of the 14th arrondissement on Crane's behalf, pleading the case for poetry—since French sensibilities were vulnerable on that theme—rather than for one drunken and American poet. They paid the fine, Crane would be released. Caresse and Harry, along with McAlmon and Kay Boyle, were at the bistro A la Bonne Santé opposite the prison gates to celebrate Crane's return to freedom. The sobered poet waved to them jauntily enough as he came out past the sentry box, but during the celebration at the bistro Crane was evidently shaken and unnerved by his experience.

Hart Crane's masterwork *The Bridge* was no closer to completion than when he first came to the Mill, but he was ready and eager to make use of the gift ticket Caresse passed unobtrusively to him, Second-Class passage on the S.S. *Homeric* bound for New York. The party in Paris was over for him.

When the Crosbys returned to the Mill after seeing Hart Crane off at the Gare St. Lazare, the house and grounds were empty, for once, of guests, and the place seemed almost ominously quiet. Caresse, beside the millstream where she was gathering mint, could see Harry atop the Sun Tower removing his Charvet dressing gown. It was the time of day when Harry offered himself nude to his adopted deity, holding aloft the chalice of gold with a ritual offering of champagne. She could not hear his prayers nor guess at the desperation of his intended enterprise, but could only wonder what next.

X

In the month following the Great Crash on Wall Street—when so many Americans were sailing home from the doleful end of a ten-year binge, Harry and Caresse were aboard the *Mauritania* bound for New York. Although the Crosbys had not been so badly hurt financially as many of their fellow passengers, Harry was scheduled for a talk with his father, and with Uncle Jack Morgan, over the dangerous hemorrhage in his trust funds from the constant and reckless withdrawals of cash. Actually, if Harry had held onto the cash from the sale of stocks, it would have been a sensational market coup: he could now have repurchased the same securities for a fraction of their former value. But the cash had gone for such items as champagne for the cellar at the Moulin du Soleil and the diamond necklace for Caresse. Caresse could not fail to notice that Harry, despite the prospect of a hard lecture on husbandry, was in the most ebullient of moods—and she knew why.

On the same ship was Constance Coolidge, still his Lady of the Golden Horse, and once again tangled in Caresse's hair. Not only did Harry enjoy the rare pleasure of having both wife and lover aboard ship, but he was the adored recipient of shipboard cables of affection from the Sorceress he had left behind in Paris, and from the Fire Princess who awaited him in Boston. Caresse was by now out of sorts with the revival of Harry's open liaison with Constance—and she was unaware of the wireless messages coming in from the woman he had left behind and the woman he was to meet in Boston. She had imagined aboard ship she would have Harry's sequestered affection, and she was disturbed over the close proximity of a dangerous rival: Constance was only a few staterooms away. For once she was unable to reconcile herself to this traveling *ménage à trois,* but she would not give in either to tears or rage (it was not her style; besides, what was the use?) so she simply left Harry to himself or to spend what time he cared in the arms of the Lady of the Golden Horse. Caresse remained alone in their cabin for most of the voyage, reading, perhaps for the irony, a popular treatise called *Beating the Stock Market* published just prior to Black Tuesday.

After the years of dissipation, her husband, at thirty-one, was returning home apparently in perfect health, looking remarkably youthful and fit. He was tanned from his long hours of sun worship at the Mill and his still-handsome visage showed little trace of sexual excess or of the drugged and drunken escapades in Paris. It occurred to Caresse that Harry's favorite novel had come to life, the protagonist personified in himself: Harry, like Dorian Gray, would remain forever the splendid young man she had married, and the real portrait was hidden away in their steamer trunk.

Harry's reassurances of devotion were small consolation in mid-Atlantic, but when the *Mauritania* docked and the Crosbys removed to the Savoy-Plaza—Constance nowhere in sight—Caresse's spirits began to match Harry's own. Caresse had always shown remarkable resilience during any domestic crisis, and could rally with amazing aplomb when she had regained her husband's undivided support. He had even suggested that they marry again here in New York, to reaffirm that original romantic ceremony, and it was this play-acting of a second honeymoon that brought them close once again.

Meanwhile there were the eccentric moments, the disturbing rituals. For three consecutive sunsets Harry had been staring out their west-facing window, and each time remarked on the significance of the fading golden glow.

"Lovely sunsets," said Caresse, amiably agreeing with her husband's sensitivity to the spectacular effect of the light.

"We're twenty-seven floors from the street, did you know?"

She knew they were on the twenty-seventh floor, but had never been concerned about the distance from the street.

Next morning Harry was more specific: "Give me your hand, Caresse. Our window is open wide. Let's meet the sun-death together."

There was no joking Harry out of such somber pronouncements;

he was as serious as he had ever been. "But why? Why, Harry, when we have so much to live for?"

It was impossible for Caresse to continue in the mood of a second honeymoon if Harry was going to be like that.

The Lady of the Golden Horse did not disappear from their lives, as Caresse expected and hoped, after the ship docked in Manhattan. According to Harry's journal he had celebrated Thanksgiving Day with Constance, not Caresse: "dreary luncheon waiter's dark hand green glass sliced oranges"

"I love three people," he told Constance. "Caresse, you, and Josephine." Did she love him enough to die with him, he wondered: "One is not in love unless one desires to die with one's beloved."

"I love you, too," Constance assured him, but as for the sun-death pact he proposed, her answer was no.

Josephine, then. Harry and Josephine Rotch Bigelow made a trip to Detroit together, a trip Caresse knew nothing about. "She cries," Harry noted. "Many opium pills and all night we catapult through space, J and I in each other's arms visions security happiness."

Whatever Harry's desire for the return, Caresse looked forward to seeing old friends, especially those of the literary set she had cultivated in Paris: they were all back in the States now. Hart Crane gave a reunion party for Caresse and Harry at his Brooklyn apartment with its view of the Bridge. e. e. cummings would be there, Harry's fellow escapee from Boston puritanism: they had served together in the Norton Harjes ambulance corps. Crane also invited William Carlos Williams, the Malcolm Cowleys, the photographer Walker Evans, and two sailors Crane had picked up at the Brooklyn Navy Yard. One of the sailors was shuffling a deck of cards when Caresse and Harry arrived at the apartment; the sailor fanned open the deck and extended it to Harry. "Pick a card," he said, "any card."

"Not any card," said Harry. He crossed himself, then said, "The ace of hearts." The card he flipped out of the pack was indeed the ace of hearts.

To the others, the random selection of an ace of hearts was a party trick, or a coincidence, but Harry did not indulge in tricks or live by coincidence. Caresse would think about that ace of hearts forever after.

After the initial shock of her son's rash marriage to Polly Peabody, Henrietta Crosby had become the ideal mother-in-law. Caresse had eventually been accepted by the Crosbys in more than the formal sense, and Harry's mother became an understanding companion and genuine friend to her errant daughter-in-law. By now the two women shared a large affection and perpetual exasperation over the erratic son and wayward husband, Harry—with an occasional ambivalence and sometime Freudian confusion of their roles. They were one in their acceptance of this grown man and small boy whose mischief however extreme could elicit the tolerance born of love.

Mrs. Crosby had come down to New York from Boston, and was staying in the room opposite theirs at the Savoy-Plaza. She and Caresse sat waiting for Harry to join them at J. P. Morgan's house on Madison Avenue: they were to have tea together, and Harry was unconscionably late. Perhaps he was anticipating another lecture on fiscal responsibility, since he had already endured one such grim session with his father in Boston, and was putting off the sour prospect of another for as long as possible. Caresse and Mrs. Crosby were bewildered and disturbed; both were trying not to think what Harry *might* be up to—for his mother knew him, from his wild letters, as well as did Caresse. It was difficult to make excuses to Uncle Jack, for Harry was the most punctual of men: he could not tolerate being kept waiting himself, and was scrupulous about being on time. A little after 6:00 P.M. Caresse realized they would have to leave; they had a dinner and theatre engagement with Hart Crane.

Nor did Harry show up at the Caviar Restaurant where the four of them were scheduled to dine together. Before they ordered, Caresse decided to put in a call to Stanley Mortimer, a friend of Harry's who sometimes turned over his studio at the Hotel des Artistes for Harry's use.

"Have you seen Harry this afternoon?" It was a violation of her husband's privacy to make such an inquiry, but Caresse had become desperate.

"Yes," said Mortimer, but he was evasive about when and under what circumstances. "I'll try to locate him and have him call you back."

Caresse told Mortimer they were at the Caviar Restaurant having dinner, and then would be at the Lyceum Theatre. The meal was an ordeal of agonized waiting.

"It's so unlike Harry," Mrs. Crosby would say, then Caresse would say the same thing.

Hart Crane tried to be witty and distracting, but obviously both his dinner companions were too upset to respond with any animation. Crane, for once, managed to drink very little during dinner. He then escorted the two women to the Lyceum Theatre, where Caresse left word at the box office that they were expecting a call. Hart Crane took the call in the middle of Act I of *Berkeley Square.* It was then his tortured obligation to inform Henrietta Crosby and Caresse that Harry was dead.

Stanley Mortimer had indeed lent his studio to Harry, and with Harry was his Fire Princess, Josephine Bigelow. After the telephone call from Caresse, Mortimer went to the Hotel des Artistes on West 67th Street and knocked for some minutes on the bolted door. He called out to Harry but got no answer. Finally he was obliged to ask the building superintendent to help him break into the studio; the superintendent called the police: the door had to be smashed open with an ax.

The inert bodies lay fully clothed, but for their bare feet, across the bed. Dangling from Harry's lifeless hand was a .25-caliber Belgian pistol with a sun symbol engraved on the handle. The first bullet had passed through Josephine's left temple; an identical gaping bullet hole had shattered Harry's right temple. Their shoes, Harry's socks, and Josephine's stockings were neatly ranged alongside the bed. Josephine was wearing a gay corsage of orchids, and Harry had with him, at the end, the gift from his fellow ambulance drivers, a whiskey flask. There was no note.

For a time Caresse was numb, with a sense neither of time nor place, hearing only the name Harry, Harry, Harry. She heard the name Josephine—or was it Jacqueline? "Harry," Crane was saying. The words "Josephine" and "Jacqueline" kept shifting in and out of her consciousness. Jacqueline was the illusory love partner Harry had sought all his life, an imagined perfect dreammate he called "the Grey Princess," a name he sometimes murmured in his sleep. Jacqueline did not exist except in Harry's mind and she was the only woman Caresse had been truly jealous of all along.

"Harry," Crane was saying, "and Josephine."

e. e. cummings wrote the epitaph:

2 boston
Dolls; found
with
Holes in each other
's lullaby and

No note, how strange—Harry wrote down everything. The missing note was a natural challenge to his poet friends: Hart Crane called the suicide imaginative, "the act of a poet," and not long after he wrote an elegy for Harry Crosby, *The Cloud Juggler,* Crane slipped over the side of a ship in the Caribbean, his body never found.

It had been determined that Harry shot Josephine at least two hours before he took his own life. Much would be made in the police report of this lapse of time. Had he murdered her in a suicide pact, the newspapers speculated, then lost his nerve? In her heart of hearts Caresse knew that Harry would never have lost his nerve—whatever he did, he did with deliberate calm. The two hours alone with Josephine's body were merely the interval Harry allowed himself to ponder the eternal mysteries, to savor the ultimate thrill.

xi

"So you're Caresse Crosby," said Scott Fitzerald.

"And you are *you,*" said Caresse.

They met at her hotel in New York, just after Christmas of 1931; the trunks and most of the luggage had already been sent on to the ship. Polleen was waiting for her at the dock, but Caresse on sudden impulse had telephoned Fitzgerald. He was one of the few important American writers she had seen little of in Paris; he might—though she had not called him for that—consider a reprint of one of his novels, as Hemingway had, for her new publishing venture, Crosby Continental Editions. Scott's expatriate years had also ended in tragedy: his wife Zelda was in a sanatarium in Asheville, North Carolina. "She went to pieces," said Scott, "that last year in Paris."

That last year in Paris, thought Caresse—but Paris that last year had not been poisoned for her as it had been for Scott. He looked ill, and sat with his fingers interlocked over one crossed knee, trying to appear jaunty or to keep his hands from trembling.

Fitzgerald was resigned to the prognosis for Zelda: schizophrenia, with little hope of recovery. He was trying to write about that last year in Paris in a new version of a novel he had been working on for years; and he was planning to make a new life for himself, expatriation again, but this time in Hollywood.

They talked around their separate tragedies, and moved on to the casual present. Caresse had taken up where she had left off in 1929, and was expanding the Black Sun Press to compete with the large German firm, Tauchnitz, the only other Continental firm publishing inexpensive classics in English. Her co-publisher was Jacques Porel, son of the French actress Réjane. The Black Sun Press had been the large fulfilling enterprise of her Paris, and she had returned to its unfinished promise. Though their talk was of Paris and Paris was over for Scott, their meeting was gay, easy, playfully flirtatious, with no serious consequence implied.

At thirty-nine, Caresse was the center of male attention again. She had always taken pleasure in the company of men; ironically, she had consulted Constance Coolidge about her need to be with a man again: "Am I being disloyal to Harry?" "Of course not," said Constance. "Have anyone who suits you, whomever might please you. Just don't aim too low."

After Harry's death, Cord Meir, the Aviator, had asked her to marry him, quickly, to take her away from the world, family, Boston—to protect her from the columns of scandal smeared across the pages of newspapers. (But the newspapers had long lost interest, and the story had diminished to shocked whispers since.) On that first return to Paris, Armand de la Rochefoucauld had met her at Le Havre.

"I'll never marry again," Caresse had told the Aviator. "I'm still married to Harry."

She intended to perpetuate Harry's name, to publish his journal *Shadows of the Sun* at Lescaret's little printshop in the rue Cardinale. And as soon as she got back to Paris, she began her own version of those same shadows and suns, *The Passionate Years.* While the Rotch and Bigelow and Crosby clans—except for Harry's mother who, in her profound grief, wrote a touching letter of condolence to Caresse—might never pronounce the name "Harry Crosby" again, Caresse hoped to create posthumous recognition of Harry's protean mind and vivid personality, the larger recognition that had eluded him in life.

"Another beer?"

"I'm going slow these days," said Scott. "I take one drink every afternoon, and I've had that."

There was a champagne bottle resting in a bucket of melted ice, but it was empty, and Caresse had called room service for Scott's beer. They drank only the one beer each in the hotel room with the bureau drawers left open, empty after packing. The one small suitcase Caresse would take with her to the ship lay upon the unmade bed. Polleen was waiting.

Fitzgerald knew about daughters; he had one of his own, Scottie, to take care of now.

Polleen had been shattered by the death of her stepfather, and unbearably saddened since. She needed her mother more than ever after the tragedy, yet drew away from her, still too close to the memory of childhood neglect to forgive the early Paris years. She now thought of Caresse as the Merry Widow, looking prettier than ever, dressing up for men: "Scores of gentlemen in rows deep on the doorstep, and she had an absolute ball."

Scott and Caresse took a cab together to the dock. Polleen was already aboard, and Scott felt a need to linger: he saw Caresse to the cabin.

"I could go with you," he said suddenly, a half-sincere reflection stated aloud. "To Paris again." His brow was creased; she could not know what he was thinking. But then he made a joke of it by patting his pockets, saying, "Ah, but I forgot to bring my checkbook."

Caresse was remembering Harry's impetuous stowaway voyage

aboard the *Aquitania* to New York, when he came to marry her, a knight errant come to rescue his princess in a tower. Harry had proved something about money then, and something larger about love, and Caresse would forever remember and still consider what the proofs were all about.

Scott was leaving the ship at the All Ashore warning when Caresse discovered a pair of chamois gloves he had left behind in the stateroom. She ran to the gangplank in time to catch up with him and return them.

Scott kissed her goodbye once again, then stuffed the gloves into his pocket.

"I'll never wear them again."

ZELDA FITZGERALD,
shortly before her marriage
to Scott in 1920.

IV

Zelda Fitzgerald

1900–1948

I don't want to think about pots and pans and kitchens and brooms. I want to worry about whether my legs will get slick and brown in the summer.

"Did ums see de pwetty pictures?"

Often Scott could lighten her mood with his playful repartee, but this time Zelda did not want to play. The Fitzgeralds were walking through the Luxembourg Gardens after having trekked through the Palais looking at paintings. Zelda did not like to walk, nor was she interested in the art work, many of the paintings by the Impressionists, willed to the Palais du Luxembourg by Gustave Caillebotte where they were to be hung until posterity decided they were important enough to be moved to the Louvre. Zelda did not care if the paintings were ever enshrined in the Louvre—she had been there too, where the sense of time past appealed to her, but her mind wandered. She knew when the setting was wrong for her, or the timing was off, as it was here in Paris. Now, coming out of the Palais du Luxembourg, she glanced at Scott and realized he was as hungover as she was, but Scott always looked worse the day after than she did.

It was the spring of 1921, and the old woman in black might have been in mourning from the Great War not long past, the war Scott missed though he had been a lieutenant at the time of the Armistice. The old woman was sitting on one of those little metal chairs positioned along the graveled walk, feeding the birds from the crusts and crumbs of this morning's leftover *baguette:* her chair reminded Zelda of a soda-fountain chair at a drugstore in Montgomery, Alabama—it was the first thing in Paris that reminded her of home. When Scott and Zelda slumped down on a bench nearby, the woman gave them a distasteful look—the only kind of look the Fitzgeralds seemed to earn from the French—since they did not know that the old woman was the guardian of the metal chairs, *la chaisière,* and when the

Fitzgeralds chose to sit on the public bench she was cheated of the rental of two of her chairs.

Bunny had talked them into this trip, or partly; Bunny was Edmund Wilson, Scott's close friend from Princeton, and like Scott a new and important name in the world of letters. Bunny had been saying how culturally important France would be, again, now that the war was over. Not that Bunny had come to Paris for its culture—the paintings of the Impressionists, the works of Anatole France—he had a more urgent reason to be here (one that Zelda well understood): he was in amorous pursuit of the lovely but elusive Edna St. Vincent Millay. How could he resist the violet-eyed poet as brilliantly articulate as himself? He had told the Fitzgeralds that once, passing through this same park, seeing the keep-off-the-grass sign *Pelouse Défendu,* she had the wit to say, "*Mais nous ne pelousons pas!*" It was the kind of spontaneous remark Zelda might have made to Scott, if Zelda had known French, and Scott would have recorded the witticism in his notebook that night.

In another part of the Luxembourg Gardens, young Ernest Hemingway walked often with Gertrude Stein and her dog, to sit beneath the bust of Flaubert or at Miss Stein's feet, to hear her tell how she had been inspired to write "pigeons on the grass alas" in this very park. Gertrude Stein and Ernest Hemingway were not in the Gardens that afternoon or Zelda would have noticed them, especially Gertrude Stein in her thick peasant-like garments and sandals, for Zelda had a keen eye for the eccentric, a writer's eye in fact, though Scott was the writer. The Fitzgeralds did not yet know Ernest Hemingway or Gertrude Stein and had only just met James Joyce, who was genuinely startled—but Zelda merely amused, for she knew Scott's stunts—when Fitzgerald declared in one breath his everlasting homage to the author of *Ulysses,* and in the next threatened to leap from Joyce's window as a demonstration of his sincerity. Nora Joyce had stationed herself in front of the window in case the exuberant Irish-American fellow was drunk enough to do what he said. Joyce persuaded him not to. As soon as the Fitzgeralds had left, Joyce said to Nora, "That young man must be mad." "Just drunk, Jim," said Nora, "and you should be knowing about that."

Scott hoped to render similar homage to Anatole France. His

admiration for these writers was genuine, Zelda knew, but Scott needed to play an exaggerated role of naive sycophant to older talents. The French author was either not at home or not at home to visiting Americans: the Fitzgeralds haunted the quarter, even camped on the great man's doorstep for an hour—an hour being the limit to their anticipation of any such encounter—but the door never opened. If it had, and Anatole France appeared in the doorway to invite them in, neither Scott nor Zelda was capable of speaking a word of his language.

No one knew them in Paris and they knew no one there but Bunny, and Bunny was otherwise occupied. Where were the parties, anyway?—the somber mansions flanking the park were walled in behind cut stone or lance-tipped grillwork, the windows thickly draped, a discouraging exhibit of impenetrable facade. The streetside dwellings were guarded, they discovered, by sharp-tempered *concierges* with the same scowl as the *chaisière* feeding birds in the park, the dragon-guardians of Paris. The residential quarters were wrapped in an unearthly calm, the quiet public parks like this one so formal the children behaved like adults. Only the traffic, and the cafés, were animated enough to give off big-city vibrations—the rest of Paris was so private and *défendu.*

Two months ago, on Valentine's Day, Zelda had discovered she was pregnant, so they decided Paris was their last chance to have fun before the baby ruined her shape and spoiled her humor. She could shop for clothes, but who came to Paris to buy maternity wear? Anyway, the fashions were dated, with old Poiret dictating the trend with his dead hand. Frenchwomen had not yet caught the flapper craze from America, or taken to bobbed hair, but Chanel was starting to change all that, and was raising hemlines too. You still saw all that ankle-length drapery and passé aigrette feathers, especially on the tired crowd at Maxim's and at the Ritz, a waxworks of celebrities only the French or a few ancient waiters remembered from before the war. The Ritz was a shade gayer and more up to date than Maxim's, with a newer crowd coming in, but not yet American enough for Zelda's taste. Where Americans were beginning to show up was at the Folies-Bergère—a show Scott and Zelda had seen, but Zelda, proud of her own showgirl figure, was made uneasy by any flamboyant display in which she herself did not shine. Against the old myth and Bunny's new opinion that "they do things better in France," Zelda had to wonder *what* things?

"Europe," Scott said, as he had said to Bunny, "is of antiquarian interest only."

So they had trekked with numb indifference through the galleries of the Louvre and along the mirrored corridors of the Palais de Versailles looking for the cultural importance Bunny raved about. They hired a taxi to take them to suburban Malmaison to see the château where Napoléon had installed Impératrice Josephine to waste away once he had shed her from his life. At a clinic not far from the château the president of France, Paul Deschanel, was being treated for an evident mental collapse after an unpredictable pattern of bizarre behavior made his continuance in office questionable. They passed the clinic without knowing that the president of France was under treatment there, or that Malmaison might someday represent the first grim sanctuary during Zelda's own distressing breakdown.

Thus the Fitzgeralds brooded for part of an afternoon in the Jardin du Luxembourg, contemplating a city's vacuity, vegetating on a park bench. There had been no such idle pauses in New York, where Scott and Zelda were the golden couple of the Jazz Age, the gay cut-ups riding the hood of a cab, Zelda as streamlined and glamorous as the silver ornament on a Rolls-Royce. When the excitement waned or the pace slowed, they whirled through the revolving doors at the Savoy-Plaza, whirled and whirled nonstop for half an hour—Scott of course could not stop before Zelda did, and Zelda could not stop before Scott—drawing a crowd of guests grown dizzy from watching, but applauding their performance. They were romantically beautiful personages each, and here they were just as golden a picture as at home, but the frame was wrong. This side of the Atlantic nobody knew of *This Side of Paradise,* Scott's best-selling success that had made their passage, First Class, to France possible. Scott needed the attention his celebrity status earned in America, and Zelda missed the reflected glory of her husband's sudden fame. Paris was indifferent to the rays given off by the golden couple. If Zelda had leaped on impulse into the *bassin* opposite—as she had done in New York, into the fountain in front of the Plaza—she would have excited no stir except in the tame children sailing their miniature boats, or she would merely have startled the nursemaids in their starched white caps and collars. At their Right Bank hotel, Zelda had fastened the rickety cage of the pneumatic elevator to their floor with two of Scott's belts, so that the elevator would always be at their disposal—the management was not amused, there was no applause in the lobby.

At the far end of the Gardens stood the original nine-foot model for Bartholdi's Statue of Liberty, a statue beloved of patriotic Gertrude Stein, but the sight of that relic only made Zelda nostalgic for the States. What she missed she could not say, for it was not the soda-fountain chairs of her hometown—Montgomery was over when she married Scott, and "no power on earth," Zelda wrote in *Save Me the Waltz,* "could make her do anything," she thought, frightened, "any more, except herself." She had got over the frightening prospect of doing exactly as she wanted, and got used to being celebrated for it.

They might go on to Rome, or they might go back to England (Scott had a letter of introduction to John Galsworthy). Scott informed Bunny that Paris as a center of culture was washed up: New York was destined to be the great metropolis of all that mattered because "Culture follows money." Zelda did not know about that, and did not pay any particular attention to the relationship of culture to money. However, she cared about what money represented in practical ways: she had turned Scott down as a poor prospect in 1919 when he earned $800, but married him in 1920 when *This Side of Paradise* and Scott's stories for popular magazines brought in $18,000. What Zelda did know at this moment was that she wanted to go back to the place where they used to sing "Ain't We Got Fun?" It was obvious to her, if not to Scott, that they had shown up at the wrong party, or before the party started—or the champagne had gone flat when they got there.

Manhattan was where Scott was the Prince Charming of all the sad young men and Zelda was his belle of the ball, but they were yet to learn that their New York party was over. Zelda was right, their timing was off. Paris was waiting.

ii

The villa Marie at Valescure was set in the deep gray-green of olive trees and umbrella pines on the Côte d'Azur just above St. Raphael. The view through the luxuriant foliage was of the town and the Mediterranean, and to the west the faint stone tracery of Roman ruins, the remains of an aqueduct and part of the circle of a coliseum. In *Save Me the Waltz,* Zelda wrote of David (Scott) telling Alabama (Zelda): "We are in Paradise—as nearly as we'll ever get." Alabama agrees, but is haunted by associations, remembering the grasshopper existence of the past year. "People can't really jump from one thing to another, I don't suppose—there's always something carried over." "I hope," says Alabama, "it's not our restlessness, this time."

This time was four years after their first misbegotten trip to France, and they were spared the restlessness of skipping from city to city or the desperate pace of New York. Removed to the perfect dreamscape in the South of France, Scott could work steadily at last: he was euphoric about the new novel; his best yet, he was certain. In Paris, before coming down here, Zelda had hired a treasure of a nanny, Miss Maddock, who also served as majordomo in the household Zelda could never manage, and dealt with the French servants Zelda could not face. The Fitzgeralds bought a six-chevaux Renault for $750. Zelda was a foolhardy driver—she had eviscerated their Marmon in Great Neck, driving over a fire plug—but here the roads were empty of traffic and the little French car would get her to the beach and back, two kilometers away. "If Zelda can't swim," Scott was always telling friends, "she's miserable."

Zelda, Scott, and baby Scottie turned nut brown under the southern sun. Scott grew a mustache and worked every day; Zelda idled at the shore in St. Raphael while Miss Maddock took care of Scottie. The beach had become Zelda's private domain: no casual tourists came to the Côte d'Azur then. There were roses on the breakfast trays and the sun rose from the direction of Cannes, the morning light a little to the left of their dining terrace, a steady, reliable, golden portent. Evenings came on slowly as the western sky grew pink then scarlet behind the Roman ruins at Fréjus, then to blue-green shadow before the moonlit nights became heavy with the perfume of jasmin and genêt.

"Everything's idyllic," Scott wrote to Tom Boyd, "and for the first time since I went to St. Paul in 1921 (the worst mistake I ever made in my life) I'm perfectly happy." It would appear that Zelda was happy too, though Scott made no mention of her, for her legs were getting "slick and brown in summer."

So many places like St. Paul had gone bad, or something (themselves?) had gone bad in the places: Montgomery, Westport, Princeton—the honeymoon visit Scott made, to show off his bride, three days of disaster; even the shore at Great Neck, the opulent setting of Scott's new novel, had failed them. How wrong they had been about France that first visit, and the belief that New York, the city of ambition and success, would restore the high delight of their days and nights of honeymoon—that had been the largest disillusion of all. But now they were going to begin their new French adventure all over again, simply and sensibly, and "live on practically nothing a year."

Scott's highest hopes for the new book were justified this time. True, he was writing as well as he ever would again, but Zelda's ambivalence about Scott's writing took another form: the discipline and accomplishment began to dismay her, and she was envious of the elation after a successful day's work inspired in him. The cold-blooded application of a daily ritual removed him from her space and aura; his earned euphoria only cast her in shadow. She felt compelled to insert herself into his realm, put his hat on her head as she passed his open window, sneak up on him and pull his ear. She had to come between him and that implacable stream of written words. At least she could join him for the celebration and reward at day's end; he needed and wanted her then.

All too often it was Scott himself who inaugurated the first drink of the day long before the change of light hinted at sunset. An alcoholic release was the sure way of coming out of a writer's trance and easing into a better one, a filmed-over suggestion of fun and now. Zelda, if she was back from the beach in time for the first, was anxious to join him then; if he was still at work, she was even more anxious to inaugurate *their* ritual at the sideboard crowded with bottles. And she was proud of the triumph of a story finished, a chapter completed that very day—and wanted them both to celebrate, with a drink. The drinks were so good here, all those funny-colored apéritifs in the oddest bottles, and the champagne, better than the suspect speakeasy cocktails at home. They were drinking together, just the two of them now; and it was so quiet when they drank, with only their two voices echoing through the salon at the Villa Marie when Miss Maddock put Scottie to bed.

Even alone at the beach Zelda could smile her cat's smile of secret satisfaction, knowing she was central to what he wrote. In St. Paul when she was coming out of the anesthesia, she murmured in stream-of-consciousness nonsense: "Oh, God, Goofo I'm drunk. Mark Twain. Isn't she smart—she has the hiccups. I hope it's beautiful and a fool—a beautiful little fool." Scott remembered, and now he was putting her words into his new book. She knew he had ransacked her diary and made notes of her bon mots: she wanted him to know these secrets and use those personal parts of herself. In that way she gave herself up to him in his work, and became a vital part of his private world.

Scott had this trick of memory, even when he was apparently drunk, of storing away the most amazing but finally useful trivia for fiction. Zelda had an odd sense of recall, too, but with a different inventory and no place to insert her shrewd accumulations except to offer them to Scott. She and Scott were so different, but strangely and often enough came to identical conclusions and shared the same observations, simultaneously, as if they could read one another's minds. But Scott went on to fashion his conclusions and observations into stories; he was the writer who closed himself off to do that mysterious thing only he could do, the thing he had to do in secret and alone. When Scott wrote, Zelda felt herself the discarded half of a perfect pair.

"You see, Scott," she confessed to him, "I'll never be able to do anything because I'm much too lazy to care whether it's done or not—and I don't want to be famous and fêted—all I want is to be very young always and very irresponsible and to feel that my life is my own—to live and be happy and die in my own way to please myself." Actually, Zelda had prefaced this confession with the news: "Yesterday I almost wrote a book or story, I hadn't decided which, but after two pages of my heroine I discovered I hadn't even started her. . . ."

Scott was welcome to any random thought recorded in her diary; much of what he knew about the mind of a Jazz Age flapper had come from there—but the time of recording exploits with beaux (including the adventure of her off-and-on engagement to Scott) was over, and she was no longer keeping a diary. Someday she thought she might write, like Scott, and know for herself how the discipline felt and what the letting go was like at the end of a writing day.

What she would do meanwhile, when there were no parties or people, Zelda was not sure. In *Save Me the Waltz,* David Knight becomes exasperated with Alabama's negligent housekeeping and chronic boredom: "I don't see why you complain of nothing to do, you can't run this house satisfactorily."

"What do you expect me to do? Every time I try to talk to the cook she scuttles down the cellar stairs and adds a hundred francs to the bill."

So Zelda watched her legs grow sleek and tanned beside the Mediterranean while Miss Maddock knitted in the shade and watched over Scottie. During the long hours when Scott worked, Zelda read alone on the beach, like Alabama reading Henry James or Edith Wharton in the long afternoons—she bathed in the tideless sea and worked at her dream of being young always. But the novels of Henry James, and especially of Edith Wharton, made her feel older than she wanted to feel. Mornings there was seldom another soul in sight along the shore, and Zelda grew impatient with the empty landscape. By noon the little train of only two *voitures* passed beside the beach on its way to the other end of the Côte d'Azur at Menton, and Scottie always waved at the passengers. Sometimes in the afternoons a contingent of three or more officers in the French Air Force—"the beautiful brown people," she called them; "They seem so free of secrets . . . "—came to swim for a little while.

The beautiful brown people were French Air Force officers from the nearby base at Fréjus. For a change, Scott was at the beach with Zelda and saw how interested she was in the newcomers. Across the top of Edith Wharton's *The Age of Innocence* Zelda was staring at an officer with "the head of the gold of a Christmas coin"; she was fascinated by the officer's broad shoulders and the strength implicit in his rigid military bearing. Scott was built on the same slim line but on the smaller scale that had kept him off the Princeton football team. And Scott was too slack about the chest and biceps to compare with the officer Zelda was beginning to think of as a young Dionysius. Naturally Scott's observant eye did not fail to notice his wife's dreamy gaze fixed on the Greek god of the trio. He good-naturedly warned her off.

But Scott was not present when Zelda at last met Edouard Jozan. Evidently the young officer had studied Zelda just as carefully. One sun-drenched afternoon—with Miss Maddock at some distance under a beach umbrella with Scottie—Jozan introduced himself and his two fellow officers. With cinematic French gallantry, he drew Zelda's hand to his lips and kissed it. The strictly formal gesture was an unusually suggestive and sensual encounter to Zelda, for they both stood close in damp bathing costumes. Zelda immediately felt in control, sure of herself in a familiar situation: it was as if a distant Montgomery afternoon were being replayed, Zelda the center of interest surrounded by Camp Sheridan's officers, especially since Jozan's face bore that adolescent look of a young officer unexpectedly, as she put it, acting out in public something he had long rehearsed in private. Because of Scott's apprehensions and chronic jealousy, Zelda felt, with her hand pressed to Jozan's lips longer than the gesture of homage required, that "she had been caught red-handed in some outrageous act."

The outrageous act set Zelda's pulse racing, and was exactly the tension she had so missed these first weeks in France. To alleviate or perhaps play on the delicious sense of guilt she felt about having finally met Jozan, she announced that evening to Scott that she had talked briefly with the trio of aviators. She could not resist singling out Jozan. "He looks like you" (would that satisfy Scott's vanity?) "except that he is full of the sun, whereas you are a moon person."

In all innocence, or distraction—consumed for once in a work that meant much to him—Scott easily accepted the young aviators, since he was accustomed to and often flattered by the attention young men paid his wife, and somehow as a group of three they appeared less of a threat than the gold-headed Jozan alone. The three officers became part of the new circle of friends the Fitzgeralds began to assemble at the Villa Marie, which now included Gerald and Sara

Murphy who were living at the Hôtel du Cap farther along the coast, at Antibes, while their Villa America was being renovated. The officers, René Silvy, Bobbé Croirier, and Edouard Jozan—Jozan forever misspelled "Josanne" by Scott, for he took notice enough of the handsome pilot to include him in journal notes—joined the Fitzgeralds for fêtes and dinners; for them the Villa Marie was a welcome change from the officers mess at Fréjus, though Jozan's interest extended beyond a change of dinner tables.

Zelda knew little French and Jozan had only a few lycée lessons in English: now for the first time since coming to France, Zelda felt compelled to learn the language. She was tediously picking her way through *Le Bal du Comte Orgel,* as if in that posthumously published novel by twenty-one-year-old Raymond Radiguet she could penetrate the mysterious facade of the French psyche—and at the same time learn to communicate with Jozan.

"I love France," she told him, in a burst of spontaneous affection for a country she had known for less than a month.

"You cannot love France," he replied, and made the suggestive assertion that to love France she must love a Frenchman.

Despite this chauvinistic insistence, Jozan had purchased a French-English dictionary, meaning to approach this *américaine* halfway. His other attentions were less subtle: Scott, at work, was annoyed to hear a low-flying French biplane pass noisily overhead; Jozan was buzzing the Villa Marie, just as the pilots from Camp Sheridan had done, stunting over the Sayre house to attract Zelda's admiration. (One pilot was said to have been killed stunt-flying to impress Zelda: she used this incident in *Save Me the Waltz,* with Alabama murmuring dreamily how brave the man had been, and for her sake.)

Gerald and Sara Murphy had occasion to meet Zelda's pilot friends, and Sara immediately divined the situation between Zelda and the slender officer with golden hair. At the beacn and on the villa's shaded dining terrace Sara noticed that their eyes invariably met: Jozan and Zelda were surreptitiously together, even when posed at some distance from one another. Eventually others began to notice. "I must say," said Sara later, "everybody knew about it but Scott." Scott was at the time fretting over a pair of field glasses that showed two visions instead of one, and writing to friends in New York to find a new pair. He wanted to see the ruins at Fréjus clearly from his terrace, while remaining unusually myopic about the human spectacle at closer focus.

Though they had only known the Fitzgeralds for the few weeks they had been at St. Raphael, Sara Murphy made a keen analysis of the crisis. Zelda, she believed, had been obliged since her marriage to tag along after Scott in a much-diminished secondary role, shadow to her husband's substance—surely frustrating to a woman of Zelda's high spirits and vivid presence. Zelda had for too long been accustomed to a spotlight of her own. For the moment her affair with Jozan made her a star again, if love affair it was. It may have been an idle flirtation, for Zelda was a congenital flirt—at the same time, Sara noticed that Zelda was obsessed with a need to lure Scott from his absorption in the novel-in-progress, and the flirtation was part of her desperate strategy. Meanwhile Scott was too caught up in the hazardous aberrant loves of his characters in *The Great Gatsby* to perceive or admit to similar aberrations in his own marriage.

"I suspect it wasn't much," said Gerald Murphy of the affair, and beyond the words of affection exchanged during their public seaside trysts, Zelda was perhaps replaying nothing more than the adolescent celebration of The Kiss, the fleeting commitment to the affair of the moment revealed in her Montgomery diary. Even this token infidelity would have greatly disturbed Scott, with his "strange mixed-up Irish Catholic monogamy," as Ernest Hemingway noted. When Zelda was still engaged to Scott she confessed to having kissed a new pilot just transferred to Jackson Field, explaining to her outraged fiancé that she had never kissed a man with a mustache and she wanted to know how it felt. Ironically, Scott was growing a mustache at St. Raphael. Jozan had no mustache, but Zelda wrote of another sensation: the electric excitement of Jozan's body beneath his linen uniform.

In *Save Me the Waltz* the Jozan character is transferred to Indochina before the love affair is consummated, leaving behind a letter of farewell to Alabama whose French has not progressed to the point where she can decipher his parting sentiments. Whom could she trust to translate? She can only tear up the letter and the photograph he has enclosed, the torn bits blowing into the sea. *Whatever it was she wanted from Jacques, Jacques took it with him.* Madame Paulette, an acquaintance from the seaside café where the aviators and Alabama met over drinks, notices how distraught her American friend has become after Jacques's transfer. " 'I am very sorry for you,' Madame said. 'We had not thought it was so serious an affair—we thought it was just an affair.' "

Sara Murphy had considered it a serious affair all along, and she and Gerald took the affair seriously indeed when Scott appeared at their door sick-faced and trembling, a candle in his hand: Zelda seemed to have swallowed a lethal dose of sleeping capsules. "We went along with him, and Sara walked her up and down, up and down, to keep her from going to sleep. We tried to make her drink olive oil, but Zelda said, 'Sara . . . don't make me take that, please. If you drink too much oil you turn into a Jew.' "

The confrontation between Scott and Zelda had taken place on the eve of Bastille Day, documented only by a cryptic note in Scott's journal for July 13 of that dangerous summer: "The Big Crisis," and in one of Zelda's letters, years later: "We were alone and gave big parties for the French aviators. Then there was Josen [sic] and you were justifiably angry." The end of the affair was unlike either of the romanticized versions in Scott and Zelda's separate novels set in the South of France.

Before Scott could turn the Big Crisis into the stuff of fiction for *Tender Is the Night,* he would tell shifting and exaggerated confessional bits to Hemingway, "as though trying them for use in a novel." In a journal note during the aftermath of his wife's romance with Jozan, Scott admitted: "That September 1924 I knew something had happened that could never be repaired."

The nightingale haunted the environs of Valescure. Its poignantly romantic mating call heard through the open windows of the Villa Marie became the motif for Zelda's *Save Me the Waltz* and Scott's *Tender Is the Night:* the nightingale, a lyric evocation of romance. Zelda had listened to the nightingale's song all her young life, always, before Scott, eager to respond to its suggestion and promise; now, easily involved with the shining sun person instead of the melancholy moon—but the nightingale's call had been a deception.

For a time Zelda drew back into her secret self, this time with no diary to confide in. One solitary pursuit was a return to the reading of Henry James; James's novel *Roderick Hudson* suggested Rome to her as a possible sanctuary for the winter, a relief and a change from the Riviera. But the Italian sojourn was a completely unsuccessful detour and more of a disaster than their first tourist trip to Paris, a grim adventure that set off Scott's loathing of Italy forever. He got into a drunken brawl with a taxi driver, was jailed and badly beaten by the police, an episode he would use to illustrate Dick Diver's downward spiral in *Tender Is the Night.* There was no respite from St. Raphael's nightmarish mood, only continued nightmare. Zelda's impression of their return to France was one of nothing more to lose:

They were on their way to Paris. They hadn't much faith in travel or a great belief in change of scene as a panacea for spiritual ills; they were simply glad to be going.

iii

The hurried swing to Paris led the Fitzgeralds to a fifth-floor apartment in the district of l'Etoile at 14, rue de Tilsitt, just off one of the busy spokes of traffic spinning around the Arc de Triomphe. An American colony of well-to-do expatriates had settled in the district bordering the Champs-Elysées, choosing to inhabit what would seem the very center of things Parisian. James Gordon Bennett had established the Paris *Herald* at 120, Champs-Elysées in his Second Empire townhouse around the corner from the Fitzgerald apartment: this was the newspaper that kept the English-language-reading public informed of celebrity visits to Paris, and its columns welcomed Scott and Zelda to the expatriate colony. Actually the literary and artistic center of expatriate life was elsewhere, on the opposite bank of the Seine in Montparnasse, where Scott and Zelda would have been much more at home and at far less expense. The new flat was overpriced for its questionable amenities, and Scott already owed Scribner's, his publisher, $6,200, but living lavishly gave the Fitzgeralds the illusion of fiscal well-being, even of stability.

Visitors, and the tenants themselves, deplored the apartment and ridiculed the furnishings: unwieldy chairs and tables, bric-à-brac and fringes and overcarved frames in the department-store style of Galeries Lafayette. Winter was gray grim with rain and frigid mist, and living quarters even in the *beaux quartiers* were crankily heated and the crude chimneys without flues. That first Paris winter was especially miserable for Zelda, confined to an apartment she described as smelling of a church chancery because it was impossible to heat and ventilate.

Adding to the damp and chill, Scott was despondent over the slack sales of *The Great Gatsby* and Zelda was infected with his low spirits; she had also picked up a physical infection following an operation in Rome. (The medical intervention was apparently to facilitate pregnancy.) Perhaps because she was still unsettled and fretful over the episode in St. Raphael, she suffered a return of her chronic colitis. The earlier introduction to Paris had been dismal enough; this second try was equally unpromising—again, because the Fitzgeralds' circumstances and state of mind refused to merge with the city's particular ambiance.

Scott had invested his usual exaggerated hopes in this new novel, and Zelda had also to contend diplomatically with his dramatized sense of failure. He correctly considered *The Great Gatsby* his masterwork, and that estimation was confirmed by the most laudatory notices he had ever received, along with letters of praise from his bedazzled contemporaries. A flattering letter from Edith Wharton had raised his spirits for part of a week, at least. But where were the financial rewards that accompanied such success? Zelda had also shared Scott's illusion that immediate financial solvency would result from the most sustained artistic accomplishment of his career. Though the author was cynical enough to contrive mass-market stories for *The Smart Set, Vanity Fair,* and the *Saturday Evening Post,* writing for the large and often excessive sums these stories generated, he would be forever frustrated by the ironic disproportion a book of literary distinction represents, even naively so. After the fluke best-selling success of his first novel, *This Side of Paradise,* no other book came close to supporting the extravagant way of life Scott and Zelda had chosen for themselves.

Zelda's mock review of Scott's second book, *The Beautiful and the Damned*—"To begin with, everyone must buy this book for the following aesthetic reasons: First because I know the cutest cloth of gold coat for only $300 in a store on 42nd Street. . . ."—was not as tongue-in-cheek as readers assumed. Scott set the standard by his gift of a diamond and platinum watch when he and Zelda became engaged: now Zelda wanted and needed the expensive tokens of her husband's affection. For Zelda, Scott must forever be the "gold-hatted, high-bouncing lover" (from the epigraph for *The Great Gatsby*), the lover to conjure excitement and find the wherewithal to satisfy her whims and fancies. In that important respect Zelda could never accept the traditional role of self-denying helpmeet in time of economic setback or crisis of morale. But Zelda had been open and frank about this failing when she broke off the engagement with Scott, and her husband no longer nourished any such illusions or expectations. Zelda, he was aware, would never settle for less—and he would not have wanted it otherwise. For her sake—and in some distorted way, for his own sake—he must contrive to wear the gold hat always.

Of the two keen observers of scene, Zelda's private response to Paris and awareness of the city's beauty and mystique was the more sensitive. Whatever her complaints and crankiness, despite illnesses and a new disappointment with Paris as a way station for killing time between highs, her evocation of that time was an example of subtle observation and tender recall, the mood of Paris filtered through a mood of her own: " . . . the grey sky came down between the chimneys . . . dividing the horizon into spires and points which hung over their unrest like the tubes of a vast incubator. The etching of the balconies of the Champs Elysées and the rain on the pavements about the Arc de Triomphe was all they could see from their red and gilt salon."

Zelda Sayre of Montgomery, Alabama, was evidently one prototype for Daisy Fay in *The Great Gatsby,* the practicing flapper who meets and falls in love with a young Gatsby in uniform, stationed at a nearby military camp. The setting is identical to Zelda's moonlit magnolia-scented South, and the romantic encounter—with its eventual deflection and breakoff—the same traumatic experience that so unsettled Zelda and Scott. For Daisy, like Zelda, "began to move again with the season; suddenly she was keeping half a dozen dates a day with half a dozen men, and drowsing asleep at dawn with the beads and chiffon of an evening dress tangled among the dying orchids on the floor beside her bed."

While Jay Gatsby, the fiancé of no noticeable prospects, is out of sight and mind overseas, Daisy marries Tom Buchanan to acquire a mate of substantial family background and affluence. The representation of Zelda's own materialistic streak is cynically evoked in this portrayal, but the author does display a larger understanding of his all-too-human Zelda, with her childlike worldly needs. Gatsby has tracked down his beloved Daisy, and hoping to impress her with his bootlegger's opulence, the *bourgeois gentilhomme* begins tossing his lavish collection of tailormade shirts before his lost love's eyes. Moved by the realization that she was meant for Gatsby all along, for now he can truly afford her, but also moved by deeper and subtler responses to the golden moment, Daisy bursts into tears: "They're such beautiful shirts," she sobbed, her voice muffled in the thick folds. "It makes me sad because I've never seen such—beautiful shirts."

Scott could be objectively chilling in his dissection of the adolescent side of Zelda's nature, but even as he exploited these weaknesses in print he saw beyond her flaws and failings the enchantment of a truly loving and lovable being. For her part, Zelda presented equally shrewd insights about Scott. She was reading Scott's mind and mood when she said of David Knight in *Save Me the Waltz:* "David was older than Alabama; he hadn't really felt glad since his first success." Scott confirmed Zelda's assessment of that early success when he wrote about himself: "I remember riding in a taxi one afternoon [1920, the year of *This Side of Paradise* and his marriage to Zelda] between very tall buildings and under a mauve and rosy sky. I began to bawl because I had everything I wanted and knew I would never be so happy again."

The sky had changed from mauve and rosy to depressing shades of gray: his editor's cable—SALES SITUATION DOUBTFUL—further shadowed the author's days, even though the second part of the message read: EXCELLENT REVIEWS. Scott's swift reply expressing grave disappointment provoked Maxwell Perkins's fatherly consolation: "I know fully how this period must try you: it must be very hard to endure, because it is hard enough for me to endure."

Thus *The Great Gatsby* was written off by its author as a failure, and in the mood of crippling disappointment the author and his wife began their expatriate life in Paris.

14, rue de Tilsitt became another of those ill-chosen temporary shelters for the directionless, unsettled Fitzgeralds. The faded gold-and-crimson wallpaper in the flat was no worse than the damp sheets at the Quirinale in Rome; Zelda's sense of household remained as absentminded as at any of their hotel rooms and borrowed apartments and rented houses on either side of the Atlantic. The closets were stuffed with soiled underwear, ashtrays overflowed, and drink rings stained the varnished surfaces of tea tables and bureaus where the abandoned cocktail glasses awaited the attention of a maid. The most inspired of Zelda's concerns for living arrangements occurred when she engaged a laundress to sort through the discard and disorder of the clothing scattered from one end of the flat to the other.

The majestically ordered pattern of living at the Murphys' Villa America had impressed Zelda and Scott, but neither of the Fitzgeralds could have emulated the Murphy sense of gracious living. In his hero-worshipping way—like Harry Crosby with Joyce and Lindbergh—Scott so admired certain men he wanted to be like them, and chose Gerald Murphy as his current model of male distinction. Zelda did not choose models: for all her admiration of Sara's stylish hostessing and household management, she had no intention or need to do likewise. In fact, Zelda did not much like women. Sara Murphy was a notable exception—and women did not often take to Zelda, so she had no close women friends in Paris. Scott thought the Murphys' sense of living well had something to do with money (both Sara and Gerald had private incomes, but the Murphys actually had less ready cash to draw from than Scott in his high-earning period), but Zelda knew it had more to do with style. Zelda also knew it was a style and outlook impossible to imitate.

It would seem that Zelda and Scott chose to set their course in Paris not by the Murphys' example, but in the way of the Crosbys, whom they had yet to meet. Paris offered its particular brand of sybaritic pleasures the Fitzgeralds had only begun to discover in New York. The profligate Fitgerald style matched the Crosby style, with far fewer means by which to support the profligacy: by now, with the disciplined labor of *The Great Gatsby* behind Scott—the far too faint applause already fading, Zelda without occupation or direction—the Fitzgeralds began a jaunty forced march toward the glorious lark they felt Paris owed them.

In the careless spirit of Gatsby's "interesting people, night and day . . . people who do interesting things," Scott and Zelda fell in with the growing American presence in Paris. The Fitzgeralds had their ideal audience; they had their party, night and day; as Zelda observed: "There were Americans at night and day Americans, and we all had Americans in the bank to buy things with. The marble lobbies were full of them."

Also in the marble lobbies Zelda heard the name "Fitzgerald" bandied about, unlike the silent first visit when the name was unknown. She could again take delight in celebrity—"You heard his name in bank lobbies and in the Ritz bar, which was proof that people were saying it in other places"—though her part was a borrowed share in the celebrity, that was enough for now. They had at last emerged from the reclusive vacuum of St. Raphael into stage center. The promise of excitement vibrated in the atmosphere of Paris in the 1920s, and Zelda could be forgiven her insouciance about certain altered circumstances: she was a mother now; and her husband, whose name she heard whispered at the Ritz bar, had reached a depressing deadlock in his artistic career. Yet Scott donned the gold hat and bounced high for Zelda before reflecting on the inevitable penalties: "It was a year of 1,000 parties and no work."

iv

This young writer in Paris, an American, was a Left Bank habitué named Ernest Hemingway: Scott thought his work first rate. The meeting with Hemingway took place at the Dingo Bar on the rue Delambre in Montparnasse. Zelda was not present at this famous encounter, nor was Ernest's wife Hadley, which allowed for Scott's embarrassing insistence on asking highly personal questions at a first meeting:

"Tell me, did you and your wife sleep together before you were married?"

"I don't know."

"What do you mean, you don't know?"

"I don't remember."

Scott certainly remembered sleeping with Zelda before they were married, and their pregnancy scare, when he sent her pills for an abortion and she wrote back: "I wanted to, for your sake, because I know what a mess I'm making and how inconvenient it's all going to be—but I simply *can't* and *won't* take those awful pills . . . I'd feel like a damned whore if I took even one."

"But how can you not remember something of such importance?"

"I don't know," Hemingway said. "It is odd, isn't it?"

In Hemingway's version of this opening conversation, recorded in *A Moveable Feast,* Scott is incapable of knowing how stubbornly gauche his interrogation could be. The Murphys complained of this same rudeness in Scott. When the awkward discussion with Hemingway came to its futile conclusion, Scott drained a single glass of champagne, perhaps too quickly, and suddenly lost all color, then passed out on the floor of the Dingo.

Nothing in Scott's behavior was propitious for beginning a friendship with Ernest Hemingway. Men did not exchange intimate information about their wives, and an even stronger principle with Hemingway was that a man should be able to hold his liquor. Worse still was the reaction of Scott's far too handsome visage, that pretty mouth and those long eyelashes. The two men were natural incompatibles, but eventually Hemingway entered Scott's gallery of heroes and Hemingway did share Scott's literary interests: both were fiercely respectful of the art and craft of writing. That, and Scott's willingness to help advance Ernest's career, made possible this most unlikely of liaisons.

Scott was anxious to display his latest discovery to his wife. The two couples were to meet over lunch at the rue de Tilsitt flat, which Hemingway found "gloomy and airless." There was nothing in the apartment that seemed to belong to Scott and Zelda except for the expensively bound copies of the Fitzgerald novels. Zelda's dark-blond hair was temporarily ruined by a French permanent, "and her eyes were tired and her face was too taut and drawn." The occasion was superficially friendly, but neither Hemingway nor Zelda was aware how antagonistic each was to the other. Zelda used a practiced strategem in such instances of first meeting. "That was one of the ways [from her story "The Girl the Prince Liked"] she established social dominance over people: she would sit and watch until she frightened them, and then suddenly be friendly and free and just as charming as she had been formidable."

With Hemingway, Zelda did not arrive at the friendly-and-free stage, nor did she frighten him. According to his account, Zelda was suffering a hangover from a café crawl in Montmartre the night before. She expressed her unhappiness with Scott by the accusation: "When you two can go off and have such simply wonderful times together, it only seems fair I should have just a little fun with our good friends in Paris." To his uneasiness over Scott's mouth, Hemingway added his suspicion of Zelda's hawk eyes. "Watching her face you could see her mind leave the table and go to the night's party and return with her eyes blank as a cat's . . . and she smiled happily with her eyes, and her mouth too, as he [Scott] drank the wine. I learned to know that smile very well. It meant she knew Scott would not be able to write."

The self-serving reports by Hemingway on Scott and Zelda could never be trusted other than to reflect his own attitudes toward the Fitzgeralds. His questionable claim to have recognized, at that very first meeting, that Zelda was certifiably crazy "if not yet netable" was one of those early diagnoses of insanity apparently based on an observer's "intuition" strongly fortified by hindsight. Of Zelda's incipient streak of madness, John Dos Passos said: "It was only looking back on it years later that it occurred to me that, even the first day we knew each other, I had come up against the basic fissure in her mental processes that was to have such tragic consequences"; and Rebecca West asserted that Zelda's craggy homeliness (the only assessment of Zelda that did not consider her particularly beautiful—though Dorothy Parker thought of her as "candy-box pretty") was a feature one found in studies of the insane by Géricault. But Hemingway's perception that Zelda took secret pleasure in Scott's incapacity for work would appear intuitively accurate. Zelda's assessment of Hemingway, however, was the more immediately conclusive, expressed just after meeting him for the first time: "Nobody is as male as all that."

These two wary rivals undeclared, friend and wife circling one another and Scott in the Paris orbit, met smiling socially but loathed one another from the first.

For Hemingway, the association with the Fitzgeralds was initially rewarding—Scott promoted Hemingway's work with the energy and ardor of a paid agent—but ultimately disruptive when he discovered that Scott and Zelda, in their idea of social exchange, could be completely inconsiderate of any convenience but their own. In Hemingway's opinion, Zelda was the instigator of most of the Fitzgerald stunts and nonstop partying. She could hold her liquor better than Scott (for that he could admire her) and would deliberately lead Scott to drink beyond his capacity, wanting him to become ruinously drunk and unable to work next day. Indeed, Zelda was jealous of Scott's literary endeavors, but the jealousy did not take the malignant form Hemingway asserts. If Zelda did lead or mislead Scott into benders without end, Scott was equally to blame for the destructive waste in their common pattern of behavior. He outlined his own self-destructive tendencies in a series of articles for *Esquire,* called "The Crack-Up," admitting to character flaws and naive misconceptions as the origin of his nervous breakdown at age thirty-nine.

"For sixteen years I lived pretty much as this latter person, distrusting the rich, yet working for money with which to share their mobility and the grace that some of them brought into their lives." He was referring to Gerald and Sara Murphy in particular, but sharing their mobility and aspiring to their grace led him to the apparently irrational pattern of exhibitionism, wasteful extravagance, and alcoholic excess. His wife shared these destructive episodes, and paid an even greater price, but in none of the *Esquire* articles does Scott refer to Zelda, nor to what might have led to her own crack-up.

"We lived in the rue Tilsitt, in red plush," wrote Zelda, "—and went to the markets with the Murphies. There were [a list of drinking companions] . . . and rides in the Bois at dawn and the night we played puss-in-the-corner at the Ritz. There was Tunti and nights in Mont Martre." The memories of seeing Eva Le Gallienne and the Murphies and the obscure Tunti were a tender recall of *les années folles,* but all was not a ride through the Bois de Boulogne at dawn; later, when they lived on the rue de Vaugirard, Zelda's reminder to Scott turned bitter: "You were constantly drunk. You didn't work and were dragged home at night by taxi-drivers when you came home at all."

Zelda was frequently aware of the darker side to their life in Paris, but she kept the nights of nightmare to herself to be expressed later, in a written record, while Scott's Paris bore the fuzzy imprint of fun and games only, as in his nostalgic revisit in *Tender Is the Night:* "The party that night moved with the speed of a slapstick comedy. They were twelve, they were sixteen, they were quartets in separate motors bound on a quick odyssey over Paris." For all his protest and regret over their ruinous odyssey in Paris, Scott was forever impressed by its glitter. One of the "motors" was the private limousine of the Shah of Persia, with silver wheels and radiator, the inside of the body inlaid with gems, marten fur on the floor. The revelers set up a "waiter trap" in the lobby of the Ritz constructed of piled-up lobby furniture—for in fiction, as in life, waiters and taxi drivers invariably suffered drunken indignities at the hands of the Fitzgeralds and company, but were lavishly tipped for their trouble, and that made it all right. In the novel, Dick Diver was compelled by his very nature to bedazzle Rosemary Hoyt, his love interest of the moment; in the real Paris of the moment, Zelda was Scott's constant object of bedazzlement. Successfully distracted—or relieved for the moment of the memory of consequence—Zelda could think of Scott as darling Goofo, and cry out *bravo* and "Ain't we got fun?" The show ran for night after night after night.

Yet the fun could be an aesthetic treat of permanent value, an insightful delight earned by those sensitive to the magic city's subtler vibrations. One dawn the Fitzgeralds returned home on a carrot-laden market cart from les Halles: "the six of us, oh, the noblest relics of the evening . . . riding on top of thousands of carrots smelling fragrant and sweet with earth in their beards." These were the golden moments of Paris the effects of alcohol and exhibitionism could not diminish or corrupt.

The complimentary letter from Gertrude Stein to Scott was in effect a royal summons from the Left Bank's most famous expatriate. Stein's work was considered the great modern breakthrough in literary experiment, even if, at the time, her writing was virtually unpublished and unknown beyond the Left Bank colony of English-speaking expatriates. Her personal claims to genius were often considered the local joke—but she was generally respected as a critic of art and literature, and her inspired remarks made instant and remembered effect. Almost alone she had introduced the work of avant-garde painters like Picasso and Matisse to the world outside Paris.

To Zelda there was something almost sinister about the two women at 23, rue de Fleurus. They were lesbians, and there were plenty of *those* in Paris, but there was something more disturbing here, and anyway the company of women was anathema to Zelda. While Scott felt perfectly at home in that salon atmosphere, the hermetic little world of Stein's studio so oppressed Zelda she thought she might have an asthma attack.

"In your dedication," Stein was saying, "I liked the melody of 'Once again to Zelda.' "

What a silly thing to praise, thought Zelda, who had been shunted off (as wives invariably were) to the Keeper of the Flame, Alice Toklas, and had to catch scraps of the real conversation by eavesdropping from across the room. Mention of the dedication did bring Zelda into the picture but not into the discussion. Just as well. She would as soon contemplate Alice Toklas's noticeable mustache with silent irony as listen to the "sententious gibberish" of Gertrude Stein.

During Alice's polite chatter Zelda contemplated the art work displayed on the studio's water-stained walls. Zelda had begun to discover Picasso—as had all of intellectual Paris by then—and considered his work more idea than painting, but she had been inspired by those ideas. For whatever the paintings were worth, Gertrude Stein seemed to have collected the Picassos worth having, in particular the *Demoiselles d'Avignon,* which worked some strange emotional response in Zelda. Lately she had thought about taking up painting—she had dabbled in art before her marriage—and the Picassos awakened that desire again.

Meanwhile Scott was being impressed and obsequious, as only he could be in the presence of certain persons, and Gertrude Stein was saying in her run-on sentences: "You make a modern world and a modern orgy strangely enough it was never done until you did it in *This Side of Paradise.*"

"You just say that . . . " said Scott.

I have got to get out of here, Zelda thought. An asthma attack was imminent.

Scott came back to the flat with that waxen look and perspiration on his chin. It was not from the five-flight climb, Zelda knew, and too early in the day for those familiar symptoms of psychic exhaustion from drink. Nor could it have been the aftershock of Scott's impossible driving: Teddy Chanler had driven Scott to the Pavillon Colombe and back.

Zelda had flatly refused to go forty kilometers out of Paris just to be condescended to by that hidebound old dowager, Edith Wharton. The *grande dame* of American letters had sent Scott one of those letters of praise for *The Great Gatsby,* so of course Scott would accept the invitation, with or without his wife. Scott could not resist showing off for an audience he had yet to impress, and at the Pavillon Colombe would be the faubourg set Edith Wharton collected for her teas.

"Fine," Scott replied, when Zelda asked him how it went. He did not look so fine.

Zelda made no attempt to pry the story out of him: she knew Scott would, soon enough, blurt out what had happened to him, and he did. On the way out to St. Brice-sous-Fôret, he and Chanler had stopped off for drinks at roadside cafés, stops not too distantly spaced. Zelda knew how badly Scott had wanted to make an impression, to create a glowing show with himself centerstage. With that crowd he would have to fortify himself first. Sitting down to tea with all those snobs, he had wanted to shock them out of their superior airs: he intended to be the worldly observer of a Paris they would never know.

"So I told them when we first came to Paris we lived in a house of prostitution."

"Whatever for? All we did once was visit that House of All Nations cathouse, and backed right out again."

"She said—Edith Wharton said—the story lacked data. 'Tell us, Mr. Fitzgerald,' she said, 'What did they *do* in the house of prostitution?' "

"I guess that knocked the wind out of you."

"They beat me," he confessed: the sweet promise of the moment to shine had been soured by a humiliating putdown. Lowering his pale face into his arms, Scott said again, "They beat me they beat me."

V

Paris had become impossible, for Zelda, in that damp apartment: she had suffered a series of colds, asthma attacks, and now colitis. So the warm invitation from the Murphys in the South was a second chance to live sanely and sweetly and to turn brown in the sun. "Just a real place to rough it," was Scott's idea of the Villa America. Yes, St. Raphael had been a disaster, but the episode with Edouard Jozan had faded from mind, or rather, had been folded back into some tuck of memory, as vague as yesterday's hangover.

Anyway, they had tried to live in the South of France too soon, like the time they tried Paris alone, before their own set had settled in. The trend was to the South, the Riviera was being discovered. When Scott and Zelda had been at St. Raphael the first time, the Côte was still the winter enclave of British tourists, retired French civil servants, and the infirm. A new generation was bypassing the birthday-cake hotels in Cannes and Nice to seek out unpopulated stretches of sand and undiscovered fishing villages along the sun-drenched shore. Affluent beachcombers like Coco Chanel, Pablo Picasso, Cole Porter, and Raoul Dufy commuted overnight in the unfashionable summer months by *Le Train bleu* from Paris to the Côte d'Azur. Slightly ahead of the crowd, Gerald and Sara Murphy had staked out a seaside sanctuary on the cap d'Antibes.

It was a "real place," but there was no question of roughing it here. With her special flair for living well, Sara had renovated the fourteen rooms of their Moorish villa in pure *style moderne*—influenced as much by Chanel's latest fashion statement, "le luxe dans la simplicité," as by the hard-edged design of a Léger painting. The American luxury in this reductive French simplicity was the baths (Americans in Europe could never adapt to French indifference to modern plumbing), a feature especially appealing to Zelda, who had a fetish for bathrooms and at parties would often sequester herself in the bath for long hours while the party went on without her.

The soft evenings on the cap d'Antibes allowed for outdoor

dining under the massive linden tree, the late sun glowing against the villa's beige walls and yellow shutters. It had been Sara's idea to use metal garden furniture inside and out, avoiding the stuffy clutter dear to the French, a decor favored by the earlier expatriates Mary Cassatt and Edith Wharton. Sara hung Japanese lanterns outdoors and painted the iron work with bright silver radiator paint. Both Zelda and Scott were impressed with Sara's taste and flair, though Scott persisted in believing all had been accomplished with American dollars.

Gerald had studied landscape gardening as an escape from family pressure to join the Mark Cross leather-goods business, and applied his expertise to the grounds and gardens, with tasteful restraint. Little of the original growth required alteration or addition to create this private Eden: there was a palm garden with eucalyptus trees, orchards of lemon and tangerine. The parties were held in the blue-shadowed garden, as described in *Tender Is the Night*: "where there were lanterns asleep in the fig trees and a big table and wicker chairs and a great market umbrella from Siena. . . ." A Provençal farmhouse had been converted to guest rooms, but the Fitzgeralds took a place of their own, the Villa Paquita, at nearby Juan-les-Pins, though their social life circled around the Villa America. The MacLeishes were there, and Charles Brackett had just left; other guests coming or going were Dos Passos and the silent film star Rex Ingram—the Fitzgeralds would also meet Mistinguette and Alice Terry, E. Phillips Oppenheim and the former premier of Italy, Orlando. The Hemingways were due to arrive any day now.

A close friendship was sustained between the Murphys and the Fitzgeralds during this first lengthy exposure to one another. Gerald would say of their four-way compatibility: "My God. How rare it is. How rare." And Scott reversed his opinion that they do things better in America, with his remark that "No one ever makes things in America with that vast, magnificent, cynical disillusion with which Gerald and Sara make things like their parties," for the Murphys' perfect parties were what Scott and Zelda now lived for. The best of all possible worlds had been created here on the Mediterranean shore. America was the backwash, and France glowed with new possibility: "America's greatest promise," wrote Scott, "is that something is going to happen and after awhile you get tired of waiting because nothing happens to people except they grow old, and nothing happens in American art because America is the story of the moon that never rose."

Evenings on the cap d'Antibes now evolved in harmony with Scott and Zelda's glamorous imaginings. They could linger late in the Murphys' magic garden watching together the glorious promise of a new moon rising from behind the ancient ramparts of Antibes.

Scott was working on a new novel, but in sporadic bursts and not to the extreme of excluding his wife from the greater parts of the day, or failing to share his thoughts about work-in-progress. "Scott's book is marvelous," was Zelda's rare comment on her husband's writing. The novel, *The World's Fair* (an early version of *Tender Is the Night*), was partly drawn from the Fitzgeralds' sojourn in Hollywood, when Scott was offered a contract to write a film script for Constance Talmadge. Zelda had not found Hollywood to her taste: "the glitter was shrouded by midnight, the parties were staring matches between rival stars," the opposite effect the cap d'Antibes was having on her. (In her warm missing-you letters to daughter Scottie, she wrote that she was "crazy to own a house," and expressed a nostalgic longing for Paris: "The weather here [in Hollywood] makes me think of Paris in the spring and I am *very* homesick for the pink lights and the gay streets. So is Daddy," she added, "also for the wine and the little cafés on the sidewalk.") Scott's screenplay had come to nothing, but at least he could turn the experience into art: he had taken up with a teenage Hollywood starlet named Lois Moran, an affair that had also come to nothing, though the starlet was the inspiration for the character Rosemary Hoyt in his new novel.

The idyllic setting at cap d'Antibes was perfect for a period of recuperation for whatever Zelda felt about Scott's Hollywood fling with Lois Moran. She had made no issue of the affair during that cinematic interlude, but on the Twentieth Century Limited speeding east, Zelda did react, dramatically: she threw her diamond bracelet from the train, Scott's engagement gift to her, purchased at large sacrifice during their troubled courtship, received with the tenderest display of affection by Zelda at the time: "I've turned it over four hundred times to see 'from Scott to Zelda.' " The wound from Scott's flirtation with his "icle durl" was healing, but Zelda was plagued anew by the illnesses that had begun in Paris. The dampness seeping through the villa's walls affected both Zelda and Scott, as had the damp and airless Paris apartment. Scott complained that he could not push forward on his manuscript because of the dampness. Zelda suffered colds, colitis, and finally abdominal pains diagnosed as appendicitis: the Fitzgeralds returned hurriedly to Paris, where Zelda's appendix was removed at the American Hospital in Neuilly.

Ironically, the financial picture brightened at exactly this morose moment. *The Great Gatsby* had become a moderately successful play on Broadway, leading to a $50,000 screen offer for the book. In this oblique way Scott actually scored the fiscal reward for *The Great Gatsby* he had originally banked upon, and he gathered in the largesse he had so recently pursued in vain. Yet he could never erase the feeling of failure because of the disappointing sales of *The Great Gatsby* when it had first appeared. It was this nagging regret that kept him from moving forward on *The World's Fair,* rather than the dampness at the Villa Paquita. He came up with an odd complaint—remembering and regretting the diamond bracelet?—that now so much money was pouring in, Zelda did not even have a pearl necklace to show for it.

From the damp confines of the Villa Paquita the Fitzgeralds moved to the commodious Villa St. Louis "on the shore with a beach and the Casino not 100 yards away. . . ." The beach was a comfort to Zelda, but the Casino was perhaps too close for comfort, considering the well-stocked bar. Then the mistral began to blow, an inconvenience of nature the Fitzgeralds took as a personal piece of malevolence: the southern wind was what now kept Scott from working, or so he said. Zelda was beginning to understand a more important reason for the break in Scott's literary flow: when earnings outweighed the pressure of debt, Scott had no spur to drive him on to production. After every successful financial coup, Scott's work went into decline, except following the good fortune of *This Side of Paradise* when he was desperately writing stories to "win his girl" and buy her a diamond bracelet. It was not in Zelda's nature to urge—she would have thought of it as "nag"—Scott back to his desk. Scott might advise Zelda to do something creative in her life (as he had, foolishly, using Lois Moran as the example of a dedicated professional, disciplined in her craft), but he could never accept the same counsel from her. Anyway, she was not inclined to advise Scott, or spur him on. Zelda could more happily share Scott's periods of careless abandon; she grew restless—as in St. Raphael—when Scott was driven by the creative urge. There were fresh new dollars rolling in, money that seemed all the easier when converted into deflated francs.

If Zelda did not nag, Scott's Catholic conscience did. But then, both he and Zelda could rationalize an interval of slackness; the winnings represented hard effort in the past, and they felt a constant need to renew themselves with the reward of Right Now. Zelda had Scott back, they could celebrate the largesse together: the Casino was only one hundred yards away.

To welcome the Hemingways to Villa America, the Murphys made the grand gesture of arranging a gala champagne dinner at the Casino. Scott became petulant with jealousy: there had been no such extravagant welcome when the Fitzgeralds came down to the Riviera. But if anyone had cause to be annoyed by the Casino fête, it was Zelda, who disliked Hemingway from the first. She, however, was passively agreeable to the dinner party. Neither the Fitzgeralds nor the Murphys were aware of a brooding crisis: Ernest's entanglement with fashion-writer Pauline Pfeiffer, whose tense presence at the Villa America would bring the Hadley Richardson–Ernest Hemingway marriage to an end.

Zelda was rather fond of Hadley Hemingway for her quiet charm, and out of sympathy for what she considered Ernest's bullying of his wife. It was evident that she was blindly in love with Ernest—well, so was Zelda in love with Scott, but she did not and could not accept being cornered in a domestic role by a preening-superior male. Zelda even remarked to Hadley that it was easy to see who was boss in the Hemingway menage. Hadley made no reply. It was Hadley's fault, if she put up with it, but Zelda did not brood over Hadley's unhappy fate.

She did enthusiastically admire and approve of Sara Murphy: to observe the harmony of Gerald and Sara's relationship, and to watch them together create a household of grace and wit and uncommon good sense was one of Zelda's constant pleasures. At some level she might even have seen Sara Murphy as a model—not in the way Scott manifestly looked up to Gerald—and she might well have taken on Sara's virtues had it not meant sacrificing her own high spirits and sense of self. What she could *not* understand was how Sara, as perceptive as she was outspoken, did not see behind Ernest's facade of all-knowing bluster—though she did not share Scott's jealousy over the Murphys' apparent favoritism.

At the Casino party for Hemingway, Scott complained noisily: "Champagne and caviar are in excess of good taste," while consuming the Murphys' champagne in excess.

Up to a point, the Murphys had a remarkable tolerance for Scott's adolescent behavior. Unhappily they watched him play his staring game with a woman at a nearby table, until her escort sent for the headwaiter. Admonishment only brought out the worst in his childishness. When he began tossing ashtrays across the table, Gerald Murphy got up and walked out of the Casino. "Scott really had the most appalling sense of humor," Gerald said, recalling the dinner party. "Sophomoric and—well, trashy." Zelda kept her thoughts to herself: in any case she could not have stopped Scott from behaving as he did, and she may have been secretly pleased to see the Hemingway party spoiled.

From time to time the Murphys were obliged to chastise Scott and Zelda as they would their own children—who were exceptionally well bred, and needed far less attention than did the Fitzgeralds. At one point Scott was juggling the Murphys' hand-blown Venetian glass tumblers in the garden, then casually tossed the glassware over the garden wall. Gerald stopped him after the loss of two valuable pieces: "I think that was the time I told him he couldn't come back for awhile."

Banned from the graceful living at the Villa America, Scott and Zelda hovered outside the garden wall while a typical Murphy party was in progress: the Japanese lanterns swaying in the light evening breeze, the Murphy children singing to the guests "Au Clair de la Lune." To call attention to their exile and disgrace, the Fitzgeralds began throwing empty wine bottles over the wall, then dumped the contents of garbage cans onto the party terrace.

Scott instigated the crudest of their stunts, while Zelda went along playfully enough, or offered the mild restraint of a moment's wit. Whenever Scott "kidnapped" a waiter to create an evening's diversion, he would threaten to saw the man in half (with a musical saw), but Zelda responded, why bother?—all they would find inside a waiter was broken china, old menus, and tips and pencil stubs. Her style of showing off was completely different from Scott's, an exhibit of reverie and remove. Once, at the Casino, Zelda faded into her secret self—eyes turned inward, as Hemingway noticed—and appeared to leave the company as she drew up her skirts and stepped up on the table from her chair: she began a slow dance among the bottles and glasses and buckets of ice. All those around her fell silent, and the orchestra caught the mood, then played to her as she dreamily danced, transported, alive to herself only. Scott too fell silent, reminded of the first glimpse of his wife at eighteen, dancing at the country club in Montgomery, as alone as she was now.

Zelda had wisely given up driving, but Scott was an abysmal driver of the "rat Renault" Sara dubbed their little runabout, an automobile at the center of many of their misadventures. On one driving excursion Zelda suddenly wanted the wind to blow through her hair, so at the next garage Scott had the top of the Renault cut away like a sardine can. Such stunts as Scott perpetrated were born of drunken impulse, to show off to Zelda or the Murphys, but Zelda's carefree pranks were becoming more and self-destructive. She once grabbed the steering wheel from Scott and swerved the car to within inches of the edge of the Grande Corniche. The car spun and stalled at the dropoff: the Fitzgeralds survived—Zelda could offer no explanation for the feeling that had come over her when she reached across Scott for the wheel.

Other close calls came of naïveté and negligence. They were like children in their disregard of danger, and were, it appeared, destined to be spared the normal consequences of human folly. One remarkable instance of the benevolent providence that watched over them was when a passing shepherd discovered the two sleeping Americans in a car parked precisely across the SNCF tracks, and awakened the curled-up innocents minutes before they would have been crushed by the passing *Train bleu.*

Sara Murphy was present the night Scott and Zelda quarreled

in the car and Zelda suddenly flung herself from the Renault and stretched out prone beside the front wheels, screaming at Scott to run over her. Hysterical, she meant it—and Scott meant to run her over until the Murphys managed to stop him and drag the sobbing Zelda to safety.

Hemingway was convinced that Scott initiated the drunken stunts (that seldom came off as the comic turns he intended), but Zelda was responsible for the riskiest ventures. It was she, he believed, who led Scott astray in follow-the-leader escapades and irrational dares. Sara Murphy would have agreed to this when she witnessed the game Zelda played with Scott on the driving cliff off the Grande Corniche. The cliff was directly over a perfect swimming cove where saw-toothed rocks jutted out of the water near the shoreline. "One needed to have a perfect sense of timing," Sara recalled, and neither Scott nor Zelda was in any shape to dive from the vertiginous height: both had been drinking and Zelda had not long recovered from her appendectomy in Paris. "Zelda stripped to her skin and very quietly asked Scott if he cared for a swim . . . I was with them and he was absolutely trembling when she challenged him, but he followed her. It was breathtaking." Zelda executed her dives with a grace inherent in the daring, taking each dive from the next niche up the cliff, five, ten, twenty feet. "They would return from the sea all shivering and white," for the night was lit by the southern moon, and Sara had fallen under the spell of their ghostly suicidal spectacle, unable to call a halt. "They took a dive . . . until the last, the one at thirty feet. Scott hesitated and watched Zelda until she surfaced; I didn't think he would go through with it, but he did."

When Sara shook herself free from the paralysis of enchantment, she admonished the two of them for their recklessness.

"But Say-ra," replied Zelda with her coy drawl, "—didn't you know, we don't believe in conservation."

"You know," said Gerald, "in their early days they were two beauties—I mean that—Scott's head was so fine, really unbelievably handsome. They were the flawless people."

Gerald Murphy could find in himself a large respect for Scott, since he understood something of the torturous way an artist trod

(Gerald had tried to be a painter, and was good at it), but with Zelda he was half in love. "Her beauty was not legitimate, thank God . . . she possessed an astounding gaze. If she looked like anything it was an American Indian." Edmund Wilson had already spoken of Zelda as a barbarian princess; and Hemingway had remarked on Zelda's strange eyes as well, but he thought the disconcerting gaze evidence of an incipient madness. Even Sheila Graham, the Hollywood columnist who fell in love with Scott in his last years, could not forget "the very intent, piercing look in [Zelda's] marvelous eyes."

"But Zelda could be spooky," said Sara. "She seemed sometimes to be lying in ambush waiting for you with those Indian eyes of hers." At one of the parties at Villa America, Sara watched Zelda greet guests pleasantly enough, then overheard her mutter under her breath as soon as the guest moved on: "I hope you die in the marble ring."

Intrigued as Sara was by the Fitzgeralds, fascinated by their unique attitudes and energies, her tolerance for the essential folly of their lives had its limits. What could not be forgiven was Scott's prying into her personal life. "What he wanted from a woman," Sara remarked, meaning when he wanted especially from Zelda, "was her *story.*" He wanted Sara's story too, charming her all the while he scrutinized and expropriated. If she had known the result of Scott's relentless interrogation, she would have been all the more guarded in her replies, and might have ended their friendship before it matured. The Murphys were being probed and analyzed, then refashioned to the demands of fiction. Gerald and Sara, along with Zelda and Scott himself, were to become the composite models for Nicole and Dick Diver in *Tender Is the Night.*

Zelda's life was beginning to take the form in which she would appear as the mentally disturbed persona—with Sara Murphy as the balanced, practical half of the prototype—for Nicole Diver. Zelda, of course, knew she was being used, as so much of herself (with her consent and approval) had been expropriated for Scott's work all along; but she did not predict nor could she possibly imagine in what way or to what extent she would be reborn as Nicole. Her breakdown was that tragic-fortuitous crisis Scott had been waiting for to give his sprawling and detoured novel a center that would hold. In Zelda's last completed manuscript, *Caesar's Things,* she wrote of Scott again as the painter Jacob, who could not stand the grit of life and tried to worry and shape people into their proper story versions "till it all made acceptable continuity with what he thought it ought to be dramatically." For the last great novel Scott completed in his lifetime, the dramatic continuity of Zelda's story would reveal itself in the days to come.

vi

A recurrent symbol in Zelda's unsettled life and divided mind was the Trunk. This was the trunk of her life, a trunk full of clothes and accessories that followed Zelda from house to villa to apartment to house again. The Trunk contained the Jean Patou suit Zelda had felt obliged to buy in New York just after her marriage, when Scott was so dismayed at her "frills and furbelows" trousseau from Montgomery, Alabama. (The suit was never worn, and eventually was devoured by moths: ". . . so relieved," said Zelda, "to find it devastated at last.") During their next sojourn in Paris, the Trunk would contain her dance workclothes and ballet slippers. Before the Fitzgeralds left the Riviera, the Murphys would see the Trunk outside the door at the Villa St. Louis: Zelda and Scott were quarreling more and more often, violently at times, and after each outburst Zelda would move her trunk outside, ready to leave. They would make up in the interval, or drunkenly sleep off the aftermath of a row—but the poison lingered in the bloodstream and the Trunk remained outside, all night, and once in a dawn drizzle the Murphys saw it dragged back inside by the two together.

Irregular and unpredictable as was the Fitzgerald pattern of living, Zelda's nostalgia for Christmas persisted, and she celebrated the holiday in whatever makeshift fashion possible. In the Trunk were the Christmas-tree ornaments that followed the Fitzgerald peregrinations: often the ornaments did not catch up with the holiday preparations at the latest address, as was the case when Scott and Zelda took an apartment on the rue Vaugirard. It was another tasteless, uncomfortable, and unlivable flat—reminding Zelda of a waxworks tableau—so to cheer the place that Christmas Scott bought an evergreen and Zelda decked the tree with gilded champagne corks and champignons-de-Paris from the market on the rue de Buci.

Scottie was five, and old enough to want to select Christmas gifts. With Nanny she made a shopping tour of Bon Marché department store for a present for Maman and Papa: the odd but darkly significant choice was a garbage can.

"And there was that lone and lovely child," Zelda wrote, "knocking a croquet ball through the arches of summer under the horse-chestnut trees and singing alone in her bed at night. She was a beautiful child who loved her mother."

The Fitzgeralds had chosen the new apartment for that lone and lovely child, who was at last becoming a consideration in their lives. The apartment was just opposite the Luxembourg Gardens where Scottie could play—if ever the winter rains ceased—and watch the outdoor marionette performances. As Scott and Zelda's relationship became more and more strained, Scottie was an increasingly important element in holding their marriage together. Until now she had been left to the care of nannies and mademoiselles; when Zelda attended to her daughter she treated her more like a baby sister, a child to play with for intervals of mutual amusement. Because of her own indulged and undisciplined childhood, Zelda had no clear concept of child rearing; Scott had strong opinions and patriarchal theories about children in general, but his sense of being a parent was slack and sporadic, as impulsive as Zelda's. On one occasion Sara Murphy came on the scene when Zelda had decided to occupy herself with the bathing of Scottie, but was bathing her in the bidet. Sara suggested it was an unsanitary tub for a child's bath: Zelda had never realized the bidet's exact function. After that, she told Scottie never to touch the thing, it was a fire extinguisher.

"I'm raising my daughter to be a flapper," Zelda once declared at a time when she was not raising her daughter at all. "I like the jazz generation, and I hope my daughter's generation will be jazzier. I want my girl to do as she pleases, be what she pleases, regardless of Mrs. Grundy." In her earlier pattern of occasional motherhood, Zelda might spend hours on the floor with Scottie making papier-mâché puppets from old theatre programs, or cutting up lace cuffs from the Trunk to make detail-perfect queenly gowns for her daughter's dolls.

Scott would volunteer his collection of lead soldiers for the elaborate tableaux of fairy-tale playlets Zelda invented for Scottie. The Murphys, who frequently observed Zelda at play with Scottie, were inclined to wonder if the mother were creating an imaginary world for the daughter or herself.

"I want her to be a flapper," insisted Zelda, at age thirty when her own flapper days were fading, "because flappers are brave and gay and beautiful."

In the neighborhood of St. Sulpice, Zelda was "much alone," and "the church bells tolled incessantly for funerals." By accident Scott discovered that Ernest Hemingway and his new wife were living in the same neighborhood, but Ernest had been keeping his address secret from the Fitzgeralds as a precaution against Scott's drop-in visits (Scott admitted that when he was drunk and buttonholed friends, "I make them pay and pay"). Nevertheless he was hurt by what he considered this latest barrier to the solid comradeship he had forged with Ernest, and he could reflect on the irony of Ernest's "Poor Scott" accusation that Fitzgerald had a compulsion to suck up to money. His second wife, Pauline Pfeiffer, was a woman of wealth, and the Hemingways were living in an impressive townhouse on the rue Ferou, opposite the cathedral. Zelda's wry observation was that the Hemingway establishment was convenient to Confession: Ernest had converted to Catholicism for his marriage to Pauline, and Zelda had got the odd notion that the conversion was not to please his new wife but merely a cynical strategy to ease the way to a divorce from Hadley.

Just as Ernest Hemingway was shrewdly disengaging himself from the Left Bank café scene, the Fitzgeralds were joining the expatriate set in its final orgiastic months before the Fall. Paris was ever there, an escape from the macabre apartment and the tolling of funeral bells, and Zelda wandered the city on her own, observing women at luncheon at Duval's, who "went to the foundries and had themselves some hair cast and had themselves half-soled with the deep chrome fantasies of Helena Rubinstein and Dorothy Gray . . . they drove the men out to lose themselves in the comparative quiet of the Paris streets which hummed like the tuning of an invisible orchestra . . . people spent fortunes in taxis in search of remote."

Drink was now the essential Fitzgerald bond of pleasuring, and

Paris nights the common adventure. Their antagonisms had become old and familiar wounds; personal clashes of the brooding kind instead of such violent flare-ups as when Zelda called Scott's father an Irish cop and Scott slapped her so hard her nose bled, and then turned to the company and asked: "Is there any man present who has not struck his wife in anger?" An unsigned cease-fire kept the marriage nominally intact, but there were no longer the reconciliations at next evening's apéritif hour or screaming recriminations made up tenderly in bed.

"I have just begun to realize," wrote Zelda much later, "that sex and sentiment have little to do with each other. . . . You said you wanted nothing more from me in all your life . . . you made no advances toward me. Twice you left my bed saying 'I can't. Don't you understand'—I didn't."

Scott had always nourished doubts and dreads about his masculinity. Zelda's complaints fueled these anxieties, even drove Scott to confide in Ernest Hemingway, worrying about penis size and satisfying his wife. Fitzgerald and Hemingway checked the genitalia on the male figures in paintings at the Louvre, compared penises in the W.C. at Michaud's, Ernest leading him on in a mocking companion-confessor episode he would exploit later, in *A Moveable Feast,* to ridicule Scott—a comic-sad commentary on the author's own insecure sexual attitudes. When Scott had tumbled drunkenly into bed after a night's café crawl with Hemingway, murmuring, "No more, baby. . . ," Zelda, who had always considered Ernest "a pansy with hair on his chest," could now declare that Scott and Ernest were lovers. She knew where Scott was most vulnerable, for she believed that "when a man is no longer custodian of his vanities and convictions, he's nothing at all." Zelda was striking back, in her failure to be loved, with whatever blunt instrument came to hand.

But she no longer dragged the Trunk outside. Instead, Scott donned the gold hat, or Zelda placed it on his head, and they swung onto the carousel of nightclubs from the place Vavin in Montparnasse to the rue Fontaine in Montmartre anticipating the magic that had once touched their lives and would set them aglow once again. Energies drained, bodies sufficiently number by alcohol to forget, they returned to sleep together in their separate stupors and widening differences.

"I think a woman gets more happiness out of being gay, lighthearted, unconventional, mistress of her own fate, than out of a career that calls for hard work, intellectual pessimism and loneliness. I don't want Scottie to be a genius." But what did she want for herself? Zelda truly believed in being mistress of her own fate, but she now took on the demands of her husband's career, which did call for hard work, intellectual pessimism, and loneliness. In New York she had tried her hand at lightweight feature articles for the magazines that published Scott's work; she had the touch, and the Fitzgerald name helped. In Paris she discovered she had a flair for a certain kind of flapper story as well, derived from Scott's formula and her own experience. There was evidence of a natural talent and an original voice, and she knew how far she could carry this voice and talent. The story ideas she could not handle, like "The Ice Palace," triggered Scott's long-dormant talent for popular writing, and he worked up the story himself.

For a time Zelda worked this vein of inspiration with what seemed a casual approach to the metier. Some of the stories were entirely of her own conception, several were edited by Scott or suggested by him; in one or two instances they collaborated on a story: closer as joint authors of magazine fiction than they had become as man and wife. At one time Scott had ransacked Zelda's diaries and letters, and especially her conversational remarks, for story and novel material; now that Zelda was engaged in writing of her own, there was the touchy matter of by-line to consider. Sometimes they both signed the collaborative efforts, but often only Scott's name appeared for publication, since his name was known to the reading public and would draw higher fees. With apparent indifference, Zelda allowed Scott to decide which name to use. At first Scott was rather proud of Zelda's stories: "they have a strange haunting and evocative quality that is absolutely new."

Zelda was an amateur, but with certain literary gifts. Essentially a writer of background and contemporary attitudes, she could create place and mood rather than tell a story of believable people, though some of her story-lines were clever in the manner of Scott's own tales of hip flasks and flappers. Of the women in Zelda's stories, Nancy Milford said, "they suffer from a boredom of the spirit." Zelda was herself suffering a spiritual malaise at the time, though far more profound than the boredom expressed by her characters.

Scott had long nagged her about the lack of direction or discipline in her life, but now that he was drying up as a writer of popular fiction, Zelda's production of slick fiction was an alarming contrast to his own lack of direction and discipline. His earlier pride in her endeavors began to sour, but he could hardly complain about her productivity. He was now sending the stories to Harold Ober, his agent, and the Fitzgeralds were beginning to depend upon the sales. In the winter of 1928–29 Zelda completed a series of stories for *College Humor,* though Scott signed his name to many of them: he maintained that the stories and articles Zelda wrote were inevitably drawn from "their common store of material." (Zelda Fitzgerald's "The Girl with Talent" and her "The Girl the Prince Liked" were simply, he said, lifted from his notebooks.) If both Scott and Zelda signed as authors, Ober could sell the stories for as much as $1,000; if Zelda's name stood alone, the price dropped to $500. The *Saturday Evening Post* wanted to publish "A Millionaire's Girl" but did not even want Zelda's name on the story: the price was $5,000, and the story was credited to Scott.

Zelda expressed no regret or complaint at Scott's expropriation of her stories under his own by-line. The stories were written in haste, then hastily turned over to Scott: the work meant money in the bank, a means to pay for life in Paris, to provide dance lessons for Scottie. As a child, Zelda had studied ballet, but the classes brought on the first of her asthma attacks. She did not want her daughter "to be a genius," but she thought now was the time to introduce Scottie to the ballet.

Diaghilev's Ballets Russes was the new and exciting cultural phenomenon in Paris, and Zelda had been introduced to the spectacle by a performance of *La Chatte* in the company of Gerald and Sara Murphy, who knew many of the dancers and could recommend Madame Lubov Egorova as Scottie's teacher: Madame Egorova had taught their own daughter, Honoria. Zelda decided to take lessons from "Madame" as well, perhaps to encourage Scottie; but Scottie's interest soon lagged and Zelda, at age twenty-nine, continued dance practice with an uncharacteristic intensity. She practiced with devotion and rigor, sometimes eight and nine hours a day, yet managed betweentimes to produce the stories Scott was sending to Ober. She installed a practice barre with mirrors in the apartment. The dance had grown beyond her interest in writing: Zelda did not feel divided between two demanding artistic endeavors, because only one was art for her. She had come to believe that ballet was the meaningful center of her life, the career she had long denied she wanted, the discipline Scott insisted she lacked.

It gave Zelda special pride to be able to buy flowers for Madame Lubov with money she had earned herself. She added a collection of tutus to the Trunk for the glittering prospect ahead: the dance had become a pursuit worthy of all the empty wasted years gone by. Zelda was transformed with the new outlook, her changed behavior a mystery beyond Scott's easy solutions.

A visiting friend remarked to Scottie: "What a lovely child."

"She's *not* a lovely child," Zelda snapped. "Look!" She took hold of Scottie's leg and raised it to an awkward ballet pose. "Look how terrible she is!"

When the friend left, Scott launched a quarrel that lasted for the rest of the day. Later he reflected, "I didn't realize she was ill. How could I have been so blind?"

Before Mademoiselle took her to the Luxembourg Gardens each day, Scottie paused to examine her parents' garbage can, the gift she had given them at Christmas, to see what scraps of their disorder they might have thrown out—if anything.

vii

Madame Lubov Egorova, the princesse Troubetskoy, had been *première danseuse* with Diaghilev's Ballets Russes; the Murphys had met her when they volunteered to help the insolvent ballet company survive by painting the drop curtains and flats for *Pulcinella.* Gerald had originally recommended Madame Egorova to Zelda as "a better teacher than a dancer," and in any case a dancer past the age of performance. Her studio was on the rue Caumartin around the corner from the Olympia Music Hall, and shared a courtyard with the Olympia's stage entrance, an animated *allée* where the two theatrical worlds crossed: Zelda could feel the thrill of stage life emanating from that narrow passageway. Gerald Murphy was considering Scottie's ballet training only, and was soon astonished to discover how serious was Zelda's involvement with the dance, and he was altogether unprepared for her driven intensity at practice. Eight daily hours of dance was hardly enough, and if Zelda missed a day of practice she was too distraught to appear in the street. He was dismayed to think of his part in what was to become Zelda's unnerving obsession: what would have served as an admirable pastime and escape from her restlessness had become a troubling midlife fetish. "She wanted," Gerald realized, "to dance for the world."

To Zelda, "Madame" was the soul of Russia—"The Russians!" she wrote, "suckled on a gallant generosity and weaned on the bread of revolution, they haunt Paris!" Madame Egorova became her icon figure, the spirit of the arts concentrated in a single inspiring personage. Madame's relative poverty—so in contrast to the means and money available to the Fitzgeralds—inspired Zelda all the more. She wanted to be like Madame even to sharing her deprivations, thus to acquire an artistic purity exemplified by her teacher. Zelda could not renounce her own high standard of living (Scott's earning power was not hers to renounce), but she could at least deny herself the comfort, waste, and indolence the money represented. What income she dredged from magazine writing, working in bursts of forced overtime, would serve as sacrificial payment of her ballet lessons. Also, she arranged with the Marché aux Fleurs on the quai de Corse to deliver bouquets of white gardenias to Madame daily, paid out of her own earnings, the white flowers a symbol of her teacher's pure spirit.

Scott had his heroes—James Joyce, Gerald Murphy, even Hemingway for certain qualities—and wanted to be like them, but Zelda not only aspired to the qualities of her role model, she directed all thought and energy to that end. No one had ever imagined Zelda as a fanatic acolyte, striving to make herself into a dancer of the first rank—least of all Scott. He was of a divided mind about his wife's late-blooming ambitions, at first approving of what appeared to be a positive transformation, then troubled by the consequent removal of Zelda from his sphere. Zelda saw in his attitude a latent jealousy: "You did not like it," she later reminded him, "when you saw it made me happy."

No, he did not like Zelda's total absorption in an art that completely escaped his appreciation or comprehension. There was a distance between them now that not even their bitter and hysterical fights had ever brought about, and the jealousy Zelda perceived in him had to do with her love for the Russian teacher who was now the largest influence in her life. Zelda was so passionately drawn to her teacher she had even come to Scott with the confession that she feared she was falling perversely in love with Madame. What was happening to her? In this instance Scott was supportive; he reassured her "she was not that way." Zelda's all-consuming passion, he realized, was more complicated than that.

Later, when Zelda wrote *Save Me the Waltz,* she struggled with her delayed insights in the characterization of Alabama, who had also taken up ballet in Paris: "She would drive the devils that had driven her—that, in proving herself, she would achieve that peace she imagined went only in surety of one's self—she would be able, through the medium of dance, to command her emotions, to summon love or pity or happiness at will, having provided a channel through which they might flow." In the ballet studio, and in her own studio at home, Zelda had at last, or so she thought, found a way to confound her personal demons; like Alabama, "She drove herself mercilously" as a way of dancing her devils to exhaustion.

When Scott was puzzling over the deeper consequences of Zelda's current state of mind, he complained of the inconveniences like the sweat-smelly worktights draped over the chairs in their bedroom. He saw the practice sessions as farcical waste. His visiting cousin, Cecelia Taylor, observed Zelda at the barre, and her report confirmed Scott's private misgivings: Zelda appeared to be hypnotized by her practice music, dancing without letup like the doomed compulsive dancer in *The Red Shoes*—and since Cecelia herself had studied dance, Scott accepted her snap verdict of Zelda as "a dreadful dancer." (Cecelia confronted Zelda privately, perplexed at Zelda's ambition to be a dancer, since "You already have a husband.") Scott complained to "Ceci" that the music Zelda practiced to, *The March of the Wooden Soldiers,* was engraved on every organ he possessed.

Since the Murphys were the original introduction to Madame

Egorova, they felt obliged to attend Zelda's first dance recital at the studio, a large bare room equipped only with a piano, a phonograph, and rows of hard chairs. The tall mirrors behind the barre, and the uptilted angle of the stage (the Murphys sat in the front row), only distorted an awkward performance all the more. It was evident to Gerald and Sara that Zelda was straining beyond her powers for a grace she did not possess. "One held one's breath until it was over," said Gerald.

Perhaps for the first time, Zelda was deeply shocked by Scott's behavior. She had always been coolly indulgent of his pratfalls in public, but the dance studio was Zelda's own shrine, and Scott lay sprawled boorishly before her icon. He was to have picked up Zelda after her class, but he arrived early, in an advanced state of intoxication, and climbed merrily up the stairs to the studio while the class was in session, introduced himself to Madame Egorova, then collapsed at her feet.

To make up for this first disastrous impression on Madame, the Fitzgeralds invited her to lunch at the George V. Zelda feared that the sumptuous luncheon might further dismay her teacher by emphasizing the contrast in their circumstances—Zelda had invited Madame on her own to a simple Russian cabaret, and filled her champagne glass with daisies—but Madame Egorova, the former princesse Troubetskoy after all, was regally *chez elle* in the George V dining room. Here was a reminder of her former priveleged life, swept away by the Bolshevik Revolution of 1917. Most of the titled White Russians had fled to Paris, their rubles valueless in French francs, reduced to commonplace employment: princes served as maîtres d'hôtel or drove taxicabs, princesses sewed for couturier houses, became governesses, or taught, like Princess Troubetskoy, the arts they had acquired before the Revolution.

What did surprise Zelda was Madame's coquettish response to Scott's gallantries. Scott could assume a calculated charm, especially with elderly women, a "trick of the heart" Zelda knew all too well. To her dismay, Madame became flirtatious in turn to Scott's playful and flattering attentions. As far as Zelda was concerned, the luncheon had completely shifted from her intent to render homage to her teacher; the party had become one of Scott's performances, and Madame had succumbed to his charm. As Scott and Madame lightheartedly clinked their flutes of champagne together and an animated contingent of obsequious waiters came bearing salvers of pâté, saumon, and sole *à la Russe,* Zelda twisted her napkin wondering why she had come.

Later, in private, Scott sought Madame's frank assessment of Zelda's potential as a professional dancer. He was not surprised at her report.

"Madame, *votre femme,* has begun the study of dance far too late. She is devoted to the ballet, and determined—which counts for much—but . . . she will never become, as she so ardently hopes, a *première danseuse.* Not possible at her age, at her stage of development. However, as a member of the corps de ballet . . . and there are small roles she might dance, in secondary companies, though not possible at l'Opéra, not possible at the principal ballet companies she hopes to join."

If Zelda had the least inkling of Madame's discouraging opinion she did not truly believe its negative prediction. ("I can do anything exactly as I please," she once told Scott. "Anything! I can sleep when I'm awake if I want to!") Zelda was elated over the visit of a delegation of agents to Madame Egorova's studio, for they especially scrutinized Zelda's sample performance. In the wake of Josephine Baker's incredible success, American dancers had become popular with Parisian audiences, and the agents had come from the Folies-Bergère looking for shimmy dancers—nevertheless, Zelda convinced herself the men represented the Ballets Russes.

At another tête-à-tête with Scott, Madame Egorova said, "I am very fond of Madame, *votre femme.* She has perhaps suffered an illness?"

None that he knew of, Scott replied.

Madame then told of a visit to the Fitzgerald apartment, invited there to tea by Zelda. In the course of this visit, Zelda's voice and facial expression shifted in ways difficult to explain or describe: Madame hardly recognized her pupil. Suddenly Zelda was babbling in a tumble of meaningless words and phrases, a desperate and disconnected monologue in English, a language Madame could not follow. Zelda had then thrown herself at her teacher's feet and clung to her legs like a frightened child. With some difficulty and considerable embarrassment, Madame managed to disengage herself. With a sharp rebuke she restored Zelda to some semblance of control.

"Has she not, Monsieur, appeared to you . . . ill?"

In Paris, before I realized that I was sick, there was new significance to everything: stations and streets and façades of buildings—colors were indefinite, part of the air, and not restricted by the lines that encompassed them and lines were free of the masses they held. There was music that beat behind my forehead and other music that fell into my stomach from a high parabola. . . .

Scott no longer complained of the disarray of dance workclothes in their bedroom: Zelda was now sleeping with her feet through the bars of the iron bed, "her toes," as she said of Alabama, "glued outward" to improve her turn-out. She registered wildly unpredictable mood swings and extreme agitation as if she were some human Richter scale for disturbances beyond the nervous system—alternating phases of inappropriate laughter, then brooding suspicion. Zelda's responses had always been original, spontaneous and unpredictable, a mystery to her friends and a delight to Scott, but now it was hard to fathom her remarks.

She once turned to Gerald Murphy and offered in profound confidence: "Gerald, don't you think Al Jolson is greater than Jesus?"

Gerald could only think Zelda was trying out another of her provocative non sequiturs. In the climate of the stock-market crash on Wall Street—which had its cataclysmic effect in Paris—it was hard to discern the dangerously bizarre from the common agitation. The American colony in general was behaving in unpredictable fashion, the mood having swung from Emile Coué's formula: "Every day in every way I am becoming better and better," to a spirit of depression and despair. The Fitzgeralds were very little affected, financially, by the Wall Street crash since Scott had never managed to put aside even a fraction of his earnings or to invest in securities. But the grim mood of the new year, 1930, had its metaphysical effect. Scott and Zelda continued on in Paris as if Black Tuesday had never occurred, yet knowing in ways other than stock-market news that their glorious spendthrift years, the Roaring Twenties, had come to a disastrous end.

A dancer could not afford the least show of extra flesh, so Zelda fell into an anorectic pattern of eating: by New Year's Eve she had lost fifteen pounds. Her cheeks were sunken, the bones of her fine face were now pronounced as if Rebecca West's unfair reference to Zelda's "craggy homeliness" as a bride had been a prediction of the Zelda a decade later. Her pallor was ghostly, all the more obvious from the lip rouge and kohl of the dancer's makeup she wore whenever she went out, and she was reluctant to go out, to go anywhere but to Madame Egorova's studion on the rue Caumartin.

The Fitzgeralds invited Morley and Loretto Callaghan to Les Trianons, James Joyce's favorite restaurant, opposite the Gare Montparnasse. Callaghan, a young Canadian writer, hoped to be introduced to the great James Joyce, or at least to catch a glimpse of the Irish master. Joyce came so often to les Trianons, his dining there was almost a ritual, but he did not appear that night. Scott could no longer force a facade of buoyancy and extrovert fun; he had been depressed over his inability to do any writing on his novel *The World's Fair,* so the dinner became a solemn and disappointing occasion.

While the two writers kept watching the door for Joyce's anticipated appearance, Zelda was alternately silent or agitated. "What will we do next?" she kept asking, then, "Let's all go roller-skating," she said without a smile, her Indian eyes watching each of them in turn.

"You're tired," Scott informed her.

"Not too tired to skate. Let's all roller-skate together."

Again Scott told her she was tired and should be in bed. He went across the street to the train-station queue for a taxi. When the cab came Zelda meekly wished the Callaghans goodnight, like a polite little girl before being sent off to bed. Then Zelda went home alone.

Morley asked Scott what the trouble was, and Scott said that Zelda was studying ballet and worked far too hard at it.

"Why does she do it?"

"She wants to have something of her own, be something herself."

By the spring of 1930 Scott knew that Zelda would find no salvation in dancing, or in anything else. She had become paranoid about what people whispered behind her back, what "Scott's friends" were saying about her; then, when she reported hearing messages carried to her by doves in the bird market, Scott could no longer trust her to wander about Paris alone.

In 1920, their first week in Paris, the Fitzgeralds had visited Malmaison to tour the château where Josephine Bonaparte had languished for the remaining years of her life after the divorce from Napoléon. Now they went back, to the clinic at Malmaison, the most reputable psychiatric facility in the vicinity of Paris (Paul Deschanel, the president of France, was under treatment there at the time the Fitzgeralds first visited the suburb). Zelda was admitted for treatment, apparently under her own volition, though slightly intoxicated and flirting theatrically with the admissions doctor. One week later she abruptly checked herself out of the hospital against the advice of her psychiatrist.

During the week Zelda was at Malmaison, Scott had taken the untenanted Murphy apartment on the rue Pergolèse, and alone, drifted into the downward spiral of incessant partying again. On the very evening Zelda returned unexpectedly from the hospital, Scott was hosting a boozy evening at the Murphy flat. The disordered apartment had been the setting for more than that night's party; Zelda had returned to join a new series of desperate nights, random guests, and meaningless celebration. It was as if she had never been away for treatment. Within three weeks Zelda's condition was compounded by a psychosomatic eczema, attacks of asthma, and recurrent delirium.

"What role does your child play in your life?" the doctor asked.

"That is done now. I want to do something else."

In a letter of reminiscence to Scott, Zelda wrote: "Our ride to Switzerland was very sad . . . I was completely insane and made a decision: to abandon the ballet and live quietly with my husband. I had wanted to destroy the picture of Egorova I had lived with for four years and give away my tous-tous and the suitcase full of shoes and free my mind from the thing."

Zelda agreed to enter Les Rives des Prangins, on Lake Geneva in Switzerland. Her condition was diagnosed as acute schizophrenia, a term only recently invented by Dr. Paul Eugen Bleuler, her consulting psychiatrist. The prognosis was clouded, hope of recovery slight.

Zelda's breakdown, confinement, and treatment were the basis for Nicole Diver's schizophrenia in *Tender Is the Night.* Scott had his theme for the novel at last, but at a terrible price. Even Zelda's mysterious eczema was described, in the symptoms of an unnamed and unknown female patient who mercifully dies after days and nights of constant torture. Nicole Diver recovers from her illness, and there is the suggestion of a new and happy life for her apart from her husband. No such happy ending was reserved for Zelda.

While still at Prangins, Zelda wrote long letters to Scott, with flashes of insight about her condition—she would never be a whole person again—intermingled with passages of recollection:

> Was it fun in Paris? Who did you see there and was the Madeleine pink at five o'clock and did the fountains fall with hollow delicacy into the framing of space in the Place de la Concorde, and did the blue creep out from behind the Colonades of the rue de Rivoli through the grill of the Tuileries and was the Louvre gray and metallic in the sun and did the trees hang brooding over the cafés and were there lights at night and the click of saucers and the auto horns that play de Bussey—
>
> I *love* Paris. How was it?

Paul Colin's famous kiosk poster, heralding Josephine Baker's arrival in Paris with *La Revue Nègre,* 1925. *(Bibliothèque Nationale,* Paris, courtesy of poster archives, Posters, Please, Inc., New York)

V

Josephine Baker

1906–1975

I'm not immoral. I'm just natural.

The poster was a stylized eye-catching caricature of three jazz-time Negroes, cocked hat, conked hair, and cartoon rows of teeth like piano keys. In the tradition if not the style of a Toulouse-Lautrec lithograph that appeared on these same street-corner kiosks a quarter of a century before, the poster for *La Revue Nègre* titillated the passer-by, then lingered as provocative after-image. The model for the wide-eyed sassy dancer was the star of the black troupe from America playing at the Théâtre des Champs-Elysées: she was all lips and hips in this blatantly primitive rendition of her persona—but the primitive was only one of the essences of Josephine Baker.

As far as Parisians were concerned, Paul Colin's striking poster for *La Revue Nègre* broadcast merely another *divertissement,* an entertainment somewhere between the Ballets Russes and the Cirque Médrano, or perhaps as distracting as a six-day bicycle race at the Vélodrome. It was 1925, the year of the International Exhibition of Decorative Arts, when Art Déco replaced Art Nouveau—since nothing remained *nouveau* for long in Paris—a style that attracted the multitudes to the spectacle of exhibits along the quais between the pont Alexandre III and the pont d'Alma. Jaded Parisians had already been introduced to *surréalisme* that year; first by the writings of André Breton, then at the first group show of Paul Klee, Hans Arp, and Miró at the Galerie Pierre—dreamscapes and Freudian artifacts after the shock waves of *impressionisme* had subsided, *cubisme* and *fauvisme* had faded, and finally the insolence of Dada had jolted French sensibilities. The central attractions of Paris by night were the Art Déco illuminations: Lalique glasswork fountains designed as crystal chandeliers, waterspray pumped from the Seine lit in color by the sensational new effect known as *néon.* Neon, too, illuminated the Eiffel Tower, for André Citroën had managed to obtain permission for CITROEN to appear in huge letters along the length of the tower, introducing the age of *publicité* with one master stroke. It was a fortuitous time for publicity's star, Josephine Baker, to arrive on the scene.

The preamble to a presentation of black vaudeville in Paris was the African Pavilion at the Arts Déco exposition, especially the displays of strange and affecting African sculpture. Pablo Picasso had already experimented with the Negro theme and motif when he painted his Dadaesque parody of Manet's *Olympia,* the reclining odalisque made black; now the catalyst exhibit of African artifacts—equal to the effect of the Japanese print exhibit on the Impressionists—confirmed his earlier inspiration from tribal masks for the seminal work, *Les Demoiselles d'Avignon.* African art and the theme of negritude so captured the Parisian psyche that another painter, Fernand Léger, returned from the African Pavilion and, rightly interpreting the climate of excitement, passed on his revelation to the impresario André Daven, whose half-filled Théâtre des Champs-Elysées was on the verge of bankruptcy.

"Give them Negroes," advised Léger. "Only Negroes can excite Paris."

Daven was at the station to meet the troupe of blacks imported from the United States: "Out spilled a little world," he recalled. The spill was a riot of color and animation: polka dot and bright stripes; black women were actually dancing along the quai of the Gare St.-Lazare, gesticulating arms waving through the train windows at startled Parisian commuters, one pair of arms extending a brassy trumpet trumpeting a circus fanfare to workaday Paris. The talk was mumbo-jumbo to Daven, who thought he knew English, American jive talk that could have been an African dialect half-sung half-shouted between explosions of raucous laughter and the drumbeat of suitcases hitting the platform. A motley crew of dancers and mixed chorus tumbled out of the boat-train compartments flashing their ivory smiles, glad-handing their greeter, easy in their astonishing costumes. *Comme c'était vif!*—how *alive* it was: the color and sound of a burst of *feu d'artifice* under the sooty gray glass panels of the station roof.

One member of the troupe immediately caught Daven's eye, a figure apart. She was a slim teenager lighter-colored than the others, a mulatto one shade darker than honey, standing with the storklike awkwardness of her young years that nevertheless implied a special grace, an engaging presence. Her eyes were open as wide as they would go, and she was talking to herself: through the laughter and tumult, Daven heard her say, "So this is Paris."

"Yes," said Daven, "this is Paris."

Immediately he bused the troupe and their baggage to the place they would feel most at home, his Théâtre des Champs-Elysées, from whose roof Josephine Baker, the numbed and disoriented newcomer, could see for the first time the essential symbol of the city itself, the Eiffel Tower. The theatre building was not on the Champs-Elysées as its name suggested, but several blocks from that lively thoroughfare, on the sedate and fashionable avenue Montaigne. Significantly, the bas-reliefs representing the muses of dance were modeled from the classic form of an earlier Parisian favorite and Josephine Baker's predecessor at that theatre, Isadora Duncan.

Initial word-of-mouth publicity for *La Revue Nègre* was a daily open-air rehearsal on the Art Nouveau theatre's flat roof in open view of the windows across avenue Montaigne, at the crosspoint of the place d'Alma and the decorated quais of the Art Déco exposition.

The first-night audience included theatre buffs, critics, authors, artists, and tastemakers—Fernand Léger (of course, the show had been his idea), Jean Cocteau, Colette, Darius Milhaud, the princesse Murat, Mistinguette (current star of the Folies-Bergère, assessing the competition), Gerald and Sara Murphy, and Janet Flanner, who was writing her "Letters from Paris," under the pen name Genêt, about just such personalities as Josephine Baker and events like *La Revue Nègre* for *The New Yorker*—a mix of art, aristocracy, and a list of celebrities known as *le tout Paris.*

Versions of the opening-night performance differed from report to report, but the composite impression was one of fast-change Dixieland and Harlem tableaux in music-hall format; in fact, *La Revue Nègre* was just that, an all-black revue following a series of music-hall turns, Japanese acrobats, and Tara Bey, a fakir who was pierced by the knives and hatpins that sprinkled his white robes with blood, but who uttered no outcry. (At the end of his act, when the house lights dimmed, Tara Bey cleaned himself of gore and slipped quietly into the audience for the real show.)

The curtain-raiser was a crowded riverboat scene, the wharf packed with cotton bales against a backdrop designed by Mexican muralist Miguel Covarrubias and Frenchman Paul Colin imagining the American South for a Parisian audience. Instead of the original tap-dance routine that attracted so much attention when rehearsed on the theatre roof, the entire troupe swung into a Charleston, jazz band onstage, the dancers bandannaed and barefoot, bursting with an exuberance unfamiliar to French sensibilities. Choreographer Jacques Charles had wisely opened with the Charleston, which was a new excitement to the French, instead of the *claquettes* (tap dancing) he considered noisy and graceless—for Parisians from that night on decided to dance *le Char-less-ton* themselves: the Revue cast became dance instructors, and other dancers like Orrea Waskae (specialist in the Black Bottom) or Bricktop or the Charleston Boys were in demand to demonstrate the free-swinging hip twist and un-French knee bend and "fan" of thighs.

According to Jacques Charles, the show itself could not be allowed a moment's lag after the first engaging burst of color and jazz: the sharp upbeat pace was one of the choreographer's shrewdest contributions to the otherwise essentially American ensemble. Charles staged a sequence of fast-moving shifts of scene with teasing glimpses of Josephine Baker flashing in and popping out of dance turns as a cross-eyed ragamuffin minstrel or a rubber-legged waif in tatterdemalion. The only let up in the animation was a subdued blues number by Maude de Forrest—originally billed as star of the show—singing the solos Josephine Baker had always wanted to sing but could never master. The blues were out of sync with the frenetic style of the revue, and de Forrest was overwhelmed by the delirium of jazz band and dance, upstaged finally by Josephine's comic gifts and her extraordinary performance in the finale.

After the kaleidoscopic effect thus far, Jacques Charles intended to close with the unexpected and *très sauvage.* The curtain opened on the solitary clarinet played by Sidney Bechet against a backdrop of surreal Manhattan skyline. A trumpet fanfare broke through the mellow clarinet melody as Josephine Baker was borne onstage, upside down, on the back of the troupe's giant Joe Alex. She was wearing a girdle of feathers, but the effect so much a chimera of nudity that Janet Flanner would remember only the fluff of a single feather—and not, as others mistakenly recalled, the suggestive sheath of bananas that later became the Baker motif. Joe Alex circled the stage with his human cargo, than swung and lowered the birdlike burden to the stage as Bechet's snakecharmer melody turned sinuously suggestive. Josephine Baker's hair was cropped and lathered flat against her skull; she slithered down the length of her muscled transport onto all fours, her barely feathered derrière cantilevered in the air; then, to the accompaniment of clarinet and drums, she weaved and coiled around the great planted trunks of her partner's legs in a ritual of serpentine coupling.

When the shock effect subsided, a shrill whistling from one part of the audience began. Members of the cast of *La Revue Nègre* had played the black vaudeville circuit, where raucous whistling was an extension of applause: in France the *sifflet* was the equivalent of hissing or booing. Nevertheless, real applause was generously mixed with the whistling, and eventually the clapping hands overcame the outraged whistlers. This mixed chorus of audience reaction was typical of the first-night near riot any new and original spectacle provoked. The disapproving and insulted made their noisy exit down the aisles while the enthusiastic majority applauded for more. With its closing number, *La Revue Nègre* had aroused the same uproar as the demonstrations at the Dadaist lectures, the George Antheil concert, the opening night of Stravinsky's ballet *The Rite of Spring.*

The beat became frenzied, and Josephine twisted and shook at the same accelerated beat with the speed (noted by at least two critics) "of a hummingbird." Her movements however swift were so fluid the music appeared to originate from the dancer herself—or so her witnesses and fans believed. In consensus, those who remained throughout Josephine Baker's initial performance saw the dance as stylized primitive art that did not breach the thin line between erotic and pornographic. Without the dancer's natural grace, instinctive control, and extraordinary presence, the spectacle would have deteriorated into the very Pigalle-cellar performance the *siffleurs* insisted it was. The last great roll of applause was said to have so frightened Josephine she ran backstage in tears; but it was not so—the dancer was as brash and cocky as her dance. If she wept, they were tears of knowing, without knowing the term, she had created a *succès de scandale.*

The American colony in Paris made up a large and faithful audience; Sara and Gerald Murphy were among the early fans, and Gerald said of the show: "You'd go to each night's performance and find everybody else there too." Expatriates in France who would not have attended the same show on Broadway were caught up in the French spirit of revelry and release this black production inspired. Maria Jolas (co-founder of the avant-garde magazine *transition*) was one of the few dissenters, and summed up the Josephine Baker attraction as: "She just wiggled her fanny and all the French fell in love with her." Her report was based on second-hand information, for she refused to see the show; also, her remark failed to take into account the many Americans who fell in love with Josephine, a rare coalescence of Franco-American tastes. The prevailing sentiment of the colony was expressed by Anita Loos (author of *Gentlemen Prefer Blondes*), who declared that Josephine had triumphed with her "witty rear end."

Part of the special cachet and appeal of black vaudeville to Americans was that *La Revue* was being presented in Paris. By the second week the novelty should have worn off, but the show had not: beyond the most optimistic expectations of André Daven and Caroline Dudley, the "music hall," as it was temporarily referred to in English, was packed nightly. At the fever height of the twenties, *La Revue Nègre* became the quintessential spectacle—and Josephine Baker the phenomenon—only Paris could have sustained after all else.

ii

"Why do you want me so bad for this show?" asked Josephine.

"Because you're beautiful and chic," said Caroline Dudley, "and you can dance."

Caroline Dudley had spotted Josephine Baker at the end of a chorus line in an all-black revue at the Plantation, a New York nightclub at 50th and Broadway: "She stood out like an exclamation point." Josephine was making $150 a week as a dancer who did an occasional cross-eyed specialty number, or fill-in for the star Ethel Waters. Waters was Josephine Baker's idol, whose blues style she yearned to duplicate, but Waters assessed the neophyte's singing voice as far too thin to "throw the velvet" and deliver the poignancy of the blues; still Josephine did have a flair for upstaging a chorus line, and a great comic sense. Ethel Waters filled out Josephine's dossier with the left-handed compliment, "She could also play the trombone."

Caroline Dudley was not interested in the chorus girl's voice or slapstick blackface routine: what she wanted was a lithe and electric solo dancer for a show she was putting together, a black vaudeville revue she had proposed to André Daven in Paris. Dudley, a wealthy New Yorker with a dilettante's interest in black music and dance, had been to see Daven in Paris not long after Fernand Léger first advanced the same proposal to the troubled owner of the Théâtre des Champs-Elysées.

Dudley's marriage to a foreign service officer was at an unhappy stage and she wanted some distraction from her domestic crisis: she wanted to create a project of her own, an ensemble of Negro music and dance, an enterprise she believed would flower in France rather than in the Harlem and Broadway clubs, where black entertainers had caught on but were being exploited as blatantly as in the segregated South. Her husband went along with the idea of a black revue, and even volunteered financial backing for the show, but his willing cooperation on a theatrical production did not save their marriage. Dudley was a passionate Francophile; she had lived in Paris and wanted to live there again—and she wanted to take Josephine Baker with her. She intended to assist at the debut: to introduce the comic and dancer to a public that had never seen anything like her.

Convincing Josephine Baker to leave New York—convincing Josephine Baker to do anything she had not decided on her own—was more challenge than Caroline Dudley had anticipated.

"I'm not figuring on Paris right now."

But Caroline Dudley sensed the hesitation in Josephine's voice; she played on that wavering note. She had picked up enough impressions of the dancer's early life to understand that Josephine had been rejected by her own mother, farmed out as a drudge and abused by her employers, "sent off" from home so often she truly felt herself a motherless child. Josephine was susceptible to the persuasion of a mother figure, and the thirty-five-year-old Dudley sensed she might play the role of mother to this rootless and talented waif.

When the owner of the Plantation Club learned of Dudley's campaign to take Josephine off to France, he offered to double the dancer's salary to $300 a week. Josephine liked being on this kind of auction block, and when Caroline Dudley bid the salary up to $500 a week, Josephine began to mull over the tales she had heard from black entertainers about moving on to Europe where fame and money awaited. But of course she had heard that kind of talk before. On the black vaudeville T.O.B.A. circuit ("Tough on Black Asses") she had traveled south on such sugar promise, and was stranded there in a hotel room in New Orleans sleeping three-to-a-bed with Voodoo Jones and his wife Doll. The U.S. Navy had closed down notorious Storyville, the red-light district that had spawned a flourishing colony of jazz musicians, the quarter in fact where jazz was born. Josephine's first real chorus-line job was with the Dixie Steppers, but that job collapsed—the Dixie Steppers disbanded in New Orleans—and when her roommate Doll left Voodoo for a sado-masochistic dwarf, Josephine walked out on the whole downbeat scene with enough of her pittance dance pay for a bus ticket back to St. Louis.

Meanwhile Caroline Dudley outlined another enticement: she could assure Josephine that her skin color would be no bar to the things she wanted out of life—the French, on the contrary, would love her for *being* black.

"I've heard tell," replied Josephine. "I believe that when I see it."

Throughout their tedious negotiations Dudley would have a rough time convincing Josephine Baker to leave the United States, all she knew of the world, but that world—the bleak underside of it—was hers. She'd be all alone in a foreign place where she didn't know the talk and wouldn't have a soul to talk to anyway. Dudley assured her that she would watch out for her. Josephine wanted to take her baby sister with her, whose eye had been clawed out by a dog. Impossible, said Dudley; but Josephine's husband could go along, if they could find a place for him in the show. Willie?—the only part of Willie she wanted at the moment was his name, Baker. A justice of the peace in New Jersey had officiated at the marriage of Josephine Martin

(Martin was her stepfather's name) and William Howard Baker when Josephine was only fifteen. They had lived together in a theatrical roominghouse called Mom's Charlestons in Philadelphia: Josephine's mother-in-law was greatly upset over the marriage, since reddish-haired, light-skinned William Howard had "married down" not only to an underage show girl, but to someone who was a shade darker than himself. When last heard of, Willie was working as a Pullman porter; Josephine had not troubled herself over which direction Willie might be traveling, she now had traveling plans of her own. Paris, France?

Caroline Dudley was discovering how wary and temperamental the dancer could be: Josephine changed her mind about Paris three times in the next two days. "I'll need clothes to wear," said Josephine, and Dudley said, "I'll buy them."

When she took Josephine to a Seventh Avenue designer, her protégé selected a scarlet evening gown with deep décolleté, the kind of dress that might help her achieve the Ethel Waters look. Josephine at the time aspired to a centerstage spotlight, a solo vocalist singing the blues in a floor-length dress; Caroline Dudley had other plans for her, but allowed Josephine to have her way with the gown.

The next stop was the passport office, where Josephine would have to answer some touchy background questions and fill in the legitimate statistics.

"Name?"

"Josephine Baker."

"Born?"

"St. Louis."

"Married?"

"Yes and no."

Actually William Howard Baker was neither her first Willie, nor her first husband: the first had been Willie Wells, the man she married in her Aunt Josephine Cooper's living room—a fancy enough wedding for the time and circumstances, roast pork dinner with baked macaroni: Josephine was thirteen years old and pregnant, wearing her dream gown, floor length and bridal white. When Caroline Dudley inquired about her first husband and first pregnancy, Josephine replied, "Willie? I hardly stayed with the man overnight. I broke a bottle over his head defending myself."

The grim hardscrabble life of East St. Louis, the "scum pond" of Josephine's young life, did not reckon with informal or official scrutiny of lovers and husbands and pregnancies unaccounted for. Survival was the only statistic worthy of record, and on that record Josephine was simply the illegitimate child of Carrie McDonald, part Appalachee Indian, and Eddie Carson, who claimed Creole and "Spinach" blood. Later she was adopted—no legal paperwork involved, but kept on as family—by her mother's new husband, Arthur Martin. By adoption she acquired brothers and sisters, all sleeping together, feet-to-nose along the crude bedding on the floor. The walls of the Martin house were papered with newsprint to keep out the wind that swept across the Mississippi, and Josephine wrapped her feet in newspapers in winter. Rats and bedbugs shared the living quarters, and at first Josephine was happy to be "sent off" from the Martin hovel to other lodgings. But she found herself the child slave of a white woman named Mrs. Keiser, with dawn-to-dark housekeeping chores, a Cinderella existence that fed her princess dreams—and ended only when Mrs. Keiser plunged the child's hand into boiling water when she caught Josephine using too much soap in the wash. The child fainted; a neighbor woman heard her screams, and Josephine regained consciousness in a hospital. Then Carrie kept her at home for a spell of cluttered family warmth, however miserable and degraded.

One night in July 1917, Josephine's mother jerked her out of the crowded bed, hustling the family out of the house after midnight to flee to the other side of the river. On the rumor that a white woman had been raped by blacks, white mobs had overrun the black ghetto of East St. Louis. Josephine was only eleven, terrified, but mindful of survival, and of her "babies," two puppies she had found half dead in a garbage can. She smuggled them with her to the Red Cross relief center. In a day and night of rape and pillage and burning, thirty-nine blacks and nine whites were killed, a ghetto of squatter shacks and boxcar homes burned out.

A dollar was hard to come by in East St. Louis, but Josephine earned her first with Medicine Man's decrepit wagon show, dancing between the old fraud's spiels, helping to sell Indian herb laxatives and suspect rejuvenators. She had watched her mother dance—when Carrie had time for such foolishness, before taking in laundry for a living—with a glass of water balanced on her head and never spill a drop. Josephine would dance for picnics, fish-fries, revival meetings, anywhere and whenever. At the Holy Roller church, Josephine outperformed the hysteric saved rolling down the sawdust aisles, yet her agitation was special, a hint of controlled grace coming along, coming along.

At fourteen she talked her way into a first professional job with the Dixie Steppers, wearing a hand-me-down costume too big for her thin frame. She looked like a little girl wearing her mother's long dress, and was laughed at when she tangled in its folds and tripped on the hem falling flat onstage—but Josephine turned the pratfall to comic use: she crossed her eyes and crawled upright with deliberate gangling awkwardness, playing the mishap for laughs. She earned her first solo applause when she topped off her routine with a sassy bump and grind; every gesture from then on was calculated intent. "Minute she hit the stage," said the stage manager, "she arched her back just like an animal. She'd jut that ass up like a rooster flipping his tail." The cross-eyed slapstick became her standard comic routine, the crudely staged beginnings of her later sophisticated style and engaging presence that came of a sure theatrical instinct. Most of her stage cronies thought the gifts of a comedienne would sustain the Josephine Baker career, but she had no intention of playing the clown much longer. Her idols were the stage aristocrats, the vocalists, creating the purest excitement, standing out alone in their glamour and elegance.

In 1922 the troupe traveled out of St. Louis and into the deep South in Colored cars on sooty trains or sat crowded together on laps and in the aisles at the back ends of buses passing through KKK territory, playing the back-of-town vaudeville stages, segregated audiences, admission 25¢. Audiences were hard to hold and harder to please ("You got to go some," said Sidney Bechet, "to play for black people"). Attention was turned to crying babies or distracted by kids scooting up and down the sawdust aisles, adults chatting from row to row. The main event was not Josephine Baker nor even so established a draw as Ethel Waters, who was playing the same T.O.B.A. circuit, but the drawing for door prize: the MC riffling through a bowler hat of ticket-stub numbers to announce the lucky winner of a live turkey, a smoked ham, or a gold tooth.

New Orleans was the end of the line, the last stop with Storyville, the jazz and red-light district, closed. When Josephine discovered that the sporting crowd had moved north, to Kansas City and Chicago (and to her hometown St. Louis), she skipped out on Doll and her perverse dwarf and headed north with the natural flow of jazz in that direction. In Chicago she played the South Side dance halls and illicit gin mills catering to a crowd of prostitutes, pimps, and small-time mobsters. From there she drifted East, available for any show seeking "tantalizing tans" for the chorus line, or "sepia lovelies," or "hot chocolates."

"Well, I could have been a prostitute, or I could have been somebody's maid."

When she was fifteen, she talked her way past the sixteen-year-old age limit onto the end of the chorus line in the season's hottest show, *Shuffle Along,* short one dancer for the line playing Philadelphia. Josephine was a shade darker than the "high yallers," the quadroons and octoroons, already engaged: she was café au lait, and the other dancers called her "Monkey" because of her darker color and the monkeyshines she pulled to upstage the chorus line. According to the color gauge established within black society, Josephine was just dark enough not to qualify as the next-best-color-to-white. Monkey she would be—inured to the insult and injury from both sides of the color line—and if her sisters on the chorus line played rough, she played as rough. Anyway, the chain-dance routine of the chorus was not for Josephine: she aimed for centerstage, and the affection she intended to engage was from those anonymous shadows on the other side of the footlights.

Playing Philadelphia in 1923, Josephine met her second Willie and married again. She stayed with him for about as long as the show lasted in Philadelphia: Josephine was shuffling along.

Of the troupe recruited for *La Revue Nègre*, only Sidney Bechet had been to Paris before, on tour with the Southern Syncopated Orchestra in 1919, just in time to escape the summer's wildfire of race riot. Whites were on the rampage just after World War I, in fear of the tide of "uppity niggers" and returning black servicemen looking for postwar jobs, *white* jobs, and homes of their own. When Bechet came back to America (why-oh-why ever come back, was his word to Josephine and the cast of *La Revue Nègre*), the racial divisions were worse than ever: a virulent book came out in 1920 called *The Rising Tide of Color,* as malevolent in its assault on blacks as *La France Juive* had been against Jews in the century before. Bechet praised the attitude of the color-blind French, and he especially talked up the black sanctuary in Montmartre, a jazz culture and bohemian quarter where there were "people with real talent to them, crazy to be doing." Bechet was crossing the Atlantic again, but he was going *home.*

On September 15, 1925, the cast of *La Revue Nègre* sailed to France on the *Berengaria,* with Josephine Baker aboard and feeling euphoric—new show, new setting, another tour—high on God-knew-what even though the ship was as rigidly segregated as any Southern train.

iii

Crazy-to-be-doing blacks were settling into the cheap hotels squeezed among *épiceries* and classic French brothels and nightclubs so small the dancers weaved between the tables and the bar could accommodate only ten stools. Montmartre seemed to be more black than it was, not just from the influx of American jazz musicians—"It took only two nights to see just about every Negro American in Paris," said Bricktop in 1924—but because a previous wave of blacks from Martinique and the French colonies in North Africa had also settled along the narrow terraced streets twisting up and around la Butte to Sacré-Coeur cathedral.

At the beginning of the black immigration from America came singers Gaby Delys (pronounced in French *délice,* "ravishing pleasure") and Florence Embry, the nightclub entertainers who set the style for those minuscule and intimate *boîtes de nuit* featuring black music and dance. "Opal Cooper, Sammy and Harvey White, Charlie 'Dixie' Lewis, Bobby Jones, and maybe ten other Negro musicians were the only Negro men in Paris when I got there," said Bricktop, the nightclub personality Ada Smith, who dyed her hair orange to match the freckles across her tan face. Not only musicians, but black writers from the Harlem Renaissance were making the move to Paris. Jean Toomer, who could sometimes pass for white, decided to be black in Montmartre; the poet Langston Hughes worked as a dishwasher at Bricktop's club, Le Grand Duc. The original black colony was small enough to be anonymously integrated to the local *quartier*—almost quietly so, criminal element and all. Montmartre had always been a risky neighborhood after dark: Eric Satie had carried a hammer-blackjack to and from his job as pianist at Le Chat Noir.

As soon as *La Revue Nègre* became a hit, Montmartre nightlife was in again, and lured such American performers as the Blackbirds, Whispering Jack Smith, Snakehips, the Three Pullman Porters (a trio that changed its name to Les Trois Garçons du Wagon-Lit), and Baby Darling with her new husband Mr. Legitimus. As Sidney Bechet remarked, "You couldn't walk down rue Fontaine without seeing five more colored, and you knew them all."

The most important of these to Josephine Baker was Bricktop, who had come to Paris with just as much reluctance as Josephine, but like Josephine found a warm and inviting second home in Montmartre. Bricktop was hired to play Le Grand Duc, the hip club of the colony, when Florence Embry left to be hostess and star in a new *boîte* farther along the rue Fontaine. When Bricktop took over, the tiny Grand Duc was mostly empty every night, but she brought the place back to life, less with her singing than with a forthright welcoming personality, a warmth and charm, that led the owners to change the name to Bricktop's. American celebrities, unknown in France, sought one another out at Bricktop's for the ambiance, and for being recognized or well-met by one another. Scott Fitzgerald and Cole Porter were regulars, as were Peggy Guggenheim, the Dolly Sisters, Tallulah Bankhead, and the Aga Khan. Until Bricktop's salary equaled her power of attraction, Cole Porter and Elsa Maxwell, social hostess for the well-to-do, would ask her to stage-manage their private parties, teaching the guests to Charleston for fifty-dollar tips. Cole Porter wrote the song "Miss Otis Regrets" for Bricktop and wanted no one else to sing *her* song. Cole was said to have escorted Bricktop to the Paris Opéra Ball, Bricktop dressed in the same Molyneux gown as the one worn by Princess Marina of Greece, but Bricktop denied this. "I knew my crowd and it wasn't at the Opera."

The sudden celebrity was more than the teenage Josephine could deal with at first. Descriptions of the star and her performance at the time struggled for the rational or spilled into the abstract: Josephine was "a sinuous idol that enslaves and incites mankind . . . the plastic sense of a race of sculptors come to life," declared the classic dance critic André Levinson. The critic Pierre de Regnier celebrated "the triumph of lubricity, a return to the manners of the childhood of man." e. e. cummings tried to sum up the ineffable quality of a "creature neither infrahuman nor superhuman, but somehow both; a mysterious unkillable Something, equally nonprimitive and uncivilized, or beyond time in the sense that emotion is beyond time." The mysterious unkillable Something that was Josephine Baker was going through a crisis of identity beyond the normal ego confusion of overnight stardom.

"There was one little girl who needed me a lot in the early days: Josephine Baker."

Bricktop took over from Caroline Dudley as Josephine Baker's mother hen and confidante when Josephine decided to quit *La Revue Nègre.* Paul Derval, impresario of the Folies-Bergère, had decided to lure the Black Venus (the name Colette had given Josephine Baker) to his famous music hall. Josephine knew that show-business success was often measured in salary, and Derval's offer went beyond her expectations—$5,400 a month, and star billing—but this meant *La Revue,* without its sensational star, would have to shut down.

"If you do this, Josephine," warned Caroline Dudley, "you will hurt your soul."

"Missus, I'm feeling fine."

When these negotiations transpired, *La Revue Nègre* was on tour in Germany, and Josephine announced she would have to leave the show before the end of its run: she was committed to return to Paris for fittings and rehearsals for Derval's production, *La Folie du Jour.* With decisions still hanging fire and Josephine's mood changing daily, she almost stayed on in Berlin. She had met a distinguished German stage director whose magnetism and determination (qualities of her own) impressed her as much as the large reputation she later heard about.

"My name is Max Reinhardt, and I was fortunate enough to see you in New York in *Shuffle Along.*"

Reinhardt casually mentioned his school for actors, the celebrated Deutsches Theatre, a repertory group comparable to Stanislavsky's Moscow Art Theatre in Russia. Josephine was susceptibly flattered, for Reinhardt wanted her to join his company: he saw in her enormous potential as a stage actress rather than the "feathered mannequin" Paul Derval would make of her in the Folies-Bergère. Meanwhile Derval was waiting for her return not a little anxiously when he heard the rumors of Reinhardt's offer. Josephine exulted in the most important power she had ever wielded: she allowed her three competing producers their separate hopes, moments of frustration, and intimations of bitterness each, as if dangling a trio of suitors. Josephine may have known exactly what she wanted all along, and in the end chose to return to Paris and fulfill her contract with the Folies, but not before extorting another 400 francs from Derval for each performance.

The *Revue* troupe was obliged to disband, stranded. Caroline Dudley lost $10,000 when the show closed prematurely, but paid the boat fare back to New York for any member of the cast who cared to return. In her chagrin, Dudley began a breach-of-contract suit against Josephine Baker to recover her $10,000 loss, then abandoned the futile gesture with a shrug. With the Folies contract, Josephine had begun a pattern of capricious dodges and changes of heart. She was special, Dudley knew: she had been hurt and then hardened, and she would hurt those who stood in her way.

"Who could blame her?" asked Caroline Dudley.

"She was still a kid," Bricktop recalled, "and she was one of the most vulnerable stars I've ever met. At the time, Negro female entertainers were still a rarity in Paris. She was only about seventeen years old. She brought out the mother instinct in me. She could hardly write her name and, suddenly, everybody wanted her autograph."

To save Josephine embarrassment, Bricktop had her write out her name in the cleanest, clearest script she could manage. Then Bricktop had a rubber stamp made of the signature, and that was the Josephine Baker "autograph" from then on.

Slowly, but with uninhibited élan and the broadest accent in Paris, Josephine was learning to speak French. ("She couldn't speak

American, let alone French," said Bricktop.) For a newspaper interview the melange of French and English was simply another facet of her engaging naïveté: "Très sweet, le public, and it's grâce à les journalistes that I have a life aussi agréable, understand?"

One journalist in particular made Josephine's life so very agreeable in Paris, Georges Simenon, a Belgian expatriate. He was writing for *Le Matin* mild pornographic short stories, commissioned by his editor, Colette. Josephine and Georges met at the nightclub El Garrob where he was drawn into her growing entourage: they began seeing one another steadily; Simenon, the stage-door faithful, considered their mutual attraction "un coup de foudre," a lightning stroke of immediate cinematic love. Josephine discovered an ardent lover with sexual appetite equal to her own; and Simenon even considered marriage with this princess of *le tumulte noir,* except that he was already married. He later became as famous as she, author of the best-selling Maigret mystery novels, but in 1926 he trailed after Josephine in the subordinate role of lover-secretary: she needed Simenon, not just as a partner in love, but to compose letters for her in both English and French.

With Simenon, Josephine would come to know a *quartier* as foreign from the Champs-Elysées theatre district and hillside commune of Montmartre as another city: the ancient, self-enclosed, and almost secret Marais district, where Simenon had a flat on the place des Vosges, a town square of eighteenth-century facades and arcades. Simenon had painted the door to his lodgings green, and on it his first nom de plume, Sim; and surely he pointed out to Josephine the house opposite his across the park where Emile Zola had lived before his exile during the Dreyfus Affair—though Josephine would have had to ask who Zola was.

Simenon also handled Josephine's money transactions, in French francs and American dollars, sending money orders for her to St. Louis; for Josephine had been sending money home to her mother beginning with the first pay she earned in France. Handling her affairs was part of having an affair with Josephine Baker, but the love affair did not endure. "Georges vanished one day as abruptly as he had come," Josephine confessed. "It appeared he was married." She was well aware of his marriage; Simenon's ménages à trois were open arrangements known both to wife and mistress, and Josephine would have met his wife Régine at one of their notoriously wild parties on the place des Vosges. Josephine's expression of regret at the end of the Simenon episode was directed sentimentally to her fans: "Will there always be barriers between me and those I wish to love?"

Josephine's *coups de foudre* occurred often enough from the time of her arrival in Paris. She was discovering the same easy and open sexual attitudes prevalent in the black ghetto at home where she had lived her ragged dream at night, peeking in and penny-scrounging the brothels and bars along the Mississippi waterfront. In bohemian Montmartre she found the same ripe ambiance the rinky-dink dens of jazz in St. Louis spilled out for her in exciting illumination; on the T.O.B.A. circuit she had learned early those pleasures stolen in the dark and on the run, the swift sweet compensation for what was otherwise sordid and grim.

Paul Colin, who had designed the famous kiosk poster for *La Revue Nègre,* considered himself Josephine Baker's first conquest in Paris—or rather, assumed he was her first seducer. When she came to his atelier to pose for the poster sketches, Colin told her to disrobe; and even though Josephine did not know the French term *à poil* (down to the hair) she could understand Colin's explicit gesture. Josephine's memory of the occasion was that of unfamiliar modesty—"Two thousand people were nobody, but undressing in front of a single man. . . ?"—but the artist recalled a completely different reaction on the part of his model: Josephine was standing in a pool of her discarded underclothes as soon as he made known what he wanted of her. Colin had observed many beautiful models in his professional life, but Josephine Baker's copper-colored form in an instant's insouciant pose completely disarmed him, then distracted him altogether. Josephine bestowed her engaging smile like a caress on the caricaturist; the sketches were put off, and she either suggested or permitted Colin more intimate appreciation of the occasion and his model.

Despite his belief and proud claim, Paul Colin was not Josephine Baker's first ardent Frenchman. In her memoirs she related (and possibly exaggerated) her surprise encounter with the room-service waiter at the Hôtel Fournet. Josephine was in her bath, with the door open, quite unused to the privacy of her own bathroom (the private bath, in the Montmartre of that day, is the most improbable part of the story), when the waiter came in with her breakfast tray. Josephine arose in soapy splendor from the water and an anonymous waiter was the first in Paris to enjoy the spectacle of Josephine Baker in the nude. The cafetière rattled on the tray, and the waiter put the tray of coffee and croissants to one side. Josephine had been apprised of the mythical lovemaking prowess of Frenchmen: instead of wrapping herself in the bath towel, she handed the towel to him. The astonished waiter complied with her wishes, and tenderly dried her when she stepped from the bath, then bore his unbelievable treasure to her bed.

In every matter except love, Bricktop was Josephine's loyal confidante: "She wouldn't go around the corner without asking my advice: 'Bricky, tell me what to do,' " but as for choosing men, "when Josephine needed advice the most, I couldn't do much good."

After the curtain fell on *La Revue Nègre,* Josephine would move on to spend the small hours at Bricktop's and the other all-night *boîtes* in Montmartre, restless and high from her nightly stage triumph. Bricktop observed that Josephine Baker, after the affair with Simenon, resorted to one-night stands with show-business sharks: she took up with the professional escorts of Montmartre, the hired dance partners who also served as gigolos to the loneliest women of Paris. Bricktop explained the paradox this way: "Many boys who might have asked her out were too shy, and too frightened by all the publicity she was getting."

By now Josephine Baker was being dressed by the leading couturiers of Paris. Paul Poiret's prewar reputation was waning, but he was still the important name in extravagant evening wear, and Josephine was bringing extravagant costuming back into fashion. "He and I had already locked horns," said Josephine of Poiret. "He said blue, I said pink . . . the finished dress was *pink* and the model became known as the *robe Josephine.*" Josephine Baker was a walking, posing advertisement for Chanel and Elsa Schiaparelli, later Patou and Jacques Fath, each of whom clothed her gratis and gratefully. The Baker image was now on picture postcards, outselling depictions of the Eiffel Tower. She was photographed by Man Ray, painted by Pascin and Foujita, sculpted as a mobile by Alexander Calder; Josephine Baker was being interviewed and written about in every Parisian publication from the conservative *L'Intransigeant* to radical *Paris Soir.* Not all the articles were favorable, but Josephine shrugged off the hostile comments—it was all publicity, and even the worst slurs could be turned to advantage.

Critic Robert de Fler spoke of Josephine's "lamentable transatlantic exhibitionism, which brings us back to the monkey quicker than we descended from the monkey," and she was even caricatured by "Sem" with a monkey's tail. Never mind, she had been called Monkey by the cast of *Shuffle Along,* and look where Monkey had climbed to. She would let the public know she *loved* animals and intended to perpetuate the animal mystique the critics created of her. "My way to dance I learned from watching the animals at the St. Louis zoo. Especially the kangaroos." She collected a menagerie of pets at the Fournet: goldfish, rabbits, macaws, a house-trained piglet, and the torpid boa constrictor she sometimes wore as a neckpiece that "separates the men from the boys, when they meet it." The boast, as Bricktop noted, was an idle one: often there were no men or boys to separate, and Josephine spent more nights alone with her pets than the flamboyant reputation would lead the public to believe. Later she was given a leopard to parade down the Champs-Elysées; and though the gift was from an impresario meant as a publicity stunt, Josephine genuinely loved Chiquita the leopard, loved all her animals. The addition of a pair of lovebirds to the menagerie was sentimentally significant.

In Bricktop's opinion, "She still needed a man."

iv

From high in the wings an egg-shaped cage, painted gold, descended on invisible cables until it settled centerstage and the mirrored interior slowly opened. Inside, of course, was Josephine Baker, posing majestically, arms wide and the familiar inviting smile, for the several heartbeats it took for her to receive the successive waves of applause. Then she quickly abandoned her golden shell to swing into an electrified version of the Charleston, wearing only the sensational girdle of bananas, the ultimate costume of erotic suggestion, as she crouched and sprang and made her breasts and bananas bounce to the music. When the frenzied dance ended and the applause overwhelmed the orchestra, she returned as demurely as her costume allowed to the gilded cage, which slowly ascended into the curtained-off heights backstage. Josephine Baker, at the Folies-Bergère, was a star all over again.

Taking up a block all its own on the rue Richer, the Folies-Bergère was the legendary emporium of music-hall entertainment, and above the Art Déco marquee were the letters JOSEPHINE BAKER spelled out in lights. The theatrical factory had operated for months solely to present her in *La Folie du Jour,* the production that cost nearly half a million dollars and the work of three hundred employees. Contributing to the sets was the celebrated design-artist Erté, and to the music, Irving Berlin; but only the name Josephine Baker appeared in illuminated letters twenty feet high.

Josephine could afford to glory in her exceptional triumph, but there were those who believed *vedette* status, or stardom, did not last, especially in France. Bricktop was the older and wiser guide to the fickle public supporting show-business success. She warned Josephine that an audience's adoration could not be depended upon forever, and the affection of the French could not be depended upon at all. But Josephine Baker did manage to sustain her exotic appeal through season after season; she was the darling of expatriate Americans and the *chouchoute* of the French, and her rapport with the audience was not as superficial and transient as Bricktop believed. With Parisians, Josephine Baker remained a fixed and final obsession. The love affair across the footlights was a great consolation to the ultimate star—yet Bricktop still believed that what Josephine needed was a man.

Of the many thousands of fan letters Josephine received during her two years at the Folies-Bergère, over half were proposals of marriage, wistful offers from anonymous fans. A form letter written by a publicist—like the rubber stamp for autographs—was her answer to the marriage proposals, accompanied by a photograph. She could be neither wife nor mistress, lacking serious opportunity for marriage and having no vocation for the traditional arrangement as professional *cocotte,* like music-hall stars la Belle Otéro and Liane de Pougny ("les grandes horizontales") who were kept by men of wealth and position.

Josephine did play the tease with some grizzled connoisseur of showgirls, accepting an expensive trinket from the jewel case at Lazare Frères in exchange for an assignation, then creating a scene when *le vieux* directed the cabbie to drive to his apartment after drinks and dinner at Larue's. Or she might play the role of mercenary dinner date, as she did with a young Parisian student of architecture, granted the privilege of an evening out with Josephine, and when he was about to pay the waiter she plucked the remaining thousand-franc note from his wallet: she had confiscated his month's allowance. "If you want to take out an actress you have to pay for it!" Later he may have convinced himself an evening with Josephine was a worth a thousand francs; he would, at least, have a thousand-franc story to tell.

But the bravado of these tales she told on herself, and the confessions to Bricktop or hints to the public, of constant seductions and indiscriminate couplings, contributed to the show-business myth yet did not essentially alter the truth of her solitary state. She would confess to her loneliness as well, as if to establish a countermyth of poignant despair. When she began at the Folies-Bergère, one young showgirl confided in her: she was English, red-haired, and the mother of a love child whose picture she showed to Josephine, the child for whom she worked. "I returned to my dressing room. There wasn't a single photograph stuck in the mirror. A whimper. I had almost forgotten the two-month old puppy I had bought the day before. He was plump, white and silky. I buried my face in his warm little body."

As the star of the Folies-Bergère, Josephine could not simply turn off the sparkle and retire for the night: her need to keep the excitement fueled took her from club to club until closing time. At one of these, Zelli's, just across the rue Fontaine from Bricktop's, Josephine met Giuseppe Abatino, or Pepito—"the no-account count," as Bricktop called him, for he sometimes assumed the title of Count di Albertini. Bricktop had already observed Josephine's fling with another habitué of Zelli's, Zito, a free-lance caricaturist and occasional gigolo. "Zito wasn't much of a date . . . but when a gal hits the top, it's taken for granted she's being wined and dined by some rich handsome guy." One night Josephine was introduced to Zito's cousin, Pepito, who with his suave and worldly manner was the image of Adolph Menjou. Pepito was in his thirties, some twelve years older than Josephine, and knew just how low to dip his Menjou mustache to graze the back of her hand with a kiss.

"I couldn't believe my eyes," said Bricktop when she saw Josephine with Pepito. Privately, she scolded: "What are you doing with this bum? He can't even pay for a glass of beer."

Pepito discovered that Bricktop had been bad-mouthing him, so he adroitly steered Josephine away from Bricktop's club: he managed to alienate her from the Montmartre crowd altogether. "He had a plan," said Bricktop, "and part of it was to cut Josephine off from her old friends . . . he kept her away from all the blacks in Paris. For some time afterward, whenever we met on the street, I found myself saying hello to her back."

Although temporarily sequestered, Josephine was no man's prisoner; and total effacement was no part of Pepito's strategy. He would steer her away from the rue Fontaine deadbeats and into the company of the "right people," like himself. He took shrewd account of the dancer's need to dance—one critic called Josephine *une machine à danser*—and soon enough turned Josephine's spillover energy to profit. As soon as she could change out of her costume for the finale at the Folies-Bergère, she often performed overtime at a den in Montmartre known as the Imperial, which became Josephine Baker's Imperial when she began dancing there. Pepito had the ambitious idea of arranging with one of Josephine's former loves, the well-heeled Gaston Prieur, to finance a cabaret of Josephine's very own, Chez Josephine. Prieur had made his fortune through a workman's medical compensation fraud, so Chez Josephine was actually established on illegal funds drained from French insurance companies. The origins of the investment were known to Pepito, but Josephine, he assured her, need not worry her beautiful head over such matters, nor over the lawsuit initiated by Messieurs Harot and Leonard when Josephine abandoned their Imperial for a nightclub of her own, both clubs now bearing her famous name. "Je m'occupe de tout ça" was Pepito's word: he would trouble himself over these affairs, and Josephine was *d'accord*—it was like having a rubber stamp for troublesome signatures, and a form letter for hopeless proposals of marriage.

Pepito had an instinct for the careful exploitation of this marvel that had fallen into his hands, to exploit Josephine not only to his advantage but to hers. He would promote the name, manage the performer, guide her hand on contracts, hire servants, see to her money and correspondence—even feed the menagerie for her—and love her, when she wanted love.

Pepito could explain Josephine to herself, and to her satisfaction: "You were just what people needed after the restriction of war. They craved something wild, natural, extravagant . . . you also represented freedom. The right to cut your hair, to walk around stark naked, to kick over the traces."

She considered Pepito the most astute manager in Paris; and for her interests and in her situation, he probably was. He was her shadow, a shrewd and soft-spoken manipulator of her life: she was his constant concern. For services rendered she presented him with a diamond and silver watch (identical to the one Bricktop had given her lover): Josephine did love Pepito, despite her stage-door infidelities, now kept discreetly to one side with Pepito looking the other way.

"You taught me how to speak and stand and act like a lady," she reminded him gratefully.

As a professional escort of lonely women, Pepito had been a quick study of manners and mores, and passed on these refinements to his charge. Until Pepito's coaching, Josephine was known to eat spaghetti with her fingers or crunch into a *salade de crevettes* unpeeled shrimps and all. Bricktop had begun to guide Josephine into the world of the well-to-do she was now part of, but Pepito was there to complete her training.

With Pepito's prompting, Josephine's public appearances were staged and timed for maximum effect. In 1927 when she turned twenty-one and could legally drive in France, Josephine was on display at the wheel of her new Voisin—a gift from the manufacturer—tan-colored to match the Baker skin, and with upholstery in snakeskin to match the skin of her pet boa, Kiki. The pedestrian Josephine could be photographed crossing the pont Royal with Chiquita, her pet leopard, with fur or jeweled collar to coordinate with whatever outfit Josephine wore. When Paul Poiret instigated a lawsuit for unpaid gowns designed for Mademoiselle Baker, Josephine turned the *procès* over to Pepito, who was astute enough to know the case would never reach the tribunal: it was a publicity ploy for the fading star of fashion to capitalize on the reputation of the rising star of stage.

The timing was perfect for the ultimate public relations coup: a wedding, with Josephine as bride and Pepito Abatino the groom. The Parisian press corps and photographers were assembled for the announcement, and at the press conference Pepito presented his bride-to-be with a sixteen-carat diamond ring from Cartier.

"And that ain't all he gave me, either." Josephine said she had received family jewels and heirlooms that had been in the Abatino family for generations. Pepito was perfectly aware that Mademoiselle Baker was on display, not himself, and stood modestly to one side while Josephine flashed her bejeweled finger and her famous smile, elaborating on their planned nuptials with details only her fairy-tale imagination could contrive.

"Love is the most beautiful thing in life," was Josephine's pronouncement. Her press conferences and newspaper interviews were invariably a melange of quotable beauty tips, such as "The best toilet water is rain water, it keeps indefinitely," and homilies like "It's important to achieve something in life." For the announcement of her engagement, she completely reinvented her American self, including a mythical sister in California who first encouraged Josephine to dance, and a mother and Spanish father who met at school: "Their parents didn't want them to marry. So they married anyway and they were very poor because they had no one to help them." Josephine Baker hardly needed an updated dossier when all of France and her fans everywhere were already enchanted with the original and true version of her slum-to-show-business life, but Josephine had her own psychic needs to fulfill, a myth to enlarge.

Pepito's fabricated background included his having been a lieutenant in an Italian cavalry regiment and a ficticious great-uncle, the Cardinal Celesio. He dressed and spoke and played the part of Count di Albertini, including monocle: the newspapers did not trouble to publish the discovery that Pepito was a simple bricklayer and plasterer who had come to Paris to escape the kind of poverty Josephine herself had fled in St. Louis. The cinematic dream stories Pepito and Josephine wanted told and the public wanted to read were the illusory and entertaining stuff of newspaper feature columns.

The awkwardness arose when newspapers in the United States published the report of an American black woman marrying a white aristocrat in Paris. A reaction was to be expected from a white public already stirred up by *The Rising Tide of Color,* while the black population could delight in the exceptional upward mobility of one of their own: out of the narrow options and grim prospects of black circumstances in America, somebody's dream had come true.

Meanwhile the Folies-Bergère posters on kiosks all over Paris now bore the name in bold letters COUNTESS PEPITO DI ABATINO, for it seemed the marriage was a fait accompli; according to Josephine, she had married Pepito quietly at the American Embassy in Paris on her twenty-first birthday. "I didn't have any idea that getting married was so exciting. I feel like I'm sitting on pins and needles. I am so thrilled." At first telling, the marriage took place at the American Embassy, but then the wedding shifted to the Italian consulate. Some newspapermen were gauche enough to want to check the story out: actually, the bride recapitulated, the marriage was at one of the *mairies* in one of the arrondissements of Paris, but Josephine didn't remember which. When Pepito was questioned for details, he yielded the floor to Josephine with the cold reserved smile of a diplomat. "He's got a great big family there," said Josephine, planning to spend their honeymoon at the di Albertini castello, "and lots of coats of arms and everything."

The black newspapers took issue with the establishment press, especially the English-language dailies in Paris that were beginning to cover the Josephine Baker marriage with skeptical mockery. Italian papers, it was pointed out, carried the story with as much delight and élan as in black America, where the headline COLORED DANCER MARRIES ITALIAN COUNT was considered legitimate news. The New York *Amsterdam News* was quick to make the comparison with white women cold-bloodedly "buying titles" by picking up titled husbands in the European marketplace: "Of course, Josephine, unlike so many American white women, didn't go to Europe in quest of a titled husband, and the fact that she now has one certainly must be as great a surprise to her as to everyone else."

When American journalists tried to corner the bride once too often, Josephine allowed the fable to dissipate in vague remarks until interviewers tired of the game. Quietly, Pepito allowed his assumed title to lapse, and suggested that Josephine abandon the fiction of their marriage by announcing the news, factual, that she was to play in the Maurice Dekobra film written especially for her, *La Sirène des Tropiques.* "Pepito will play my husband in the *film,* vous voyez?"

But wasn't he her husband in real life?

"Well, since it was amusing to be married, I let it out around town that I was . . . It was nice."

It was fun, she said, to be called Madame for a while, instead of Mademoiselle.

The dramatic arrival of Charles Lindbergh at Le Bourget in his fragile monoplane *The Spirit of St. Louis* briefly eclipsed the popularity of Josephine Baker as France's favorite American. Josephine herself was an enthusiastic Lindbergh fan, and stopped her own show at the Folies to break the news: "Bonnes Nouvelles! Ladies and Gentlemen. Charles Lindbergh has arrived!" Americans and French were "delirious with happiness," and Josephine joined a jubilant Franco-American crowd at the season's fashionable restaurant L'Abbaye de Thélème to celebrate the exploit. However, the gala evening turned sour when a celebrant at the table next to hers called the waiter over and protested Josephine's presence in the restaurant: "Back home a nigger woman belongs in the kitchen." The bigot's voice rocketed through the restaurant until the maître d' appeared and with French savoir faire managed to cover the incident, announcing that in France there was no distinction made between races. Nevertheless, Josephine, in one of the few moments in her life she wanted to vanish, thought: "If the floor could open up and swallow me, it would be a blessing."

As if the ugly scene at L'Abbaye de Thélème was the announcement of new and ambivalent attitudes of the French, a shock of another sort occurred when Josephine Baker and Pepito Abatino were refused a term lease on a suite of rooms at a distinguished Right Bank hotel; the reason, frankly given, was that the hotel's American clientele would resent the presence, however celebrated, of a Negro woman in the establishment.

In her second season at the Folies, in a newly staged show, *Un Vent de Folie,* Josephine was still the featured display in every ingeniously framed spectacle, but the glitter was beginning to fade. Her show-business sense told her the public had turned fickle: bare breasts and feathers and bananas aroused little excitement that season. When

Marcel Sauvage asked to co-author Josephine's "memoirs," Pepito was overjoyed, certain the publication would be a boost to her reputation at this delicate period of apparent decline and troublesome what-next.

Josephine's apartment on the rue Beaujon, near the parc Monceau, was in splendid and colorful disarray when Sauvage arrived for the first interview. A bust of Louis XIV shared a marble-topped table with a rag doll and on the phonograph was a fish bowl full of crumpled hundred-franc notes. They spoke together in the writer's scrappy English and Josephine's pidgin French amidst the designer gowns strewn across the floor, the love birds scattering seed through the bars of their cage into the heaps of discarded evening wear. Sauvage saw the charming dancer as *coquine*, mischievous, and in separately defined details: the head of a delicious little savage, with hair hastily oiled flat against her skull; animated hands with nails painted silver; the widest smile possible illuminated with thirty-two magnificent teeth—Josephine counted them for him with one silver nail.

"Memories . . . mais je ne souviens pas encore mes souvenirs." Memories—she did not yet remember her memories.

She slid into a leather armchair, then shrieked with uninhibited laughter as if laughing for the pure pleasure of living. What followed was a chaotic babble of events Sauvage could barely note or make sense of, an apparently coherent—to Josephine—sequence of remembrances, offhand comments about love and life, and the witty naïveté typical of Josephine's public relations press conferences. Sauvage managed to stitch together this scattered replay of the Josephine Baker interviews, and in some measure describe Josephine to the satisfaction of her public: *Les Mémoires de Josephine Baker* was a success in exactly the way Josephine and Pepito had hoped. But in one confession, she had made a serious blunder. She was naturally hypersensitive about her own body: form and face were essentially her stock in trade, and she ventured to remark frankly, "I've heard a lot of talk about the war. What a funny story! I swear I don't understand it all, but it disgusts me. I have such a horror of men with only one arm, one leg, one eye. I sympathize with them with all my heart, but I have a physical repulsion for everything unhealthy."

Sauvage faithfully recorded this statement. Josephine, bluntly truthful for once, had badly misjudged attitudes in her host country.

Wounded veterans of World War I were much honored in France and were a powerful lobbyist group: certain public works jobs—not always the most attractive (attendants in public toilets), but jobs nonetheless during a time of vast unemployment—were reserved for war-injured veterans, as well as designated seats on the Métro. These men were organized in several official and unofficial associations, and soon after the memoirs were published, Josephine encountered a band of wounded war veterans at the corner of rue Fontaine and rue Blanche blocking traffic, carrying placards and banners of protest, picketing her nightclub, Chez Josephine.

Josephine thought she might talk the issue to one side, as she had always done, with a press conference—but Pepito knew better. His star's love affair with the French public was in jeopardy, and Pepito was shaken. What if the pickets took up positions on the rue Richer—patrons of the Folies-Bergère would be faced with legions of *les gueules cassées* and *mutilés de la guerre* surrounding the celebrated music hall where Josephine was star. The safest course was for Josephine to deny ever having uttered any such remark about deformities, then blame her careless co-author for inserting the libelous statement in her memoirs. Before the Association of Wounded War Veterans could take action on a threatened lawsuit, Josephine announced she was suing Marcel Sauvage; neither suit was ever taken before the tribunal, but it had been a close call.

Since Josephine had always been generous with her offstage time in giving benefit performances for the working class of Paris—her last benefit had been for the children of the *pompiers,* the fire brigade of Paris—Pepito saw to it that her next gala benefit would be for the war wounded of France, a carefully staged and well-publicized apology for any misunderstanding.

V

"They didn't understand my nature at all."

When Josephine saw the rushes of her first film, she wept. Her eyes were already swollen from working under overheated lights, and she was miserable from trying to adapt her auditorium style of audience rapport to the narrow confines of close-up and naturalistic gesture. *La Sirène des Tropiques* was the crudely produced flicker-flack adventures of an innocent native girl transported from her tropical island (fleeing the threat of rape by the Great White Hunter who pursued her for a reel) to a gloriously successful dancing career in Paris. Pepito played her husband, as he had been doing for over a year; the scenario a simpleminded sample of early and primitive French film making. Josephine was unable to project her characteristic humor, charm, and vivid personality in cinematic terms; she was so out of her element as to be disoriented. "Was that ugly silly person me?" Josephine asked through her tears when she saw the final cut.

By the end of 1927, in the last frantic phase of the 1920s, Pepito had the foresight to inaugurate a world tour of twenty-five countries for his celebrated client-partner. Josephine feared she would be forgotten by her beloved Parisians, but absence, as it turned out, saved her from stalemate. Pepito had been watching from the wings as Josephine's luster dimmed: he especially noticed evidence of her decline in the yawns she drew at a benefit auction when Josephine extended her time as entertainer-auctioneer. On the outer fringes of the audience, people wandered away from the outdoor stage. Josephine ran on, and when she was ready to take her bow was roundly booed—a new and disturbing experience she had never known in Paris.

But in the year 1927 Paris was undergoing a complete change of heart in Franco-American relations. The peak moment of *amitié* had been Lindbergh's triumphant arrival; hardly had the cheers for Lindy died away than two anarchist-immigrants were executed in Boston after a highly questionable trial. Parisians reacted violently to the execution, and in the anti-American riots that followed there was as much a spillover resentment of the American-in-Paris with his spendthrift dollars as outrage against a miscarriage of justice in the United States. Even the black community, the charmed *quartier* until now, began to feel the animosity. The French romance with negritude had shifted to a protective chauvinism. Nightclubs had been dominated by all-black American jazz bands and the French now resented the monopoly: a municipal ordinance was hastily passed requiring the band of any Parisian *boîte de nuit* to employ at least 50 percent French nationals, a crippling statute in a country that would not have its own jazz artists until the 1930s when Stéphane Grapelli and Django Reinhardt appeared on the scene. The pragmatic French compromise was that clubs could hire Frenchmen to sit in during performances with prop instruments they were not to play—for decor, and regulations, only. Some Montmartre clubs were forced to close, unable to pay double salaries. The larger clubs, if they could afford to, hired separate bands, the French to play traditional dance café music, café-conc, and in alternate sets the Americans played jazz.

Until 1928, blacks had been granted considerable latitude in their particular world, that corner of Montmartre where the jazz clubs flourished, but that year at Florence Embry's club, Chez Florence, Mike McKendrick and Sidney Bechet began a fracas on the bandstand, then carried the fight outside where they pulled pistols out of their tuxedo jackets and began firing in a drunken duel. Neither man was wounded in the shootout, but one shell from Bechet's gun struck a passing Frenchwoman, causing a superficial injury and some loss of blood. If a French citizen had not been involved, the incident would likely have been dealt with leniently, but this time the letter of the law was applied. Bechet was condemned to eleven months in prison; he was obliged to serve part of the sentence, after which he was expelled from France.

During this grim period of anti-Americanism and backlash against blacks, Josephine was out of harm's way touring Eastern Europe, being discovered all over again and stirring controversy in every country—the kind of publicity, from a distance, that only enhanced her popularity in France.

In Catholic Vienna, Josephine's presence was a challenge to the Church: the liberties Josephine took in dance and costume were condemned as a "pornographic exhibition of Satan's handmaiden," and the Austrian parliament convened in special session to deal with the "Josephine Baker" issue. Throughout Austria sermons were preached against the "Congo savage" and particularly at St. Paul's in Vienna, for Josephine was performing next door to the cathedral, at Johann Strauss Theatre, having paid an outrageous theatre tax for the privilege.

Contrary to Viennese expectations, Josephine opened the revue costumed modestly enough in the floor-length evening dress she had long yearned to wear in the role of blues singer. Pepito had rightly calculated the moment to introduce Josephine as a vocalist: she made her singing debut with a modest little ditty well within her range and training, a song called "Pretty Little Baby." Overnight she became Vienna's pretty little baby instead of the devil's mistress—and at the same time she had managed an out-of-town tryout for her voice without risking the critical edge of her sharp Parisian audience.

Vienna's reaction was subdued compared with the delirium elsewhere. When fans of Josephine gathered at the station in Prague to meet her train, windows were smashed and several in the crowd were trampled underfoot. Josephine was escorted through the riot by a contingent of police officers, but as the crowd spilled beyond the station and along the streets of Prague, she was prevented from entering her hotel. The only way to satisfy the surge of spectators was for Josephine to ride through the streets atop her limousine, on parade.

At an outdoor theatre in Bucharest an unexpected downpour drenched the audience, but Josephine danced on, carrying an umbrella for the remainder of the performance. During her stay she walked the unpaved city streets barefoot, and was taken for a gypsy—then, in Madrid, she was considered a gypsy in truth, by the foremost gypsy dancer in Spain, Macarona, who taught Josephine the flamenco to add to her crowded repertoire. For the Budapest arrival, where the mobs were hostile, Pepito dreamed up the distraction of presenting Josephine transported in a cart pulled by an ostrich. Nevertheless, students threw ammonia bombs at her as she left the theatre that night, screaming "Go back to Africa!" Despite Josephine's having performed a sample Charleston for the town council board of censors who granted permission for her to appear, Hungarians continued to demonstrate against her sinful presence in their city.

In Munich the town council flatly banned Josephine from the city's theatres. There were again student riots in Zagreb, Yugoslavia, but also a large counterdemonstration of fans. Taken altogether, Pepito was more than satisfied with the stir and controversy Josephine aroused; but Josephine—for all her sang-froid in public—was shaken by the racial hatred directed against her. "They hounded me with a Christian hatred from station to station, city to city, one stage to another."

Of gossip that filtered back to France, the most intriguing to her Parisian public were the tales of Black Venus's lovelife and endless liaisons. Pepito was ever aware of the sexual mystique that created and fed on the Josephine Baker reputation, and in Bucharest he rigged a phony confrontation—contrived despite his very real jealousy—with a Hungarian cavalry officer. There was a love poem sent by the officer, a challenge to a duel by Pepito. Of course no blood was to be shed on the field of honor; after firing at one another in the cemetery of St. Stephens at the traditional first light, the two men declared themselves "satisfied" in front of a carefully assembled corps of journalists.

There were several variations in the tale of the death of Alexius Groth, a suicide for love of Josephine. According to *The New York Times,* the brooding young man had followed Josephine from nightclub to nightclub in Zagreb, besieging her with love letters and bouquets of roses. In Josephine's version: "There he sat at his usual table. After the last guest departed, he rose to his feet. Because I was leaving Budapest [she meant Zagreb] next day and we had never spoken, I followed him into the hall to say goodbye. As I searched for the proper words he gazed at me somberly. Then he reached into his pocket—for a cigarette, I assumed—pulled out a revolver, pressed it to his temple and pulled the trigger." *The New York Times* concluded with "He wounded himself, but may recover"; Josephine remembered, "It was horrible . . . there he lay, dead at my feet."

The tour ended in South America, where Josephine played to full houses in Brazil, Chili, and Argentina. Without knowing or caring the least about Argentine politics, Josephine somehow became a symbol of the government of President Irigoyen, and at her performance in Buenos Aires a riot erupted. She continued to perform while the police dragged out the agitators and the orchestra played lively tangos to drown the explosion of firecrackers thrown beneath the seats. Both right and left claimed her sympathies—or was it opposition?—whether she was supposed to be for or against Irigoyen Josephine was never to know. This was simply more of the disruption, contention, and riot that followed her around the world, almost a part of the act.

The vagaries of romance also followed Josephine around the world. On the *Lutetia* sailing back to France, she had a comic encounter with the renowned architect Le Courbusier, who had been lecturing in South America at the same time Josephine was on tour. For the ritual crossing-the-equator fête, Le Courbusier appeared at the masquerade ball with his skin blackened to match Josephine's and wearing a feathered codpiece in imitation of her Folies costume: "What a pity you're an architect, Monsieur. You'd make a sensational partner." After the ball Josephine paired off with Le Courbusier, a sensational partner at least for the remainder of the voyage.

vi

"It's time," said Pepito, "to use everything you've picked up in the twenty-five countries we've visited in the last two years."

Instead of returning to the role of "feathered mannequin" at the Folies-Bergère, Josephine was now to appear in a revue especially tailored for her at the prestigious Casino de Paris.

"It's all arranged, Josephine. All you have to do is sign."

"Sign what?"

When Pepito explained the contract to her—a show under the direction of Henri Varna, who had been responsible for the early and enduring success of Casino star Mistinguett—Josephine was eager to sign. The spectacle was to be called *Paris Qui Remue (Swinging Paris),* a welcome-home production built entirely around the talents, old and new, of Josephine Baker.

In the ranking of show palaces, the Casino de Paris was several notches higher in caliber of entertainment than the Folies and the Moulin Rouge, going beyond the sequin-spangled spectacle of topless dancers and top-hatted prestidigitateurs. Neither of the competing houses would have arranged for a jewel-studden G-string for the "lake fairy" in *Paris Qui Remue,* created by Van Cleef & Arpels and with its own security officer stationed backstage, his armored van parked around the corner on the rue Lord Byron.

In appearing at the Casino, Josephine was nudging aside La Miss, the redoubtable Mistinguett, the female *vedette* best established as the heart and soul of French entertainment—and Josephine Baker's foremost rival. If Josephine had reigned supreme at the Folies-Bergère, Mistinguett's undisputed realm was the higher-class Casino de Paris. La Miss had referred to Josephine as "cette petite négresse"—how delicious to usurp Mistinguett's very own dressing room, and further, to be awarded the services of Mistinguett's personal choreographer and regular dance partner, the American Earl Leslie. To Mistinguett, this last was the ultimate betrayal, and Henri Varna was obliged to endure an outburst of temperamental rage over the issue. Even so, *la petite négresse* prevailed.

Pepito had wisely decided no more *danse sauvage*; let Paris welcome the new Josephine Baker in a stage production of relative decorum, something of the muted display he had advised for the Vienna tryout. Her world tour had in fact calmed Josephine's hyperactivity and diminished her exhibitionism without eliminating the essential sensuality she projected onstage and off. In her subtler new essence, the refined and glamourized Josephine was preparing to "throw the velvet" for the first time in Paris, chanteuse as well as danseuse.

Though Pepito had no control over Josephine's sentimental adventuring, he was effectively authoritarian in her professional life. In preparation for the Casino show, he locked her in the apartment so that she would be obliged to rehearse: "It wasn't the first time Pepito had imprisoned me. He sometimes closed me up to make me work. Not that I was lazy . . . but what was the point of standing behind a piano practicing scales? We discussed my future by the hour. Of course I had to keep developing. 'Otherwise you'll disappear like the rest,' Pepito assured me. 'Think of all the names that *used* to be in lights. The public is like a man. We're happy to stick with a woman as long as she keeps changing!' "

So far Pepito's judgment had been infallible on Josephine's behalf: Josephine's own innate responses and instinctive sense of display accounted for the rest. Also, during the sojourn in New Orleans many years before, she had been converted to superstition by Voodoo Jones and Doll. Voodoo had sent her a rusty nail with a lock of hair wrapped around it: she depended on this lucky token, along with a rabbit's foot, to be in her dressing room always, and she wanted the names of her shows, like *Paris Qui Remue,* to have thirteen letters.

Just as *La Revue Nègre* had coincided with the Art Déco Exposition of 1925, Josephine's *Paris Qui Remue* played during the 1930 Colonial Exposition with the influx of tourists for the exhibits of French overseas colonies in Africa, the Caribbean, and Indochina. In the show's opening scene Josephine was costumed as an Indochinese singing "La Petite Tonkinoise," a plaintive and winning lament that demanded no more virtuosity than her high uncertain voice could sustain. Another number, "Dis-Nous, Josephine," was a running dialogue between Josephine and a male chorus in a song that narrated the life and times of Josephine Baker, a song she delivered wittily and well. But the number that drew the most attention was a hastily scribbed lyric by Vincent Scotto expressing a sentiment ideally associated with Josephine and her two countries, the two identifying nostalgias of her life: "J'ai Deux Amours (Mon Pays et Paris)."

"Uncork the champagne, Pepito!" The crowded spectacle at the Casino de Paris was a triumph beyond the wildest promise of Josephine's good-luck charms. She had feared the critics were "armed for the kill" this time, pens sharpened to draw blood, especially because of her evident competition with their favorite, Mistinguett. La Miss was famous for her regal entrances, the descent on a massive staircase flanked by a chorus of dancers. In the same style, Josephine made an even more spectacular entrance down the staircase redesigned as a steep metal ramp, the star moving forward as if in flight, wearing light translucent dragonfly wings.

Even if the new Josephine had not won over the critics, the audience response was an immediate uproar of adoration, especially for the Baker rendition of "J'ai Deux Amours." The show ran for over a year, and the song became so firmly associated with her that she sang it at every request and occasion. Josephine calculated that she must have sung "J'ai Deux Amours" more than a thousand times that first year alone.

In her *Letter from Paris* that summer of 1930, Janet Flanner made up for her hasty misinterpretation of the Josephine Baker mystique in the earlier review of *La Revue Nègre*: "If you can get away for a day or so, it might be a good plan to fly to Paris and spend the evening at Josephine Baker's new Casino show . . . the revue contains everything, including Pierre Myer, and practically no feathers and furs. It is, as much as the Folies' show, one of the best in years." The *Letter* went on to describe the three-ringed circus of British dancing choruses, "the four best can-can dancers in captivity," a traditional Russian ballet and an Italian ballet of high-wire artists, a cheetah, a splendid Venetian set (mixed quaintly into the French Colonial decor), and Josephine rescued in the finale by a gorilla.

There were a few sighs and regrets over the polish Josephine Baker had acquired at the expense of her native vivacity and charm. Janet Flanner best expressed this in her conclusion to the review of *Paris Qui Remue:* "Her caramel-colored body, which overnight became a legend in Europe, is still magnificent, but it has become thinned, trained, almost civilized . . . on that lovely animal visage lies now a sad look, not of captivity, but of dawning intelligence."

The "cheetah" Janet Flanner mentioned was really Josephine's pet leopard Chiquita, given to her by Henri Varna as a useful accessory to her own gift for publicity and as a striking complement to her legendary jungle nature. There was a close affinity and affection between Josephine and all of her pets, but Chiquita was her inseparable favorite. When Varna asked her if she might not be frightened of the big cat, Josephine replied, not at all: "Animals don't hide their feelings the way people do. That's what I like about them."

Chiquita appeared on the kiosk poster for *Paris Qui Remue* offering his mistress a bunch of flowers from his mouth, though the leopard, Josephine noted, "was not one to offer posies." Chiquita was still a jungle cat, though trained—and the two sleek creatures were associated in the public's mind as "la panthère avec son léopard." The animal went everywhere with Josephine, even to a performance of *La Bohème* at l'Opéra where, during Mimi's dramatic death scene, Chiquita slipped his leash (or more likely was deliberately let off his golden chain) and leapt into the orchestra pit creating the expected evening's pandemonium and next morning's headlines.

When Pepito found a suburban villa for Josephine, Chiquita could at last be housed with the entire menagerie in the woodland acreage at Le Vésinet. The country house, called Beau-Chêne for the ancient and majestic oaks on the property, was a rather overwrought and pretentious structure in patterned brick and slate turrets from the time of Baron Haussmann; it stood alone on its own private *parc* on the edge of the Bois de St.-Germain-en-Laye north of Paris. The Casino de Paris was only an hour's commute in Josephine's new Delage limousine (given to her by the manufacturer for the publicity value), but Chiquita, who appeared with Josephine in *Paris Qui Remue,* was too agitated by Pepito's Latin-style driving and had to be transported to Paris separately by cab. What trauma was wrought in Josephine's relationship with Pepito by including Chiquita in the canopied Directoire bed was never made clear.

Josephine discovered the same delights in suburban-country living that had led other expatriate Americans to seek to escape the demands and distractions of Paris city life—yet remain within reach of the place most vital to them. There was the opportunity to know the small-town French at close quarters, and Josephine began to be concerned with the welfare of her neighbors, especially the local children, in the way of a gracious chatelaine—and at Christmas their mulatto Père Noël. She engaged in gardening as if she were born to it, taking pleasure in the floral terraces (one plot of red and yellow blossoms spelled out JOSEPHINE BAKER along the edge of the driveway), and the kitchen garden of vegetables and herbs. At Beau-Chêne Josephine could drop out of character and costume to wear simple peter-pan collars and cotton pantaloons—or, as one neighbor discovered her, wading playfully through the waterlilies of the duck pond, splendidly nude. She would live at Beau-Chêne, her first and best and only real home, for the next eighteen years—years she admitted were her happiest ever.

"But what if Monsieur Offenbach doesn't think I'm right for the part?"

Pepito explained that Jacques Offenbach had died the century before: his light opera *La Créole* had never been a grand success, probably because in 1875 there was no one quite like Josephine Baker to play the West Indian title role.

"Ça ne jazze pas," was her next reservation—the music didn't "jazz."

Naturally the producers restructured the libretto to Josephine's style, a champagne-bubble plot made lighter and frothier still. Josephine had never really performed in the legitimate theatre before, and the prospect was daunting—especially with the grim reminder of "acting" in the film *La Sirène des Tropiques.* But Josephine believed in Pepito's advice and could recite his philosophy by rote: "You have to grow and change all the time. When you no longer have something new to do or say you disappear."

Fortunately Sacha Guitry, playwright and leading musical-comedy entrepreneur in Paris, volunteered to coach Josephine in stage technique. He would help her control the grand gesture and restrain the strut of the music hall to develop a technique suitable to the legitimate stage. A chorus of children was added to the production: Josephine had always found the company of children a delight; her benefit performances for children's causes were first on the agenda—and now the spontaneous good-natured spill of children into her dressing room helped Josephine overcome the fear of opening night.

Although the Offenbach operetta was never considered an important or enduring work, as a vehicle for Josephine Baker *La Créole* endured for many months at the Théâtre Marigny across from the Grand Palais on the Champs-Elysées. "The revival of Offenbach's 'Créole' starring Josephine Baker," wrote the critic for *Variety*, "finally consecrates Miss Baker as a full-fledged French headliner. Opening day of the show cinched its success, and all credit is being given to the star, not to the operetta." Janet Flanner confirmed *Variety*'s rave notice for Josephine with the remark that "her high, airy voice, half child's, half thrush's," and "superb brown thighs, especially when prancing in *Restauration* lace pantalets, seems without argument what Offenbach must have had in mind."

While Josephine was enjoying the ultimate success of appearing in an all-French *opéra comique,* starring in the most Parisian of her theatrical showcases, Pepito was still anticipating new ventures such as the cinema production of *Zou-Zou,* for which he would first have to overcome Josephine's reluctance to appear before the motion picture cameras again. By now Pepito's drive had diminished, his health erratic—doctors were unable to diagnose the source of his colorlessness and depleted energy. Despite failing health, he undertook the *Zou-Zou* negotiations with great élan and habitual optimism. Josephine guardedly said yes to the film idea, and during its production Pepito worked up an all-out advertising campaign by launching a revival of the banana motif so closely associated with the celebrated Folies costume. His successes were lackluster: few fruit stores were willing to stack pyramid piles of bananas in front of the counter with the label "Josephine Baker est Zou-Zou" on each banana. The old spirit had gone out of Pepito's strategies; he had lost the touch—or his physical condition affected his characteristic flair—for the selling of Josephine in this campaign. The stunts were too flamboyant: he failed altogether to convince cinema owners to dress their ushers in banana skins.

The film was memorable only for the appearance of Josephine's co-star, Jean Gabin. The banana revival was a flop. Never mind, Pepito had even greater prospects in mind for keeping Josephine in the spotlight, to keep her from disappearing.

vii

In 1935, exactly ten years after she had first sailed to France on the *Berengaria,* Josephine went aboard the fast new French liner *Normandie* with trunkloads of costumes and evening dresses for a return trip to New York. Pepito had worked out a contract with the Shubert brothers for Josephine to star in the 1936 Ziegfeld Follies, and Josephine agreed that this production could very well represent the culmination of her successes so far, and on her native turf.

The Josephine Baker legend preceded her, and a crowd of New York reporters and photographers were at dockside to greet Josephine with a barrage of questions while the flashbulbs popped: "Do you personally know the President of France?" "Do you think Joe Louis is greater than Einstein?" Manhattan was apparently ready to extend its hometown welcome and make as much of Josephine Baker as Paris ever had.

One of the first indications of a less than promising reception occurred at the St. Moritz Hotel, where Josephine was received cordially enough, but the manager explained that hotel policy required her to stay clear of the lobby; she would have to use the employees' entrance and the service elevator. Pepito had booked rooms for himself elsewhere, to avoid the kind of confrontation that had arisen when he and Josephine tried to lease a suite of rooms together in Paris; he may have advised Josephine to give in to this first homecoming insult, she would probably have encountered the same treatment in other such Manhattan hostelries, so Josephine bowed to "hotel policy" at the St. Moritz.

Her next shock was the discovery that Fanny Brice, the reigning favorite of Broadway, would rate exclusive headliner billing: FANNY BRICE IN ZIEGFELD FOLLIES OF 1936—*with Bob Hope and Josephine Baker* in reduced wattage at the bottom of the marquee. In ten years Josephine had never played second fiddle to any other entertainer; Pepito had promised her co-starring status with Fanny Brice—it was surely in the contract.

"This is New York," Pepito murmured, in the middle of Josephine's tantrum, "and not Paris."

Her personal wardrobe of costumes—gowns designed by Dior, Balenciaga, and Erté, meant to display Josephine's ineffable chic, Paris style—remained packed in her steamer trunks at the St. Moritz: she was to have no say in her own costuming; the Follies costumes had already been designed by Vincente Minelli. The most daring ensemble was a throwback to her pelvic belt of bananas, but instead of bananas Josephine wore a waistband of aggressively pointed silver tusks that suggested some spiked weapon rather than playful totem phalluses. Josephine did not blame Minelli, or George Balanchine, the choreographer of the show—though, as in her film productions, "they didn't understand my nature at all"—but she never recovered from her bitterness toward co-stars Fanny Brice and Bob Hope. Neither made an acknowledgment of her presence in New York; they would appear in the Follies with her, but with never a pleasant remark backstage. Their lack of cordiality may have been exaggerated: Josephine was inured to this kind of competitive disdain, and was more deeply hurt by the rave reviews both Fanny Brice and Bob Hope received, in contrast to her own.

Critical opinion of Josephine Baker in the Ziegfeld Follies of 1936 was altogether negative, the most demoralizing setback in her career. The kindest comment Josephine earned was from the Philadelphia *Ledger* reviewing the show's out-of-town tryout, which spoke tepidly of Miss Baker as a "sophisticated songstress and extravagant dancer" while complaining of her lack of material, the tired replay of "Josephine Baker imitating herself." Opening-night reviews were devastating. Pepito came to her suite at the St. Moritz with the morning papers under his arm; he tried to skip lightly over the grim news with the comment: "You rated a few polite words here and there. Fanny Brice got raves, as usual."

In Josephine's mind, the rivalry with Fanny Brice was equal to the challenge offered by Mistinguett in Paris. In the New York arena she had lost badly; it was Josephine's turn to bleed.

"Miss Baker has refined her art until there is nothing left of it," declared *The New York Times,* leading the attack. Her voice reminded Ira Wolfert in the *Journal-American* of a "cracked bell with a padded clapper," but he added that he liked Chinese music. Others could not understand her accented lyrics or resented her Frenchified pose or heard only a "dwarf-like voice eclipsed in the cavernous Winter Garden." Pepito had hired a *claque,* a scattering of paid professional applause throughout the audience to respond to each of Josephine's numbers, which inspired Walter Winchell to write: "Critics aren't fooled by noise." "Some people like Josephine Baker," said one disgruntled commentator, "I don't."

The personal attack in *Time* reviewed Josephine's life as "a washer woman's daughter who stepped out of a Negro burlesque show into a life of adulation and luxury in Paris during the booming 1920s." *Time* explained her success as undeserved because "In sex appeal to jaded Europeans of the jazz-loving type, a Negro wench always has a head start. The particular tawny hue of tall and stringy Josephine Baker's bare skin stirred French pulses. But to Manhattan theatre-goers last week she was just a slightly buck-toothed young Negro woman whose figure might be matched in a night club show, and whose dancing and singing might be topped practically anywhere outside Paris."

The racist essay on Josephine in *Time,* and the overwhelming deluge of cutting reviews from all sides, at first depressed, then stirred Josephine to rage. Her only target was Pepito, and though he had grown accustomed to her volatile temperament, he was too tired and sick to bear through this storm. He had ruined her, she declared; he had failed to get her top billing and then left her to the sharks. Pepito was no longer up to Josephine's onslaught and too weak to reason with her. This time he became angered beyond hurt, he allowed her to rage on.

She was saying she wanted him out of New York. Was that what she really wanted? Yes, out of New York and out of her life. She had said this before, but never with such vehemence. If that was what she wanted he would leave. Pepito took the next ship back to France, and instead of returning to their home at Beau-Chêne he settled into a bachelor apartment just off the Champs-Elysées, nostalgically midway between the two significant theatres in their life together: the Marigny and the Théâtre des Champs-Elysées.

On her own, Josephine opened a nightclub in the East Fifties: she would show these New Yorkers what she could really do, what she was really like in a setting of her own. But the marginal success of another Chez Josephine in Manhattan was no compensation for the disaster on Broadway. Only in Harlem was she the star of stars, applauded at every club in the black community she visited; there was a celebrity parade down 125th Street in her honor.

A homecoming trip to St. Louis lasted a restless five days, made gloomy by the news of a series of deaths in her absence: grandmother McDonald had died quietly in her sleep, but her favorite half sister with the damaged eye, Willie Mae, had bled to death after a botched abortion. Not long before Josephine revisited St. Louis, her stepfather Arthur Martin had been committed to a municipal asylum where he broke his cell window and died of intestinal bleeding by swallowing the splinters of broken glass. Depressed over the litany of calamity, Josephine tried to think of some gesture of uplift: she offered her work-wearied mother a $20,000 house, but Carrie Martin would say yes, then back off and say no. Finally Carrie said she would think it over: "We'll talk about it . . . when you come back." Her mother, and Josephine, knew that she would never come back to St. Louis again.

On the return to Manhattan, Josephine stopped off in Chicago just long enough to see Willie Baker, working as a waiter there—"I'll take her back," said Willie, "if she'll have me." But Josephine was there to work out terms of a divorce, to free herself from that long-abandoned early marriage.

Though she did not yet know it, Josephine's common-law relationship with Pepito Abatino had ended as well. All along Pepito had believed he was suffering from hepatitis, but in Paris his condition was finally diagnosed as cancer of the kidneys: he died before Josephine returned to Paris. There is no record of Josephine's reaction to the news of Pepito's death, she kept such emotional turmoil to herself, but stated publicly that she had always loved Pepito, and added, sincerely, "He made me."

On her return to New York, there was an old friend from Paris waiting to see her at the St. Moritz: Paul Derval of the Folies-Bergère. He was putting together the 1937 show, *En Super Folies,* to coincide with the new Colonial Exhibit opening in Paris. The city would be swarming with tourists again—Derval wanted his Black Venus back, and so did Paris. Josephine was mumbling to herself, and counting on her fingers. Yes, the title of the new Folies show had exactly thirteen letters.

Derval must have known of Josephine's complete failure to charm Broadway as she had fascinated Paris and much of the rest of the world. He had chosen the psychological moment, and he was ready to talk contracts immediately, without waiting for her return to Paris: this would be her first contractual negotiation since *La Revue Nègre* without Pepito's management. When Derval sat down to open his attaché case, he accidentally sat on Josephine's pet Chihuahua. Josephine gave a shriek and pulled the tiny trembling canine from beneath the portly French producer: she then took advantage of the awkward occasion by insisting that the 40,000 franc advance Derval had offered be raised to 42,500 "to cover the veterinarian's bill."

For the interior decorating of Beau-Chêne, Josephine, with Pepito, had indulged a fancy for furniture and drapery that might well have served a set designer for one of her productions at the Folies. The childlike clutter of antique and Art Déco perfectly suited Josephine's style and spirit: the principal bathroom became a theatrical showpiece of Roman-style excess; the walls were entirely mirrored, Josephine's form and face reflected from every angle under stagelights in the ceiling. But the pleasure of country living at Beau-Chêne had greatly diminished now that she lived there alone.

On her return to Paris Josephine had overseen the completion of a Temple of Love in her garden, in the stage-Roman style of *bassin* and marble pavilion supported by the trunks and uplifted arms of classic statuary in imitation of the stonework pieces in the Tuileries. She bathed outdoors in the company of stone admirers only. The closest male equivalent she had ever seen to compare with one of the gods framing her temple was a twenty-two-year-old dancer appearing with her in *En Super Folies* as one of a trio of partners who alternately intertwined with the star in a balletic skit.

Frédéric Rey was an extraordinarily handsome Viennese youth toward whom she was immediately drawn. They exchanged similarly troubled life stories, how each had overcome barriers the world had placed in their paths, Frédéric lacking only the stage triumphs Josephine had enjoyed at the end of the trail of hardships. Frédéric's most exciting adventure was the picaresque story of his illegal immigration from Austria, a history that would naturally warm Josephine's heart, until he mentioned waiting at the stage door of a Vienna music hall for Mistinguett to appear.

"Mistinguett?"

"Yes. I was just seventeen. I told her, 'I am crazy about music hall. Take me with you.' "

"Mistinguett?"

"Yes. And she did. She smuggled me out of Austria in her big wicker basket of costume jewelry and feathers."

Frédéric had become Mistinguett's regular dance partner from that time until he signed with Derval for *En Super Folies;* it was Josephine's turn to take over. She had taken young lover-companions before, the last one being Jacques Pills, who had been a small-town pharmacist until Josephine helped him advance along the treacherous path of show-business success. Jacques stayed with Josephine long enough to achieve star billing himself as part of the team of Pills and Tabet: she was heartbroken when he left her, but by then she had no illusions or faith in men as stable elements in her life. There had been Pepito, whose devotion was reliable and constant, but he had used her (though with her consent)—and now Pepito was dead. Here was Frédéric Rey. She knew the young dancer was fascinated by her and would be eager to join her in an intimate relationship; she wanted him, and she was prepared to help him.

"Do you love animals?"

"Yes," he said, "very much."

Then he would be delighted to visit her magnificent menagerie of pets at Beau-Chêne. He asked about her famous leopard, Chiquita, and Josephine lowered her head when she said, "He died."

Actually Chiquita was now in the Jardin d'Acclimatation in the Bois de Boulogne. At Beau-Chêne one night he slipped out of the compound of animals and made his way into an isolated house near Le Vésinet, badly frightening an elderly widow when he tried to crawl into her bed. Not even Josephine's prestige and good-hearted assistance to the village could sway the mayor's decision to have Chiquita confined to the zoo. As far as Josephine was concerned, her jungle cat behind bars at the Jardin d'Acclimatation might as well have been dead.

Frédéric was invited to Beau-Chêne to see Josephine's collection of pets and visit her Temple of Love, where the two could compare their bodies to the gods'.

viii

The romance with Frédéric Rey was a passing fancy on Josephine's part, a career opportunity on Rey's: when the two drifted casually apart there were no tears shed on either side. Then, under the most unlikely of circumstances, they were reunited.

As the first German troops bore down on Paris in 1940, Josephine Baker disappeared from the city. She had become a refugee herself among the thousands of frightened Parisians fleeing to the unoccupied zone or trying to leave France by way of neutral Portugal—but Josephine was neither frightened nor desperate: she was engaged in espionage work for Jacques Abtey of the Résistance, a former Deuxième Bureau officer now in liaison with General de Gaulle. When Josephine joined the Underground she declared she would never sing in Paris again "as long as there's a German in France." Both her music-hall rivals, Mistinguett and Maurice Chevalier, remained in Paris to entertain the German invaders (and were accused of collaboration after the war), and at first even Josephine was suspect to the newly organized Resistance movement in southwestern France: the gold-dust and feathered Folies star was possibly a double agent in the tradition of Mata Hari. If not a Mata Hari, Josephine was considered *pas sérieuse* by the clandestine army when she arrived in her Delage limousine, having driven south with contraband petrol stored in champagne bottles. But Abtey backed her without reserve: she was the complete actress, and invaluable in the role of spy through her prewar connections to both the German and Italian embassies. In Vichy France her celebrity was a useful screen—doors were still open to the Black Venus, closed to the rest of Europe—by which she could obtain exit visas for members of the Resistance needed for work in North Africa.

At first Josephine installed herself in the most luxurious hotel in Marseilles, draining the limited funds she had brought with her. Everyone was short of money: Abtey was waiting to collect military pay for himself and Josephine as members of the Free French forces. Josephine moved to a district near the Gare St. Charles, a red-light section of the city reminiscent of her early bohemian existence in Montmartre: her unheated hotel room (she wore her furs to bed) became a network center for exiles and refugees passing through Marseilles. One of those on the run was her Viennese lover from the Folies-Bergère, Frédéric Rey. His situation was as desperate as any, since he had entered France illegally when he was seventeen: he was without a passport of any kind and technically could be conscripted for the German Army. Josephine welcomed Rey to her secret entourage—under the circumstances they could truly be "just friends" and comrades-in-arms. She assured him she would see to his identity papers.

"Do you still love animals?"

"Yes," said he, "as much as ever."

Josephine had a favor to ask. Abtey had received orders from De Gaulle to proceed to Morocco: passports and exit visas were miraculously made available, but before Josephine would leave she *must* take with her the white mice, hamster, her monkeys, and Great Dane sequestered at her latest château home, Les Milandes. Frédéric Rey agreed to make the hazardous trip back in Josephine's Delage, then bring the animals to her for their Noah's Ark crossing of the Mediterranean to French Morocco.

There, as if the script had been written for a new cinematic adventure of Josephine Baker, she became the guest of a powerful and generously attentive sheik, Si Thami el Glaoui, the Pasha of Marrakesh. From the palace of her aging pasha, Josephine operated as an undercover liaison with espionage agents in the neutral countries of Spain and Portugal on her "entertainer's" passport. She gaily attended embassy parties, visited diplomats, cultivated men with Europe's secrets in their attaché cases, meanwhile collecting whatever information she thought useful, noted in invisible ink between the notes on her sheet music or on small scraps of paper she tucked inside her brassiere and panties. Even crossing the strictest wartime border, Josephine Baker was of course the least conceivable person subject to body search.

Wartime espionage work may have been Josephine Baker's greatest role: she brought all of her talents to that risky theatre, her showmanship and flair for daring. After the war she was decorated with the Légion d'Honneur and the Médaille de la Résistance, not only for her work with the Underground but for her North African troop entertainment tours and relentless propaganda for France Libre. Her first loyalty was to France, her great and constant love for Paris. Frédéric Rey, with her at the Folies after the disaster in New York and on tour in North Africa, may have been the first to notice Josephine's shift in intonation when she sang her theme song, "J'ai Deux Amours," changing the lyrics from "mon pays et Paris" to "mon pays *c'est* Paris."

Epilogue

i

The invitation to lunch George Biddle received in January of 1926 was a shakily scrawled note in Mary Cassatt's uncertain hand. The note was accompanied by a letter from the maid Mathilde, who said that her mistress was truly in sad condition: a fall from bed had injured Miss Cassatt in a way that made walking impossible without support; she was now bedridden except for a daily excursion in her beloved automobile, carried to and from the car by her chauffeur of many years, Philippe.

On his arrival at Beaufresne, only Mathilde was there to greet him. Mademoiselle Cassatt had been unable to eat or sleep for the past twenty-four hours. A telegram had been sent, but Biddle had not received word of the canceled lunch before setting out; since he had come such a distance in dreadful weather, a special lunch was being prepared for him, with a bottle of Château Margaux personally selected by Mary Cassatt. After lunch, Mathilde led him to an upstairs bedroom for the formal visit Mary Cassatt had insisted upon. She was propped against a mound of pillows in the great green bed depicted in *Breakfast in Bed*, one of her last tender renderings of the maternal scene George Biddle remembered seeing at Galerie Durand-Ruel. Her once carefully coiffed hair now straggled limply from beneath the lace bed cap. Her hands came alive as soon as he appeared at her beside, and the words poured forth: how had he found the wine? It was the last bottle of Château Margaux sent by her brother Aleck, long dead.

When her guest assured her the wine had been excellent, she was suddenly animated and as vital as he had ever known her. In a tumultuous spill of words she spoke of George Biddle's first visit to Beaufresne at the beginning of the Great War—also during a rainstorm—and of her fall from a horse forty years ago, but she strained to remember the name of the doctor who treated her with camphor, snapping her fingers high in the air to try to recall his name. Mathilde hovered at her mistress's pillow, pushing the loose strand of hair back into her cap and whispering the doctor's name to her.

Mathilde was to go immediately and fetch the drawing of the Cassatt family: "I was a child when it was done and the first effect of art for me was that drawing." The drawing included a sketch of her younger brother Robbie—she snapped her fingers trying to remember the city where he had died, and Mathilde whispered, "Darmstadt." Yes, she had sent to Darmstadt for Robbie's remains to be brought back to Mesnil-Théribus and buried in the cemetery, next to her mother and father; she would be buried there too, the last surviving Cassatt in the family portrait.

In the family sketch, Mary stared out wide-eyed and unflinching, the determined chin evidence of her strong will, prim in pose, with the loops of strict Teutonic pigtails at the sides of her head.

"And the jewels from Egypt, Mr. Biddle must see them." She struggled to make Mathilde understand about the jewels, her fingers grasping air.

Mathilde disappeared, then returned with the trinkets in carnelian and lapis lazuli. But Mary Cassatt was nearing exhaustion. The worried expression on Mathilde's face was a signal that Mademoiselle could not hold up much longer. George Biddle then told her that he would see her again soon, knowing they would not meet again, ever.

Her blind eyes were already turned away as he quietly withdrew. She was staring into the empty space, colorless and without mass.

ii

Not long before her death in 1937, Edith Wharton left a memorandom: "I wish to be buried at the Cimetère des Gonards, at Versailles, & have bought there a double plot, as near as possible to Walter Berry's grave, I wish a grave stone like his, with my birth & death dates (January 24, 1862–) & Ave Crux Spes Unica engraved under it. The receipt for my burial plot will be found with my other papers."

The second Great War was only three years away, but Edith Wharton was apparently unaware of the threatened devastation of Europe again as she lived out her last days, cared for by servants as always, visited by friends from Paris, but more alone than she had ever been. She was devoted to her Pekingese, Linky, and when the dog died that spring she reminisced with trembling hand in her diary about Teddy Wharton's love of animals, seeing in him a goodness she had seldom dwelt upon when they were man and wife: "He enjoyed life so." very much as she had written about Walter Berry in the same diary: "Walter loved life so . . ." She decided to destroy some personal papers; a servant burned all of the letters from Teddy—but, strangely, she allowed a fragment of erotica to survive, a manuscript known as *Beatrice Palmatto,* about father-daughter incest, written with a straightforward sexual explicitness unthinkable from the pen of Edith Wharton. The fragment had probably been drafted a few months before, unpublishable in the 1930s, but something she obviously wanted to leave behind, perhaps as evidence that the reticent Edith Wharton had not been the straitlaced *grande dame* she was believed to be.

In a long relapse following three successive bouts of influenza, Edith Wharton grew more and more fatigued. She had been to Paris to see her oculist, and had even taken up work on a last manuscript, *A Little Girl's Old New York,* a postscript to her rambling unrevealing memoir, *A Backward Glance.* On the annual journey to Hyères in the South of France, she suffered a stroke and had to be transported by ambulance to the Pavillon Colombe, her home outside Paris.

On August 11 she lay in her chaise-longue looking out upon the white garden she had created, and that evening did not awaken to her maid's voice; as tranquil and dignified a passing as she could have hoped for. The funeral was also as she wished, at the American Episcopal Cathedral of the Holy Trinity, in Paris—in contrast to the princely *pompes funèbres* of her dear friend Walter Berry, she had left the instruction: "I wish a *simple hearse,* with only two horses." At the cemetery in Versailles her casket was lowered to the sound of a bugle call from the military guard of the commune of St. Brice, veterans of the Great War who formed an honor guard around the gravesite.

iii

In Paris again, in the 1930s, Caresse Crosby revived, with some success and modest profit, the Black Sun Press. She had fallen in love with Jacques Porel, son of the celebrated French actress Réjane, and it was Porel who assisted her in creating and promoting the Crosby Continental Editions, in competition with the foremost English-language softcover editions, Tauchnitz. Yet she failed to convince American publishers and bookstores to extend her venture to the United States: she was twenty years too early with the idea to print and distribute mass paperback editions in the United States.

"I believe that Mama was truly in love with Jacques," said Polleen, who otherwise deplored what she considered her mother's Merry Widow phase. "He was on the scene much longer than most." But Jacques Porel was an incorrigible sponger and womanizer, "flirting with anyone in sight, including myself and my classmates when they came home with me." Both mother and daughter remembered Paris in the 1920s in soft-focus nostaglia: Caresse honored Harry Crosby's memory by publishing his journals, *Shadows in the Sun,* in a Black Sun edition; Polleen sadly regretted her mother's indifference to the men who had been most devoted to Caresse and kind to herself. Polleen's favorite—and most loyal still—was Gerald, Lord Lymington. "I don't know why he loved my mother so faithfully for so long, since he was sorely neglected, and in those early years, often was left alone with me and one of my dreadful governesses. . . .

(Meanwhile Mama, in widow's weeds, was dining and dancing with someone else!)"

When the affair with Jacques Porel soured, Caresse suffered the first of the heart attacks that would darken her remaining years: she fled to England to recover from both blows. Meanwhile the literary and artistic colony, along with the wealthly patrons who had supported the arts in Montparnasse, were shifting the expatriate scene from Paris to Venice and Rome, but World War II brought an end to the cultural revolution and the search for the great good place. The Black Sun Press languished during the war years, then expired (Roger Lescaret had enlisted in the French Resistance), but Caresse, ever concerned with avant-garde publishing, launched a fresh literary venture, *Portfolio: an Intercontinental Quarterly,* in Washington, D.C. As soon as the war ended, Caresse was bound for Europe on her first transcontinental flight, a BOAC transport for military personnel—except for Caresse, traveling with her Schiaparelli hat box and copies of *Portfolio.* The magazine became a truly "intercontinental quarterly" in Paris, published from Caresse's address at the Hôtel California on the rue de Berri. "The going is difficult in regard to paper, printing and getting about Paris . . . everything is full of red tape"; but in spite of all she could announce: "So in this issue we have ELUARD, CAMUS, SARTRE, PICASSO, CARTIER-BRESSON . . . and a Siamese doctor whose name I cannot spell."

After creating a One World colony on the island of Cyprus in 1967, Caresse was spending more and more of her time in Italy, so she moved the project—called World Man Center—to Roccassinibalda, a village outside Rome. When she purchased a seventeenth-century castle, with seventy-two rooms to house her one-world commune of artists and humanists, she became known to the locals along the crest of the Abruzzi hills as the Principessa of Roccassinibalda, fulfilling the first half of a prediction by a Parisian gypsy who had once accosted Caresse in the street and informed her that she would one day live in a castle, and die at the age of seventy-seven.

At Christmas, 1969, she received a nostalgic message from Gerald, Lord Lymington, from Kenya, where he had settled but now planned to leave. "I will be coming via Italy to see you in summer. Keep well my darling wench. I loved you all the years and love you just as much now. God bless you." But Caresse did not keep well, nor did Lord Lymington keep his summer rendezvous with her. In the chill of a winter's evening Caresse insisted on wearing a thin cocktail gown to dinner; she caught pneumonia and was taken to Salvatore Mundi hospital in Rome, where she died on the night of January 24: she was seventy-seven.

iv

Back in America, in the winter of 1932, Zelda Fitzgerald was under treatment at the Phipps Clinic of Johns Hopkins University Hospital, and while there—as part of her therapy and for "something to do, something of her own"—she wrote *Save Me the Waltz.* Her novel was written in counterpoint to Scott's version of their lives in France, material that encroached on what Scott felt was his exclusive literary terrain. Zelda had moments of affecting lucidity and great powers of recall: she applied the hard gaze of her nostalgias to *Save Me the Waltz,* and many truths emerged in the telling, though ultimately the novel failed with public and critics alike. Scott's reaction was at first one of relief, his professional resentment assuaged, then his feelings shaded into belated concern for the effect of failure on his mentally ill wife.

Zelda would take up painting. She would even try to write another novel, *Caesar's Things,* but the last true hope for "something of her own" had collapsed when *Save Me the Waltz* went unrecognized. At this time a family member who visited Zelda in the hospital found her dressed all in white, weighing less than a hundred pounds and at prayers beside her bed looking like a "desperate angel." Zelda asked her guest if she would forever look after Scottie for her . . . and could she please have a candy bar?

Later Zelda was treated at Highlands Hospital just outside Asheville, North Carolina. Except for short periods with her mother in Montgomery, Highlands Hospital would be her home for the desolate years remaining. In the spring of 1948 the hospital caught fire. The fire escapes were of wood and quickly aflame; Zelda was identified by a slipper found beneath her body.

V

None of the honors received—the Légion d'Honneur, the Médaille de la Résistance—nor the celebrity attached to the name Josephine Baker could prevent foreclosure and loss of her château, Les Milandes, in 1969. Despite a television appeal by French film star Brigitte Bardot, which brought in 1.2 million French francs, Josephine's debts and the upkeep of her lavish menage represented far more than the public or well-to-do friends could provide. There were postponements and last-minute reprieves, but finally the princess was evicted from her castle.

The bankrupt estate had been Josephine's most ambitious and extravagant project: she had made of the château a home for her adopted family of twelve orphaned children—of various hues and nationalities, collected in the countries throughout the world where she had played—an international family of outcast infants she called the Rainbow Tribe. The adoption of these children, saved from the neglect and poverty she had known growing up in St. Louis, was Josephine's personal gesture of active integration as well as an expression of love.

When Josephine lost Les Milandes, Princess Grace of Monaco came to her aid, and provided a villa and funds for Josephine and her Rainbow Tribe in the ancient village of Roquebrune, overlooking Monte Carlo and the Mediterranean. Josephine still made music-hall appearances at the age of sixty-nine—"I'm carrying thirty-four years on one shoulder, and thirty-five on the other—you add them up!"—and her 1975 revue at the Casino de Paris in Monte Carlo was such a success that she was asked to bring it to Paris.

Josephine's final triumphant appearance was the show of her life, *Josephine,* staged at the Bobino Theatre on the rue de la Gaité, removed from her familiar Right Bank theatrical district but mobbed nonetheless on the night of the opening, April 8, 1975, exactly fifty years since she had first aroused a Parisian audience with her outrageous semi-nude Charleston at the Théâtre des Champs-Elysées. To celebrate her return, *le tout Paris* turned out to toast the Black Venus of then and now—though *le tout Paris* had changed, and her fellow celebrants were Princess Grace, Mick Jagger, Jeanne Moreau, Alain Delon, Mireille Darc, Madame Sukarno, Sophia Loren, and Pierre Balmain. Jean-Claude Brialy read a letter of *félicitations* from President Giscard d'Estaing, and Josephine stood transfixed and tearful during a fifteen-minute standing ovation. At the second night's show—sold out, as were all performances for weeks ahead—Josephine performed with characteristic chic and miraculous élan for her sixty-nine years, with a dozen elaborate costume changes her only hurried respite; at midnight she was bubbling with energy and anxious to go out on the town, perhaps to Chez Micho where a black male performer with a comic cannibal bone in his hair did a takeoff on the Josephine Baker of fifty years before. No one in the cast had the energy to continue, so Josephine told them, "I'm younger than any of you," and retired to her apartment with the evening papers. That night she lapsed into a coma, blanketed with the newspapers' eulogies scattered across the bed.

From l'Hôpital de la Salpêtrière the long black hearse passed the southern flank of the cimetière du Montparnasse to the rue de la Gaîté where the marquee lights spelling out JOSEPHINE were illuminated in the middle of bright morning, and from there crossed the Seine to the Théâtre des Champs-Elysées, outside lights also ablaze, then made a deliberate detour to the Casino de Paris on the Champs-Elysées before circling l'Etoile and returning past the Théâtre de Marigny. Some twenty thousand Parisians had spilled back along the rue Royale to the place de la Concorde where the hearse turned and parted the crowd massed before the steps of l'église de la Madeleine. The tricolor-draped casket was borne through an honor guard to the echo of a twenty-one-gun salute.

Josephine Baker died at la Salpêtrière hospital of a cerebral hemorrhage, but there were those in the crowd at la Madeleine who said she had died of joy.

Acknowledgments

I am grateful to the following institutions for assistance with the research and writing of this book: Bibliothèque Nationale, Paris; British Museum, London; Centre Pompidou, Paris; Humanities Research Center, Austin, Texas; Penrose Library, University of Denver, Denver, Colorado; The Tattered Cover, Denver, Colorado.

I would like to express my thanks to Harold Beaver, Leo Bukzin, Rikki and Guy Ducornet, Glenn Giffin, Diane and Daniel Harlé, Michael Mewshaw, Rosemarie O'Leary, Alexandra Olsen, Bin Ramke, Don Revell, May Smith, June Spackman, for information, texts, suggestions and moral support. For the warmth and welcome of their extraordinary bookshops, I am especially grateful to Odile Hellier of The Village Voice, Paris; Margaret Lake of Bloomsbury Books, Denver; and George Whitman of Shakespeare and Company, Paris.

Bibliography

GENERAL

Allan, Tony. *Americans in Paris.* Chicago: Contemporary Books, 1977.

Aldrich, Mildred. *A Hilltop on the Marne.* Boston: Houghton Mifflin, 1915.

Barnes, Djuna. *Ladies Almanack.* Dijon: Contact Editions, 1928.

———. *Interviews.* College Park, Md.: Sun and Moon Press, 1985.

Beach, Sylvia. *Shakespeare and Company.* New York: Harcourt, Brace, 1959.

Benstock, Shari. *Women of the Left Bank.* Austin, Tex.: University of Texas Press, 1986.

Boyle, Kay, and Robert McAlmon. *Being Geniuses Together.* Garden City, N.Y.: Doubleday, 1968.

Brassai. *Paris Secret des Années 30.* Paris: Editions Gallimard, 1976.

Callaghan, Morley. *That Summer in Paris.* New York: Coward-McCann, 1963.

Crespelle, Jean-Paul. *La Folle Epoque.* Paris: Hachette, 1968.

———. *Les Maîtres de la Belle Epoque.* Paris: Hachette, 1966.

Culbertson, Judi, and Tom Randall. *Permanent Parisians.* Chelsea, Vt.: Chelsea Publishing Co., 1986.

De Cossart, Michael. *The Food of Love.* London: Hamish Hamilton, 1978.

Earnest, Ernest. *Expatriates and Patriots: American Artists, Scholars and Writers in Europe.* Durham, N.C.: Duke University Press, 1968.

Ehrlich, Blake. *Paris on the Seine.* New York: Atheneum, 1962.

Fitch, Noel Riley. *Sylvia Beach and the Lost Generation.* New York: W. W. Norton, 1963.

Flanner, Janet. *An American in Paris.* New York: Simon & Schuster, 1940.

———. *Paris Journal.* New York: Atheneum, 1965.

———. *Paris Was Yesterday.* New York: Viking, 1972.

Ford, Hugh. *The Left Bank Revisited: Selections from the Paris Tribune 1917–1934.* University Park, Pa., and London: Pennsylvania State University Press, 1972.

———. *Four Lives in Paris.* San Francisco: North Point Press, 1987.
——— (ed.). *Nancy Cunard: Brave Poet, Indomitable Rebel.* New York: Chilton, 1968.
———. *Published in Paris: American and British Writers, Printers, and Publishers in Paris, 1920–1939.* New York: Macmillan, 1975.
Gardner, Virginia. *"Friend and Lover." The Life of Louise Bryant.* New York: Horizon Press, 1982.
Glassco, John. *Memoirs of Montparnasse.* New York: Oxford University Press, 1970.
Gosling, Nigel. *Paris 1900–1914, The Miraculous Years.* London: Weidenfeld & Nicolson, 1978.
Guilleminault, Gilbert. *Le Roman Vrai des Années Folles.* Paris: Librairie Plon, 1939.
Hemingway, Ernest. *A Moveable Feast.* New York: Scribners, 1964.
Huddleston, Sisley. *Back to Montparnasse: Glimpses of Broadway in Bohemia.* Philadelphia: Lippincott, 1931.
———. *Paris Salons, Cafés, Studios.* Philadelphia: Lippincott, 1928.
Josephson, Matthew. *Life Among the Surrealists.* New York: Henry Holt, 1962.
Kert, Bernice. *The Hemingway Women.* New York: W. W. Norton, 1983.
Lanoux, Armand. *Paris in the Twenties.* New York: Essential Encyclopedia Arts, 1960.
Longstreet, Stephen. *We All Went to Paris.* New York: Macmillan, 1972.
Loyer, François. *Paris Nineteenth Century: Architecture and Urbanism.* New York: Abbeville Press, 1988.
Mellow, James R. *Charmed Circle.* New York: Praeger, 1974.
Putnam, Samuel. *Paris Was Our Mistress.* New York: Viking, 1947.
Rhys, Jean. *Smile Please.* New York: Harper & Row, 1979.
Shattuck, Roger. *The Banquet Years.* New York: Harcourt, Brace, 1955.
Street, Julian. *Where Paris Dines.* New York: Doubleday, 1929.
Wickes, George. *The Amazon of Letters: The Life and Loves of Natalie Barney.* London: W. H. Allen, 1977.
———. *Americans in Paris.* Garden City, N.Y.: Doubleday, 1969.
Wineapple, Brenda. *Genêt: A Biography of Janet Flanner.* New York: Ticknor & Fields, 1989.
Wiser, William. *The Crazy Years: Paris in the Twenties.* New York: Atheneum, 1983.

Mary Cassatt

Bazin, Germain. *L'Epoque Impressioniste.* Paris: Editions Pierre Tisné, 1947.
Biddle, George. *An American Artist's Story.* Boston: Little, Brown, 1939.
Bredin, Jean-Denis. *The Affair.* New York: George Braziller, 1986.
Breeskin, Adelyn D. *Mary Cassatt: A Catalogue Raisonné of the Oils Water Colors and Drawings.* Washington, D.C.: Smithsonian Institution Press, 1970.
Breuning, Margaret. *Mary Cassatt.* New York: Hyperion Press, 1944.
Bullard, E. John. *Mary Cassatt, Oils and Pastels.* New York: Watson-Guptill, 1972.
Burr, Anna Robeson. *The Portrait of a Banker: James Stillman.* New York: Duffield & Co., 1927.
Cabanne, Pierre. *The Great Collectors.* New York: Farrar, Straus, 1963.
Fèvre, Jeanne. *Mon Oncle Degas.* Geneva: P. Cailler, 1949.
Gimpel, René. *Diary of an Art Dealer,* trans. John Rosenberg. New York: Farrar, Straus, 1966.
Halévy, Daniel. *My Friend Degas,* trans. Mina Curtiss. Middletown, Conn.: Wesleyan University Press, 1964.
Hanson, Lawrence and Elisabeth. *Impressionism: Golden Decade.* New York: Holt, Reinhart & Winston, 1961.
Havemeyer, Louisine W. *Sixteen to Sixty, Memoirs of a Collector.* New York: Privately

printed for the family of Mrs. H. O. Havemeyer and the Metropolitan Museum of Art, 1961.

Le Pichon, Yann. *The Real World of the Impressionists.* New York: Clarkson N. Potter, 1983.

Love, Richard H. *Cassatt: The Independent.* Chicago: Milton H. Kreines, 1980.

Mathews, Nancy Mowll (ed.). *Cassatt and Her Circle, Selected Letters.* New York: Abbeville Press, 1984.

———. *Mary Cassatt.* New York: Abrams, 1987.

McKown, Robin. *The World of Mary Cassatt.* New York: Thomas Y. Crowell, 1972.

McMullen, Roy. *Degas, His Life, Times and Work.* Boston: Houghton Mifflin, 1984.

Rewald, John. *Camille Pissarro: Lettres à Son Fils Lucien.* Paris: Albin Michel, 1950.

———. *The History of Impressionism.* New York: Museum of Modern Art, 1948.

Saarinen, Aline. *The Proud Possessors.* New York: Random House, 1958.

Segard, Achille. *Un Peintre des Enfants et des Mères, Mary Cassatt.* Paris: Librairie Paul Olendorff, 1913.

Varnedoe, Kirk. *Gustave Caillebotte.* New Haven, Conn.: Yale University Press, 1987.

Watson, Forbes. *Mary Cassatt.* New York: Whitney Museum, 1932.

Winkler, John K. *The First Billion, the Stillmans and the National City Bank.* Babson Park, Mass.: Spear & Staff, 1951.

Edith Wharton

Auchincloss, Louis. *Edith Wharton.* New York: Viking, 1971.

Bell, Millicent. *Edith Wharton & Henry James.* New York: George Braziller, 1965.

Edel, Leon. *Henry James, 1901–1916, The Master.* New York: J. B. Lippincott, 1972.

——— (ed.). *Henry James Letters: Volume IV, 1895–1916.* Cambridge, Mass.: Harvard University Press, 1984.

Flanner, Janet. *An American in Paris.* New York: Simon & Schuster, 1940. ("Dearest Edith," pp. 185–196).

Kellogg, Grace. *The Two Lives of Edith Wharton.* New York: Appleton, 1965.

Lewis, R. W. B. *Edith Wharton: A Bibliography.* New York: Harper & Row, 1975.

——— (ed.). *The Letters of Edith Wharton.* New York: Scribners, 1988.

Lubbock, Percy. *Portrait of Edith Wharton.* New York: Appleton, 1947.

Painter, George D. *Marcel Proust, A Biography: Volume Two.* New York: Random House, 1959.

Powers, Lyall H. (ed.). *Henry James and Edith Wharton, Letters: 1900–1915.* New York: Scribners, 1990.

Wharton, Edith. *The Age of Innocence.* New York: Appleton, 1920.

———. *A Backward Glance.* New York: Appleton, 1936.

———. *Ethan Frome.* New York: Scribners, 1911.

———. *The House of Mirth.* New York: Scribners, 1905.

———. *Xingu and Other Stories.* New York: Scribners, 1910.

Wolff, Cynthia Griffin. *A Feast of Words.* New York: Oxford University Press, 1977.

Caresse Crosby

Boyle, Kay, and Robert McAlmon. *Being Geniuses Together.* Garden City, N.Y.: Doubleday, 1968.

Conover, Anne. *Caresse Crosby.* Santa Barbara, Calif.: Capra Press, 1989.

Cowley, Malcolm. *Exile's Return.* New York: Viking, 1956.

Crosby, Caresse. *The Passionate Years.* New York: Dial Press, 1953.
———. *Poems for Harry Crosby.* Paris: Black Sun Press, 1931.
Crosby, Harry. *Red Skeletons.* Paris: Editions Narcisse, 1927.
———. *Shadows of the Sun.* Paris: Black Sun Press, 1928.
Ford, Hugh. *Published in Paris.* New York: Macmillan, 1975.
Wolff, Geoffrey. *Black Sun.* New York: Random House, 1976.

Zelda Fitzgerald

Baker, Carlos. *Ernest Hemingway: A Life Story.* New York: Scribners, 1969.
Bruccoli, Matthew J. (ed.). *The Notebooks of F. Scott Fitzgerald.* New York: Harcourt Brace, 1980.
———. *Some Sort of Epic Grandeur.* New York: Harcourt Brace, 1981.
———, and Margaret M. Dugan. *The Correspondence of F. Scott Fitzgerald.* New York: Random House, 1980.
Donnelly, Honoria Murphy, with Richard N. Billings. *Sara & Gerald.* New York: Times Books, 1982.
Fitzgerald, F. Scott. *Babylon Revisited and Other Stories.* New York, Scribners: 1971.
———. *The Crack-Up.* New York: New Directions, 1945.
———. *The Great Gatsby.* New York: Scribners, 1925.
———. *Tender Is the Night.* New York: Scribners, 1934.
Fitzgerald, Zelda. *Save Me the Waltz.* New York: Scribners, 1932.
Hemingway, Ernest. *A Moveable Feast.* New York: Scribners, 1964.
Mayfield, Sara. *Exiles from Paradise.* New York: Delacorte Press, 1971.
Mellow, James R. *Invented Lives.* Boston: Houghton Mifflin, 1984.
Milford, Nancy. *Zelda: A Biography.* New York: Harper & Row, 1970.
Mizener, Arthur. *The Far Side of Paradise.* Boston: Houghton Mifflin, 1949.
———. *Scott Fitzgerald and His World.* London: Thames & Hudson, 1972.
Tompkins, Calvin. *Living Well Is the Best Revenge.* New York: Viking, 1971.
Turnbull, Andrew. *Scott Fitzgerald.* New York: Scribners, 1962.

Josephine Baker

Baker, Josephine, and Jo Bouillon. *Joséphine.* Paris: Editions Robert Laffont, 1976.
———, and André Rivollet. *Une Vie de Toutes les Couleurs.* Grenoble: B. Athaud, 1935.
———, and Marcel Sauvage. *Les Mémoires de Joséphine Baker.* Paris: Kra, 1927.
Bechet, Sidney. *Treat It Gentle.* New York: Hill & Wang, 1960.
Bresler, Fenton. *The Mystery of Georges Simenon.* New York: Beaufort Books, 1983.
Bricktop, with James Haksins. *Bricktop.* New York: Atheneum, 1983.
Derval, Paul. *Folies-Bergère,* trans. Lucienne Hill. New York: Dutton, 1955.
Haney, Lynn. *Naked at the Feast.* New York: Dodd, Mead, 1981.
Papich, Stephen. *Remembering Josephine.* New York: Bobbs-Merrill, 1976.
Rose, Phyllis. *Jazz Cleopatra.* Garden City, N.Y.: Doubleday, 1989.

Index